I first met Billy while doing an interview with TheBlaze. I had spent a long weekend doing press interviews in New York City and was so impressed by Billy's genuine faith and ability to unpack a story from our interview to his written words. In this book he masterfully unpacks one of the most challenging and difficult-to-understand teachings from the Bible—the end times. I have been in church my whole life, and yet there is still so much about what the Bible says about the end times that remains a mystery to me and so many others. I believe Billy's findings will shine a much-needed light on these days in which we live and remind us that the end times will lead the way to a new beginning—eternity.

—MATTHEW WEST
CHRISTIAN SINGER

I've never felt comfortable reading about the end of days. It always feels over the top. Thank heavens I have a good friend named Billy Hallowell who is willing to make it easier to face Armageddon. The language is straightforward, the concepts are made real, and the Christian message is clear. I still don't like that part of the Bible, but at least now I have a useful tool to help navigate it.

—SEAN ASTIN
ACTOR

Billy Hallowell's new book investigates the raging debate on various issues related to Bible prophecy. And he does so by direct interviews with leading proponents of the various, strongly opposing positions. That makes the book quite controversial—but it also makes it worth reading.

—DR. RON RHODES
AUTHOR, *THE 8 GREAT DEBATES OF BIBLE PROPHECY* AND
40 DAYS THROUGH REVELATION

Covering the interpretive spectrum, Hallowell conveniently juxtaposes widely differing opinions on biblical prophecy, offering the reader a unique opportunity to engage contentious issues and puzzling questions through an enjoyable writing style—an accomplishment as colossal as the debate itself.

—SHANE J. WOOD
PROFESSOR, NEW TESTAMENT STUDIES AT OZARK CHRISTIAN COLLEGE
AUTHOR, *THE ALTER-IMPERIAL PARADIGM:*
EMPIRE STUDIES & THE BOOK OF REVELATION

Though this may be his first "official" book, Billy Hallowell has been a successful and prolific writer for years. He keeps his finger on the spiritual pulse of America, fearlessly tackling essential, and often hotly debated, topics. This book is no different, as he unravels the often-confusing tapestry of end-times beliefs.

—Jeff Kinley
Author, *Wake the Bride* and *As It Was in the Days of Noah*

Really—another book about the end times? Well, not exactly. If you make the mistake of thinking that you've had enough of the genre to last a lifetime, you'll miss the true service veteran journalist Billy Hallowell has rendered in this book. This isn't another book offering you "speculative certainties" about how the future will pan out because "the Bible tells me so." If you've ever wondered why Bible prophecy is confusing, creates so much debate, and has left generations of pastors, professors, and pew-sitters throwing up their hands in surrender, Hallowell will make at least that much clear. *The Armageddon Code* gives readers the "inside baseball" talk between Bible scholars that reveals how complicated and ambiguous the Bible really is when it comes to prophecy. You already know Christians don't agree on how prophecy will work out. Billy Hallowell explains why it's even a struggle.

—Dr. Michael S. Heiser
Scholar-in-Residence, Faithlife
Corporation/Logos Bible Software
Author, *The Unseen Realm: Recovering
the Supernatural Worldview of the Bible*

I have been very impressed with the care that Billy Hallowell has given to a complicated and challenging subject and his desire to be fair to all orthodox perspectives.

—Douglas Wilson
Pastor and Theologian

Billy is a wonderful reporter who uses his journalistic capabilities in this book to beautifully weave together a variety of opinions about a monumentally complex subject matter. It's a must-read book for anyone with an interest in Scripture and theology.

—Roma Downey
Actress/Producer

T H E
ARMAGEDDON
CODE

BILLY HALLOWELL

FRONT
LINE

Most CHARISMA HOUSE BOOK GROUP products are available at special quantity discounts for bulk purchase for sales promotions, premiums, fund-raising, and educational needs. For details, write Charisma House Book Group, 600 Rinehart Road, Lake Mary, Florida 32746, or telephone (407) 333-0600.

THE ARMAGEDDON CODE by Billy Hallowell
Published by FrontLine
Charisma Media/Charisma House Book Group
600 Rinehart Road
Lake Mary, Florida 32746
www.charismahouse.com

Cover design by Lisa Rae McClure
Design Director: Justin Evans

Visit the author's website at www.billyhallowell.com.

Library of Congress Cataloging-in-Publication Data:
Names: Hallowell, Billy, author.
Title: The Armageddon code / Billy Hallowell.
Description: First edition. | Lake Mary, Florida : FrontLine, 2016. |
   Includes bibliographical references.
Identifiers: LCCN 2016008615| ISBN 9781629989211 (trade paper) | ISBN
   9781629989228 (e-book)
Subjects: LCSH: Eschatology. | End of the world.
Classification: LCC BT821.3 .H35 2016 | DDC 236/.9--dc23
LC record available at http://lccn.loc.gov/2016008615

First edition

16 17 18 19 20 — 987654321
Printed in the United States of America

Train up a child in the way he should go, and when
he is old he will not depart from it.

—PROVERBS 22:6

— — — — — — — — — —

I would like to dedicate this book to Ava
and Lilyana, as it is my hope and prayer
that you will always walk in truth.

CONTENTS

ACKNOWLEDGMENTS

I WOULD LIKE TO acknowledge and profoundly and formally thank the following individuals and institutions, as this book would not have been possible without them:

First and foremost, thank you to Charisma House for bringing this project to me, and for allowing me to explore one of the most fascinating facets of Christian theology.

I would also like to specifically thank Woodley Auguste and Todd Starnes for your friendship and guidance in connecting me with the publisher and with this project.

Megan Turner, I'm also immeasurably grateful for all of your hard work and dedication on the manuscript.

I am especially grateful to Southeastern Baptist Theological Seminary for offering me the opportunity to study Christian history and theory—a pursuit that helped to prepare me by instilling the knowledge and interest to accomplish this feat.

I would like to also call attention to the interview subjects and other instrumental individuals in this project. The following lists those individuals (and in no particular order): Dr. Ed Hindson, Dr. Sam Storms, Greg Laurie, Dr. Michael Heiser, Randy LaHaye, Tim LaHaye, Jeff Kinley, Joel C. Rosenberg, Dr. Mark Hitchcock, Rabbi Aryeh Spero, Dr. Michael Brown, Dr. Ron Rhodes, Dr. Darrell Bock, Don Preston, Hank Hanegraaff, Mark Moore, Dr. William Lane Craig, Dr. Shane Wood, Douglas Wilson, Mark Biltz, and John Hagee.

Last—but most certainly not least—is my wife, Andrea, who allowed me many days and hours away from her and our two young kids. She was a true partner in this project, and I couldn't have done it without her.

Thank you all for making this book a reality.

Introduction

OUR OBSESSION WITH THE END OF DAYS

AMERICANS ARE SEEMINGLY obsessed with apocalyptic story lines, frequently flocking to consume TV shows, movies, and books with plotlines that center on zombie attacks, worldwide weather disasters, biblical raptures, and the like—end-of-days scenarios that depict humanity on the cusp of extinction.

At a deep, visceral level there seems to be an inherent interest among the masses in exploring the terrifying "what-ifs" when it comes to potential mass calamity, with entertainment providing a typically safe venue for such consumption.

Sociologists and academics have a variety of theories about what drives these interests, with Dr. Kyle Bishop, an English professor at Southern Utah University, positing that fears in the post-9/11 world have potentially driven much of the recent fascination with zombie-themed entertainment.[1]

"Because the zombie is so simple and can be whatever people want it to be, more than any monster, it represents the tabula rasa [blank slate]," Bishop said. "A white space—it allows itself to be rewritten and reused."[2]

The professor also dug a bit deeper, though, noting that in the post-9/11 world many people began to feel unsafe, with related and subsequent events such as the anthrax and avian flu scares and Hurricane Katrina adding to those worries.

"Suddenly there was a 5-year period when people in the U.S. felt insecure, and as it so happened, the nature of those insecurities manifested in zombie narratives: Invasion, destruction, apocalypse, infection," Bishop said. "There was this intersection of these influences that made it perfect for the zombie to take over. People like monsters that manifest the things they're worried about."[3]

But that obsession has extended well beyond the five years that followed the 2001 terror attacks, with Hollywood continuing to capitalize on the end-times intrigue as those with an interest in biblical prophecy keep a watchful eye.

Even before 9/11 the end-of-days narrative was ripe in entertainment and literature with Hollywood churning out the 1998 apocalyptic film *Armageddon* and with religious publishers and production companies beginning to court faith audiences by shedding new light on interpretations of events recounted in the Book of Revelation.

In real life too people have reacted in a variety of troubling—and comical—ways in recent years when they interpret certain events as being potentially cataclysmic.

While it wasn't quite an end-of-days scenario, let's not forget people's overwhelming obsession with the turn of the twenty-first century—the event known as Y2K that led countless Americans to store water and food for fear that computer systems worldwide would essentially self-destruct. The systems, of course, didn't combust or break down, and life continued on without much of a blip.

And who could forget the hoopla surrounding the Mayan calendar that left some worrying that the world as we know it could come to an end on December 21, 2012? Of course, the earth kept on spinning beyond that date without incident, proving that those fears were patently unwarranted.

What really causes this inherent interest in the end of days? And, on the theology front, what will happen if and when the Bible's predictions about the end come to fruition?

As for the former question, Dr. Angela M. Becerra Vidergar, a comparative English professor at Stanford University, has sought to explore these paradigms, positing that the modern-day fascination with the end of the world stems from World War II, particularly America's use of nuclear weapons in Hiroshima and Nagasaki.

Vidergar argues that those events made it more difficult for people to "imagine the type of positive future that was more prevalent in centuries past, for example, during the Enlightenment or the Industrial Revolution," according to a recap of her views that was published by Stanford.[4]

"We use fictional narratives not only to emotionally cope with the possibility of impending doom, but even more importantly perhaps to work through the ethical and philosophical frameworks that were in many ways left shattered in the wake of WWII," she said.[5]

With the world not really improving much after World War II, Vidergar explained that people still find themselves struggling for answers in light of "other atrocities, other genocides and other disasters."[6]

She too noticed an increase in depictions of the apocalypse in books, movies, and TV shows, saying that these themes tend to become pervasive in the wake of events such as 9/11 as people process what unfolded.

But in a world in which instability seems to be the new norm, with radical Islam dominating the headlines and fear gripping a great many, one must wonder if people are more routinely feeling as though something isn't quite right—as though the world is off-kilter in some profound way. Perhaps people are looking for answers.

Team that dynamic with the fact that Christians themselves have believed for two millennia that Jesus Christ will one day return in His much-anticipated second coming to usher in a new heaven and a new earth, and you find yourself with a fascinating scenario.

Perhaps people are awakening. Or, at the least, feeling that internal inkling that the world is headed in an uncertain or calamitous direction—an idea that the Bible blatantly predicts.

A focus on the end times in religious circles, of course, is nothing new, but it's the extension of that theme into the mainstream culture that is quite fascinating, causing one to wonder if the events of the day are responsible for sparking a greater interest—even in fictitious and improbable scenarios—among those who aren't religious or biblically literate.

When we speak about the post-9/11 world in particular, it's important to note that the fears that emerged after the attacks never subsided but instead have morphed and evolved at a rapid rate.

Without a doubt, domestic and international events have intensified, creating increasingly troublesome conundrums over the past fifteen years: Economic woes. Wars. The rise of the incredibly barbaric Islamic State (also known as ISIS). The list goes on.

Theologians and Bible experts are looking at these events and comparing them to what's prophesied in Scripture, coming away with divergent ideas.

Many are asking: Is the world currently living in the last days? I'll be diving deep into that question in this book, exploring what the Bible says about eschatology and why so many biblical experts of goodwill come away with incredibly divergent ideas.

Chapter 1

WHY THERE'S SO MUCH DEBATE OVER THE END TIMES

THERE'S CLEARLY SOMETHING about the topic of the end of days that captivates the imagination and unites the masses, forcing every individual to consider not only his or her own impending fate but also the potential finality of the world as we know it.

Whether the plot centers on a zombie apocalypse or some twist on the Christian Rapture theory, the end times is a subject that has proven time and again to have deep interest with diverse audiences.

But as the masses consume books and films about these dynamics, there's a real-world battle unfolding among Bible experts, pastors, and theologians over eschatology—the study of the final events in the history of the world as recounted in the Judeo-Christian scriptures.

Hardly a discussion about fictional paradigms such as zombies, the ideas and theories surrounding the end times have been around for centuries, with believers looking to prophecies surrounding Jesus's first coming in the Old Testament to assist them in processing what they believe will unfold before, during, and after His second coming.

Before we dive deep into the mix, it's essential to understand that the eschatological debate is one that has led to some fierce divisions among theologians, individual believers, and denominations, as experts construct and advance various end-times scenarios, wrangling over the prophetic timelines and events.

These ideological battles are plentiful. Consider that those who believe in a pre-Tribulation Rapture—the idea that Christians will be taken up to be with the Lord and thus spared from a horrific Tribulation period on the earth—obviously think that their critics in the post-Trib, mid-Trib, and partial-Trib realms are theoretically off base and vice versa.

Other points of contention are the literal or figurative nature of the

Antichrist, Christ's millennial kingdom, and whether or not a major end-of-days battle led by an individual named Gog from the land of Magog will literally unfold in the future. (Don't worry if you're unsure of what all of these elements mean; I'll be diving into each in detail throughout this book.)

The important takeaway at this point is that there are numerous arguments that unfold in the realm of biblical prophecy. While some of these discussions are relatively benign, others can have profound implications on how Christians view the modern world.

— — — — — — —

Bridging the eschatological divide is tough, and it is difficult to understand, on the surface, why so many Christians of goodwill and sound theology end up walking away with stunningly diverse opinions about what's being explicitly said, expressed, or implied in biblical texts.

Bible scholar Dr. Michael Heiser offered a pointed response when I asked him why there are such divisions when it comes to the end times: "There's ambiguity in scripture."[1]

Prophecy expert and author Joel Rosenberg, who is no stranger to the debate, agreed that the seemingly boundless splits over the end times are both difficult and, to an extent, understandable, as "there's a degree of mystery involved."[2]

The choice of language, structure, and the information that is left out of the biblical narrative quite naturally leads to some gaps and, thus, a number of important questions, from which eschatological experts arrive at very different conclusions as they seek to fill the voids.

"[The Old Testament Prophet] Daniel was told that he was not allowed to explain certain things, and there are elements in Daniel and Ezekiel and Revelation that are described with much symbolism," Rosenberg said. "So exactly discerning what those symbols mean can sometimes be challenging."[3]

With those complexities in mind, Rosenberg conceded that good people can—and often do—disagree when it comes to interpretations of end-times scriptures.

But a lack of clarity and the dominance of symbolism aren't the only reasons for the diverse pool of thoughts and ideas about the end times. People many times fall into one of two camps.

Some struggle, for a variety of reasons, to hold to the belief that the end—and Christ's return—will one day come, while, on the flip side, others see a sign at every corner that Jesus's second coming is impending. One camp has essentially become theologically lazy, while the other is overshooting when assessing signs of the end.

"Many people actually anticipate the Lord's return at any moment, and with each new cataclysmic event, they think that the end of the age is upon us," Christian author and radio host Dr. Michael Brown told me. "But many others are skeptical simply because Jesus hasn't returned yet, so why should He come today?"[4]

He continued, "People tend to go one extreme or the other: Jesus is coming any second, meaning that we can hardly plan or think ahead in long-term ways, or Jesus won't come for many more generations, and so we become complacent and lackadaisical."[5]

An even more pervasive and related paradigm, Brown said, is rooted in how consumed people have become with "the things of this world": many are so enthralled that he believes they have simply "lost sight of eternity."[6]

"Why long for the world to come when we're so cozy now?" he rhetorically asked. "And so we think less about the return of Jesus."[7]

Rosenberg said this eschatological contention has created a great division within the Christian church—a travesty, considering his belief that this is the polar opposite of the intended purpose of prophecy to unite believers with information about what's to come during the end days.

— — — — — — — —

We'll spend a great deal of time in this book exploring differences of opinion, but let's pause for a moment to note the one element that most orthodox Christians embrace: the second coming of Jesus. It is from that point, though, that Rosenberg said that "things break down quickly into different camps."[8]

It's no secret that Christian denominations hold divergent and competing norms when it comes to what exactly they teach and preach about the Rapture, the Second Coming, and other eschatological events, leading to a smorgasbord of ideas under the Christian umbrella.

"The Rapture, for example, is not something that the Catholic Church really teaches," Rosenberg said, explaining that this is generally the case among mainline denominations as well.[9]

With ambiguity abounding, end-times author Ron Rhodes believes that these differences all boil down to the way in which Christians approach "interpretive methodology."[10] On the most basic level there are Bible scholars who interpret end-times scriptures literally—and to the contrary there are those who see much of eschatological scripture through allegory and symbolism.

Rhodes said that it is interesting to see such a profound divide considering that many Christians on opposing sides of the interpretive spectrum do agree on so much, including the nature of Jesus, the Trinity, and other related doctrines.

While these theological opponents might use similar hermeneutical, or interpretive, principles, the resulting end-times theologies end up quite different, with Rhodes maintaining that he believes some who mainly see symbolism in end-times prophecy mistakenly assume that nothing can then be taken literally.

It's this mind-set that he patently rejects.

"Just because there are symbols in Revelation, does that mean that every single prophecy must be interpreted allegorically?" he asked. "I don't think so."[11]

Rhodes cited the example of the millennial kingdom that is described in Revelation 20 to highlight the sort of split that develops from differences in interpretive methodology.

"If you believe in a literal approach to interpreting Bible prophecy, then you will hold to a literal millennial kingdom as described in Revelation 20, which is a thousand-year period over which Christ will rule," he explained. "If, however, you take an allegorical approach to interpreting prophecy, then you'll end up believing that that thousand-year period is not a literal time period."[12] In this latter case Rhodes said that adherents would view the thousand-year period as referring to either amillennialism—the rejection of a literal, ten-century-period reign of Jesus—or postmillennialism—the belief that Christ will only return after a period of Christian dominance during which the world converts; this latter period might not necessarily span one thousand literal years.

Rhodes agrees that Revelation and Daniel most certainly include some symbolism, but argues that "propositional statements of prophecy" can also be found. He embarked on a discussion of Ezekiel 36 through 39—which I will expand on in later chapters—to make his point.

"In Ezekiel 36 and 37 there's no symbolism. It just comes right out and says that Israel is going to become a nation again," Rhodes said. "And gathered from many nations around the world, many Jews will be streaming back to the Holy Land."[13]

Furthermore, speaking to what many Bible scholars believe to be an Old Testament prophetic proclamation that extends into the modern era, Rhodes cited Ezekiel 38 and 39 as stating that a coalition made up of Iran, Libya, and other nations around the Black and Caspian Seas will one day join Russia in rising against Israel.

Others, though, look at these same paradigms and come away with vastly different interpretations, which I will also present in detail.

— — — — — — — —

If one holds to the view that the Bible's presentation of prophecy is somewhat ambiguous, one wonders why this would be the case. Weighing in on this very subject, Heiser told me that he doesn't simply believe that biblical prophecy is mysterious by chance, but that it is "deliberately cryptic" in the way that it presents details and information about what's to come.[14]

Heiser explained that prophecies surrounding Jesus in the Old Testament were not as clear before His first coming as they were later on when the details could be analyzed to realize that Christ was the promised Messiah.

"It was deliberately cryptic the first time around," he said of Old Testament prophecies about the Messiah. "And it's going to be deliberately cryptic the second time around."[15]

One of the central debates about the end times centers on the notion that some eschatological theories depend on an intermixing of Old and New Testament verses, leading critics to accuse those who embark on this quest of improperly cobbling together the texts.

But Heiser pointed back to Christ's first coming, likening Old Testament prophecies about the Messiah to a mosaic of sorts that can now be put together to achieve the full picture. It's a portrait and a complete narrative that wasn't fully evident until Jesus came to encompass all of the prophesied characteristics. Heiser sees the same sort of dynamic when it comes to the Bible's outlining of the end times, claiming that it will likely "only be comprehensible after the fact."[16]

"All of the elements that we're familiar with as Christians as far as the role of the Messiah—what He would do, what He would say, where He would go, where He'd be from—all this stuff is just scattered across the Old Testament," Heiser said. "It's never put together. It's fragmented, and it's deliberate."[17]

Had the entire narrative surrounding Christ been explicit, he said that the "powers of darkness" could have simply read the Scriptures and concluded, "Oh boy, better not kill [Jesus]."[18]

Instead, the Scriptures left enough mystery so that these powers still facilitated the salvation plan without even realizing it. "When you read the Gospels, demons and other entities, they know that Jesus is there, and they know who He is. They're the only ones, surprisingly enough, in the Gospels that actually address Jesus as the Son of the Most High," he said. "They know who He is, but they don't know what the plan is."[19]

Heiser continued, "The logical thing is, 'OK, the Messiah's here, the Son of God, so He wouldn't be here unless this was a time when God is going to kick-start the kingdom of God, and that means we're in trouble. What do you think we should do? Let's kill Him. Let's get rid of Him.'"[20]

This was quite obviously the move that needed to happen, though, to facilitate God's plan, which makes exploring prophecies surrounding Christ that much more pertinent when seeking to understand end-times predictions.

"On what basis are we supposed to conclude that it'll be clearer upfront the second time around, as opposed to the first?" Heiser asked. With these ambiguities in mind, he said that he finds it "amusing" when Bible experts and believers speak as though they have definitively solved these riddles.[21]

— — — — — — —

Prophecy expert and author Jeff Kinley—who is among those who take a more literal approach to Scripture—more plainly laid out one of the most pressing challenges that he believes exists when it comes to understanding prophecy: biblical illiteracy.

"Most [Christians] are afraid of touching prophecy, because they think it's only reserved for PhDs or what I call 'PNTs' (prophecy nerd types)," he said. "Like it's written in HTML code or encrypted in hieroglyphics."[22]

What's written in Revelation, he said, can seem "far off, even far-fetched, sci-fi, or irrelevant to our lives today," but he said that he's spent time trying to encourage believers to look past assumptions to see the importance of end-times scriptures.[23]

Another major challenge when it comes to diving into prophecy is "those who scoff at what the Bible says about the end times," according to Kinley, though he said that these critics generally regard other elements of Christianity in the same manner.[24]

The author pointed to 2 Peter 3:1–9 to note that Peter predicted this very scoffing about the end of days, with the apostle explaining in verses 3 through 9 why believers can take refuge in their faith to know that God will act in His own timing:

> Know this first, that there shall come scoffers in the last days who walk after their own lusts, and say, "Where is the promise of His coming? For since the fathers fell asleep, all things have continued as they were since the beginning of the creation." For they willingly ignore that, by the word of God the heavens existed long ago, and the earth was formed standing out of the water and in the water, by which the world that then existed was flooded with water and perished. But by the same word, the heavens and the earth that now exist are being reserved for fire, kept for the Day of Judgment and destruction of the ungodly.
>
> But, beloved, do not be ignorant of this one thing, that with the Lord one day is as a thousand years, and a thousand years as one day. The Lord is not slow concerning His promise, as some count slowness. But He is patient with us, because He does not want any to perish, but all to come to repentance.

With Peter's words in mind, Kinley argues that mockery of prophecy has had an impact on "weak and biblically uninformed believers," calling for "sound, solid, balanced teaching" on the subject.[25]

As you'll see throughout this book, though, it's not just attacks coming from nonbelievers who push back at various interpretations of end-times scriptures. Other Christians too have taken aim at literal approaches to eschatology, believing that their fellow Bible scholars and pastors have crossed the line by seeing everything through too rigid and futuristic of a lens.

Some have fervently spoken out against the Rapture, among other end-times interpretations, while others have rejected the idea that there are still-unfulfilled end-times verses in the Old Testament, believing that what's presented in Ezekiel, among other texts, has already come to fruition.

The debate over the end times runs the gamut. On rare occasions there have also been instances in which faith leaders have named proposed dates for specific end-times events, including Jesus's antici-pated second coming—proclamations that have never come to fruition and that nearly every individual interviewed for this book blasted as inappropriate.

In fact, Ed Hindson, an evangelist and a dean at Liberty University, credited date setting for, at least in part, helping to fuel both debate and skepticism over Bible prophecy, saying that those partaking have "over speculated" and "over sensationalized" and, in turn, have pro-foundly harmed the discussion.[26]

"[When] these things do not come true, that creates a push back," Hindson said. "Anytime there's an excessive amount of speculation that turns out to be false, there tends to be a reaction about the whole idea of trying to understand what the Bible projects about the future."[27]

And while most Christians do not engage in date setting, Kinley added that there are some who are guilty of sensationalism and over-speculation, agreeing that this has posed some real challenges to the discussion over prophecy.

"Where I really have a problem is when authors [and] speakers capi-talize on people's fears regarding the end times, even manipulating their thoughts and emotions by going way beyond what Scripture actually says," Kinley said.[28]

He said that there's nothing wrong with "informed speculation," but that good writers are well aware that words can be powerful—and that it is dangerous to use them to lead people to the wrong conclusions about Scripture.

"Crafting communication in a way that leads someone to fear or unbiblical speculation is a form of abuse and literary irresponsibility in my mind," he said.[29]

When Kinley composes his books and writings on the end times, he said that his goal is to balance a respect for the Bible and the reader with the tough task of delving into incredibly complex subject matter.

"My objective is to maintain a high sense of integrity when dealing with a volatile subject like prophecy," Kinley said, explaining that he allows the Bible to be his guide as he ensures that his tone is aligned with what the text proclaims. "Where I believe Scripture is clear and authoritative, I want to be equally clear and confident," he said. "But when I cross over into the 'not yet known,' I strive to provide biblically informed answers without necessarily having to be definitive."[30]

Left Behind coauthor Tim LaHaye, who, like many others interviewed for this book, embraces a premillennial, pre-Tribulation Rapture worldview, said that he believes that confusion surrounding the end times is rooted in the notion that many people simply "don't know anything about Bible prophecy."[31]

"Their pastor doesn't teach it, or he teaches the wrong view of interpretation of prophecy and takes it spiritually or allegorically or some other way…instead of taking it literally," he said. "They can sit for fifty years or a lifetime under the preaching of somebody who doesn't take prophecy literally and they'll never understand it." LaHaye concluded, "It's one of the sad features of our times."[32]

It is clear that there are a plethora of reasons why there is so much debate over the end times, with rhetoric and discussion sometimes getting heated, particularly when it comes to the Rapture and the idea that there are Old Testament verses that directly applied to the creation of modern-day Israel in 1948, as well as other still-unfulfilled events.

Pastor Greg Laurie, founder of the Harvest Crusades and pastor of Harvest Christian Fellowship in Riverside, California, is careful to note that, though he doesn't understand why some theologians reject the notion that there are still unfulfilled prophecies in the Old Testament, he sees some important points of unity.

"I don't know why people hold that view, but I certainly understand that you can hold that view and clearly obviously be a Christian," Laurie, who has been teaching and studying prophecy for four decades, told me.[33]

He described the belief that some Old Testament prophecies have yet to come—a paradigm that he embraces—as a "nonessential" when it comes to salvation, though he said that one's view on the end times will most certainly impact how he or she sees a variety of issues in life. Consider, for instance, that one's belief about whether modern-day Israel is the result of prophecy or the consequence of a mere political whim would likely impact how the country is viewed in both a theological and a political sense.

"By nonessential, I mean your views on eschatology do not determine if you will get into heaven or not," he said. "That's based on your belief in Christ and turning from your sins and following Him, so these are nonessential, but they are important." In the end, he said that the main focus for all Christians should be "that Christ is coming and could come at any time."[34]

He also warned of the danger of Christians swinging "too far in either direction" when it comes to either ignoring prophecy entirely or, on the flip side, focusing too heavily on it. The former can lead people to miss the blessings that can come from studying Revelation, Laurie said.

"There's a blessing when we understand it," he said of prophecy, later adding, "There is a spiritually purifying effect on the Christian when they study and understand Bible prophecy."[35]

Mirroring what others said of the subject, Laurie added that too heavy of a focus could lead people to overemphasize eschatology, which runs the risk of becoming spiritually unhealthy if taken to the level of "date setting or something that even appears to be date setting."[36]

Regardless of uncertainties and where people land in the eschatological debate, though, Rhodes encouraged believers to educate themselves on matters surrounding the end times and to try come down on one side or the other.

Next, we'll look at the Rapture—perhaps the most contested and debated feature of eschatology.

Chapter 2

THE RAPTURE AND WHETHER IT'S BIBLICAL

THE BELIEF THAT God will supernaturally rescue Christians from chaos and destruction before the end times kicks into high gear is widely accepted in many modern-day Evangelical circles—but not everyone agrees that the Rapture is a biblical slam dunk.

Some theologians and pastors, in fact, flatly reject the idea that Jesus will usher believers off of the earth before a so-called "Tribulation period," though the vast majority of Christians embrace the notion of a still-unfulfilled event known as the Second Coming—the unknown moment in which Christ is expected to return.

However, surveys have shown that many Evangelical believers and leaders across the globe believe that the Rapture is a definitive event that can be found in Scripture, positing that it will take place at some undetermined future time.[1] That said, the theory also has many vocal critics who dismiss it as patently inaccurate.

The Rapture battle can often be a heated one, but biblical experts like Dr. Ron Rhodes, who embraces a pre-Tribulation Rapture, believe that acceptance or rejection of the Rapture has little to do with a validation or condemnation of one's overarching faith in Christ.

"You have a lot of Christians who have different opinions on a lot of this...and so I think it's a good thing to come to firm conclusions," he said. "But I don't think we need to have on boxing gloves."[2]

That's a sentiment that many theologians have embraced, regardless of where they stand on the issue. This isn't to say, though, that Rapture proponents don't believe that embracing the idea of a mass Christian exodus is theologically important. Author Jeff Kinley noted in his book *Wake the Bride* that he believes it's essential to fully understand this dynamic, especially for anyone who is alive when the end times ramp up. Summarizing why he believes exploring the Rapture is important, Kinley wrote, "If the events depicted in Revelation 6–19 are still future, and if there is no Rapture, then believers are destined to endure the horrible judgments and plagues God sends upon the earth during the seven-year period known as the Great Tribulation."[3] Thus, he concluded that the Rapture isn't something to simply dismiss or take lightly.

— — — — — — — —

Before we move deeper into the heart of the debate, let's take a brief look at the array of divergent beliefs surrounding the Rapture. These theories generally differ based on the chronology surrounding the Tribulation period, which end-times expert Mark Hitchcock described as a "time of trouble"[4] that will last seven years and that will culminate with Christ's second coming. (There's a fair amount of debate about the Tribulation as well, as you'll learn.)

Many biblical scholars consider the *pre-Tribulation Rapture theory* to be the predominant paradigm among modern-day Evangelicals. As I've said, not everyone embraces this theory, as the general debate over the Rapture is much broader and more complex than simply boiling it down to who accepts and rejects that single paradigm. In fact, there are at least five overarching viewpoints involving the Rapture.

- The pre-Tribulation Rapture theory holds that, before many of the end-times events recounted in the Book of Revelation kick up into high gear, genuine Bible-believers will simultaneously ascend from the earth, being divinely saved from unimaginable terrors that will follow. Under these parameters, those who do not believe in Jesus Christ as their personal Savior, at that time, will be "left behind" to cope with the Tribulation period that is to come—a desperate time frame that will likely be anything but pleasant. Proponents generally believe that the Tribulation period will last seven years before Christ's earthy reign begins.[5]

- There's also the *post-Tribulation Rapture theory*, in which adherents believe that Christians will remain on the earth through the Tribulation period but will be protected or shielded from the chaos unfolding around them.[6]

- A third theory adopts a middle-range approach known as the *mid-Tribulation Rapture theory*, which holds that Christians will be taken up in the Rapture in the middle of the seven-year Tribulation period.

- The theological constructs don't end there, as there is a *pre-wrath theory*, in which the Rapture happens near the end of the Tribulation period, but before God's wrath.

- There is also the *partial-Rapture theory*, in which only some believers will be raptured.

— — — — — — — —

Before we get into the debate over specific ideas surrounding the Rapture, it's probably a good idea to explain where the notion of a seven-year Tribulation actually originates—an idea that we will expand on in a subsequent chapter. What follows is merely an introduction to help readers understand the theology behind the construct.

Some Bible experts believe that the concept of the seven-year Tribulation period can be seen in the Old Testament in Daniel 9:24–27—the same chapter in which prophecy gurus believe that Daniel foretold the coming of a future Antichrist.

It is in verse 27 that the term "one week" is taken to mean that a tribulation will unfold for seven years, during which some believe that the Antichrist will "make a firm covenant with many for one week." Read verses 24 through 27 below:

> Seventy weeks have been determined for your people and upon your holy city, to finish the transgression, and to make an end of sins, and to make atonement for iniquity, and to bring in everlasting righteousness, and to seal up the vision and prophecy, and to anoint the Most Holy Place.
>
> Know therefore and understand that from the going forth of the command to restore and to rebuild Jerusalem until the Prince Messiah shall be seven weeks, and sixty-two weeks. It

shall be built again, with plaza and moat, even in times of trouble. After the sixty-two weeks Messiah shall be cut off and shall have nothing. And the troops of the prince who shall come shall destroy the city and the sanctuary. The end of it shall come with a flood. And until the end of the war desolations are determined. And he shall make a firm covenant with many for one week. But in the middle of the week he shall cause the sacrifice and the offering to cease. And on the wing of abominations shall come one who makes desolate, until the decreed destruction is poured out on the desolator.

The idea is that the Antichrist will begin to act out against Israel in the middle of the seven years (at the three-and-a-half-year mark). There are a variety of theories about what will unfold during the seven-year Tribulation period, with a mixture of perspectives about different forms of wrath being brought about by Satan, mankind, and God; one's view on the Rapture directly impacts how these forces take form.

Prophecy expert Mark Hitchcock explained that the Tribulation period—and specifically the time in which God's wrath begins—might be looked at very differently, depending on how individuals view the timeline sequence of the Rapture.

"A pre-Triber would say, 'Look, the whole seventieth week of Daniel, the whole tribulation period—that whole period's wrath.' A mid-Triber would say, 'No, only the last half is God's wrath, and the first half is the wrath of man, the wrath of Satan—a lot of bad stuff happening, but it's not God's wrath.'" Meanwhile, he said that post-Tribers would say that the wrath of God is at the end of the tribulation period. "I would say the whole Tribulation's wrath," Hitchcock said, though he called the overarching debate a "legitimate disagreement."[7]

— — — — — — — —

As we look across the landscape, opinions on the matter certainly aren't in short supply; critics regularly take aim at the seemingly more popular and prevalent pre-Tribulation theory.

Christian philosopher William Lane Craig once made no bones about his position in an interview with *Charisma News*, calling the

Rapture "made up" and detailing how he believes it became such a firm fixture in Evangelical theology.[8]

"The rapture was made up by someone in the 1800s, and the story caught on among some groups who still believe it today," he said. "The simple truth is that it is not biblical, nor was it ever the historic position of the Christian church."[9]

Craig said that the Rapture was an idea that emerged in 1827 from an Irish preacher named John Darby.[10] The preacher had reignited the belief in premillennialism at the time—the notion that Christ will return before a literal thousand-year earthly reign.[11] Critics charge that Darby developed a unique form of premillennialism, known as dispensationalism—the belief that the Bible teaches about two groups of people who have a relationship with the Almighty: the nation of Israel and the Christian church.[12] Darby also developed and touted the idea of the Rapture.

Dispensationalists do not believe that the Christian church has "replaced" Israel in the Scriptures and see the two groups as being separate entities. They believe that promises from God in the Bible are still set to come to fruition for Israel specifically—a theme that we will repeatedly explore throughout this book.[13] Adherents also see the Bible as being divided into seven dispensations—or periods of time, which we'll also cover in a later chapter.

When it comes to the Rapture, Craig believes that Darby's views were simply inaccurate and that they ended up gaining precedence and widespread acceptance after being embedded in the Scofield Reference Bible, a popular study Bible that gained precedence in the early twentieth century.[14]

"I would say that there is no such thing as the Rapture and so when it occurs is a non-question," Craig told me in an interview for this book. "I would just say that what the New Testament looks forward to is the personal, bodily return of Christ to bring about the end of human history—and that that is an actual future event that will take place."[15]

Craig believes that many of the ideas surrounding the Rapture are essentially read into the biblical text and are not fervently laid out or even remotely implied in the Scriptures, as many Evangelicals contend.

As for those who he believes have it wrong, Craig said that "the average person [is] misreading the Thessalonian letters of Paul," contending that these books are being explored out of context and with a Rapture framework already in mind. "If you come to it with this Rapture framework, one can understand how you could read 1 and 2 Thessalonians in that light," Craig said.[16]

The Christian philosopher urged people to truly step back and consider that Paul—the author of 1 and 2 Thessalonians—got his doctrine about the return of Christ and the end times from Jesus Himself.

"Paul was heir to Jesus's own teachings. It's the teachings of Jesus that need to provide the context for understanding what Paul writes," Craig said. "When you take Jesus's teachings as primary, then it's very evident from, for example Jesus's Olivet Discourse…that Jesus never anticipated this sort of preliminary return prior to His final, decisive return as the Son of Man to judge humankind."[17] It is in Matthew 24 that Jesus speaks about the impending destruction of the temple as well as the end of days, with Craig noting that the idea of a Rapture simply isn't referenced by Christ in that chapter.

Craig isn't alone in his dismissal of the Rapture, as Hank Hanegraaff, a noted Bible expert, agrees that it simply isn't a biblical construct. Hanegraaff, who expressed his belief in Christ's second coming in a past interview with me, took great care to differentiate that paradigm from the Rapture.

"Well, the Bible says…that Jesus is going to appear a second time," he said. "Those who have lived on the planet…Jesus said, do not be amazed by this…there will be the ultimate judgment that takes place, which those who have a relationship with God in this time-space continuum are given that relationship in eternity and those who did not want a relationship will have that validated in eternity as well."[18]

In discussions for this book, Hanegraaff, like Craig, made it clear that he doesn't see Scripture as backing any sort of a pre-Tribulation Rapture or other end-times ideas embraced by Rapture enthusiasts and dispensationalists; Hanegraaff claims that many people are simply "not taking seriously the art and science of biblical interpretation."[19]

"From my vantage point there's nothing in the Scripture that in any way suggests a pre-Tribulation Rapture, or a thousand-year semi-golden age with a rebuilt temple and reinstituted temple sacrifices," he said. "All of that is an imposition on the biblical text, as opposed to reading the Bible for all it's worth."[20]

Hanegraaff said that he believes Christians can definitively expect Jesus's second coming—and not the Rapture—to be the next event on the prophetic calendar.

"When that happens, the universe itself, which groans in travail, according to Paul in Romans chapter 8, will be liberated from its bondage to decay," he said. "We'll be resurrected, immortal, imperishable, incorruptible. The problem of sin and Satan will forever have been resolved, and we will enter into the eternal state."[21]

Dr. Michael Heiser, who said that he embraces no official system but is closest to historic premillennialism, took a bit of a gentler approach to the Rapture debate, telling me that he would never say that "there's no possibility, scripturally…for a Rapture," though he called it the "least likely scenario.…As far as the Rapture goes, I think it's a possibility that I think it's on the lower end of the probability spectrum," Heiser said.[22]

But some, like Rhodes, disagree with overt dismissals from Hanegraaff, Craig, and others. While he is well versed in the pre-, post-, and mid-Tribulation theories, Rhodes personally believes that the Bible fully backs the pre-Tribulation paradigm—and that many contemporary events are actually quite intertwined and intermingled with biblical prophecy about the end times to come.

For instance, Rhodes believes that increasing chaos in the Middle East is a dynamic that could indicate that the end is getting closer.

"First of all, I believe that the days we are living in, we are witnessing certain signs of the times," Rhodes once told me in an interview for TheBlaze. "The time of the end is at least drawing near and among those signs of the times would include the rebirth of Israel, which took place in 1948." He continued, "But there's other things we've witnessed—the escalation of apostasy in the church, there's a move toward globalism, a continued move toward a cashless society." Rhodes believes that Israel will become a "thorn in the world in the end" and that the Rapture could come not long after that.[23]

It should be noted that the word *Rapture* isn't in the Bible, though others, like Kinley, would argue that the concept is deeply embedded in the text.

In his book *Wake the Bride* Kinley wrote that there are plenty of other words that the Bible also never mentions, but that are still embraced by the Christian world: Bible, Trinity, missions, Great Commission, incarnation, and monotheism.[24]

Experts like Rhodes and Kinley would also argue that there are most certainly scriptures that reference the Rapture event. Here are some key verses that they would point to:

- "Two will be in the field; one will be taken, and the other left. Two women will be grinding at the mill; one will be taken, and the other left" (Matt. 24:40–41).

- "In a moment, in the twinkling of an eye, at the last trumpet, for the trumpet will sound, the dead will be raised incorruptible, and we shall be changed. For this corruptible will put on incorruption, and this mortal will put on immortality. When this corruptible will have put on incorruption, and this mortal will have put on immortality, then the saying that is written shall come to pass: 'Death is swallowed up in victory'" (1 Cor. 15:52–54).

- "But I would not have you ignorant, brothers, concerning those who are asleep, that you may not grieve as others who have no hope. For if we believe that Jesus died and arose again, so God will bring with Him those who sleep in Jesus. For this we say to you by the word of the Lord, that we who are alive and remain until the coming of the Lord will not precede those who are asleep. For the Lord Himself will descend from heaven with a shout, with the voice of the archangel, and with the trumpet call of God. And the dead in Christ will rise first. Then we who are alive and remain shall be caught up together with them in the clouds to meet the Lord in the air. And so we shall be forever with the Lord. Therefore comfort one another with these words" (1 Thess. 4:13–18).

- "Because you have kept My word of patience, I also will keep you from the hour of temptation which shall come upon the entire world, to test those who dwell on the earth" (Rev. 3:10).

Again, it is the absence of the word *Rapture* and the claim that a detailed view of the concept is not found in the text—notably in the Book of Revelation—that leaves philosophers like Craig highly critical. And considering that the Bible's final book recounts the end of days, Craig finds that dearth of material quite telling.

"[Revelation] won't be of any help to you in finding a Rapture," he said. "That's sort of interesting that it's got things in there like Tribulation and Millennium...but there's no Rapture doctrine in the Book of Revelation." Concluding his views on the matter, Craig reiterated: "It's just not anywhere in the New Testament as far as I can tell."[25]

But Kinley, who devoted two chapters to this very subject in *Wake the Bride*, rejected these arguments and urged people to think deeper about the implications surrounding the Rapture debate.

He argues that the removal of Christians before God's outpouring of wrath against "unbelieving humanity" will be a reality, explaining that he believes exempting Christians from this simply makes sense.

Kinley was also careful to note that God never promised that He would exempt all Christians from every form of suffering. But since the Tribulation period is specifically about addressing unbelief, he believes that the "snatching up" of believers is a biblical reality.

"As you look at the pattern of Scripture, we see four things that are happening that tell us that there is a rapture event coming, and I think one of them is just the pattern of deliverance and rescue throughout scripture, specifically in the Old Testament. God never promises to save his people from tribulation or hard times as it relates to the world...however, when God himself lowers his wrath and his fury on the Earth, his pattern has been to remove the righteous prior to that event."[26]

Kinley continued, "He did it, of course, with Noah before the flood. He did it with Lot in Sodom and Gomorrah, and he did it with Rahab with the battle of Jericho before he destroyed that town."[27]

Beyond these arguments, though, Kinley pointedly responded to claims that the Rapture is a theological belief that emerged in the 1800s and should thus be disregarded. He noted that it has taken some Christian ideas centuries to take root and said that this might be what happened with Rapture theology, presenting the theory that, as time progressed, so did eschatological understanding.

Some theologians most certainly accept the notion that the Rapture was always the intended interpretation, but that revelation was progressive in nature and took time to take root; others insist that the Rapture is a relatively new idea that holds little merit.

The debate will likely never be settled, as the lack of clarity has led to a variety of perspectives on the matter. Next, we'll dive a bit deeper into the pre-Tribulation view on the Rapture, which appears to be among the more popular ideas in modern-day evangelicalism.

Chapter 3

DIGGING DEEPER: PRE-TRIBULATION RAPTURE THEORY

ANY MODERN-DAY BIBLE experts embrace a so-called "doctrine of imminence"—a paradigm in which they believe that Jesus could return "at any moment in history" to Rapture Christians, according to prophecy expert Joel Rosenberg.[1]

Citing this doctrine, Rosenberg said, "The church is really called to live as though the coming of Christ—for us, to take us—could happen at any moment."[2]

Many pre-Tribulation theorists believe that the next event in God's prophetic timeline will likely be the Rapture—an event in which Christ will return in the clouds to snatch up Christians before the Tribulation begins, thus sparing believers from the anticipated chaos that will follow. Numerous Bible prophecy experts interviewed for this book, such as Mark Hitchcock, Ed Hindson, Jeff Kinley, and Joel Rosenberg, among others, said that they believe the Rapture will likely be the next eschatological event to unfold.

"The next event on God's prophetic calendar is the Rapture…it's the catching away of believers in Jesus Christ," Hitchcock explained. "The dead will be raised and their spirits will be reunited with their bodies, and those who are alive and remain will be caught up to meet the Lord in the air."[3]

Rosenberg shared that viewpoint, but offered a caveat about the potential dangers surrounding drafting and advancing definitive end-times timelines: "They can be tough" and can run the risk of being inaccurate.[4]

"The danger is that a person's going to think, 'Well, that's exactly the way it has to be,' rather than the way *we think* it's going to be, based on as much as we can understand from Old and New Testament prophecies," Rosenberg cautioned.[5]

He and others are careful in how they craft and market their end-times theories; these prophecy experts have painstakingly thought through each paradigm, dissecting and trusting Scripture to guide their interpretive journey. While their theological opponents—who have also looked to the Bible with equal respect and discernment—reject the notion of a pre-Tribulation Rapture, Rosenberg and others believe that not only will the mass exodus unfold, but also that it will end up being a "world-changing event"[6] with monumental impact.

"My end-times scenario starts with the Rapture, which ends this church age that we live in now," Hitchcock told me. "After that, in some point of time the Tribulation period will begin. This Antichrist figure—or world leader—will begin to emerge."[7]

Hindson, who explained that the church age began at Pentecost and corroborated Hitchcock's belief that it will end with the Rapture, also agreed with Rosenberg that uncertainty abounds when it comes to specific prophetic timelines.

As for the Rapture and emergence of the Antichrist, pre-Tribulationists believe that it will come at an unexpected time during which the world will be looking for someone to usher in peace and stability, with the chaos and confusion that is brought by the Rapture helping to further set the stage for what's to follow.

— — — — — — — —

As stated, among the underpinnings of pre-Tribulation theology is the idea that God will spare believers from a seven-year Tribulation period by snatching them up to heaven. Many see this concept being spoken about in 1 Thessalonians 4:16–17, when Paul writes that the dead will rise first and that living Christians "shall be caught up together with them in the clouds to meet the Lord in the air."

Hitchcock said that anyone questioning the existence of the Rapture is mistaken, citing the original Greek for the portion of Scripture that says that people will be "caught up" and explaining that the word—*harpazo*—means "to be snatched or seized."[8]

Bible expert Ron Rhodes also pointed to 1 Thessalonians 1:9–10 and 1 Thessalonians 5:9, which he said highlight a promise that God will deliver the church from the Tribulation, including His coming wrath. The former proclaims that Jesus "delivered us from the wrath to come," with the latter reading, "For God has not appointed us to wrath, but to obtain salvation by our Lord Jesus Christ." It is the collective reading of these verses that has many Bible experts advancing the notion of a Rapture that precludes Christians from facing the Tribulation period.

Revelation 16, of course, recounts a situation in which God's wrath will be poured out on the earth. (It's a scenario that is presented throughout Revelation with mentions of the seven seals, seven trumpets, and seven bowls.) Revelation 16:1–4, which focuses on the bowls, provides a partial overview of the wrath:

> Then I heard a loud voice from the temple saying to the seven angels, "Go, pour out the bowls of the wrath of God on the earth." The first went and poured out his bowl on the earth, and foul and grievous sores came on the men who had the mark of the beast and those who worshipped his image. The second angel poured out his bowl on the sea. It became like the blood of a dead man, and every living creature in the sea died. The third angel poured out his bowl on the rivers and springs of water, and they became blood.

As for the concept of believers being "caught up," Hitchcock said that the concept of a Rapture that consists of Christians meeting God in the air shouldn't be problematic or controversial, but did say that there's a legitimate battle over the timing of the Rapture, as not everyone believes that it will precede the Tribulation.

"To say you don't believe in the Rapture is denying what Scripture says," Hitchcock said. "What you can deny is the timing of it."[9]

Rhodes echoed that sentiment, saying that, in his mind, the debate isn't over whether one should believe in a Rapture that consists of Christians being caught up, but instead it's appropriate to question when it will happen.

"Most Christians will believe in some form of a Rapture," Rhodes said.[10] Hindson also affirms that there will be a "dramatic removal of the church at some point" based on his reading of 1 Thessalonians 4.[11]

Despite fierce debate over whether Jesus will return to rescue Christians before the Tribulation begins or before His second coming, few theologians I spoke with felt that acceptance or rejection of the Rapture is a "salvation issue," per se.

That said, for pre-Tribulationists the Rapture's placement in the eschatological timeline is anything but benign; it is part of a grander narrative that encompasses their assumptions about the order of end-times events and, eventually, the conclusion of the world, as we know it.

— — — — — — —

Even among pre-Tribulationists there are questions about the placement of other end-times events. For instance, if and when believers are raptured, when does the Tribulation period, complete with its great troubles, begin? How long is it until the Antichrist rises to power?

Hindson believes that the time frame won't be very long.

"Believers are always left with the sense of the imminent coming of Christ as a real potential, but after the Rapture I would envision that the time of tribulation would begin very quickly," Hindson said.[12]

He differentiated the Rapture from the Second Coming by specifically noting that 1 Thessalonians 4 references Jesus coming in the clouds and Christians being "caught up in the air to meet Him"—language that he said seems different from the concept of the Second Coming, also known as Christ's return. "The return is when the believers return with Him to the earth at the battle of Armageddon and establish His kingdom on earth literally," Hindson said.[13]

Given the complexity of the Rapture debate, it's essential to note that the disagreement does not end with the battle over the Rapture, with additional bickering continuing to rage over what follows the Tribulation.

We'll tackle that in subsequent chapters, but, for now, here's how Hitchcock recaps what he believes will happen after this period of struggle: "[Jesus is] going to set up His kingdom on the Earth, one-thousand-year reign," he explained. "And eventually that thousand-year reign will give way to the eternal kingdom of God."[14]

Hindson described the current dynamic—the time in which we live—as a "spiritual kingdom" in which "Jesus rules from heaven in the hearts of believers," and said that he believes that there won't be a literal, theocratic kingdom until Christ's return.[15]

Jesus's second coming is one of the cornerstone beliefs that almost every Christian on the planet embraces, regardless of his or her stance on the time sequence or reality of the Rapture.

Throughout the ages the question has consistently been: When will Jesus return for the Second Coming? The answer—at least based on the Bible—is that no one but the Lord Himself knows, but that a return is indeed impending.

This is the sentiment that Rosenberg invoked in pointing back to the doctrine of imminence to highlight his belief that the Rapture can unfold at any moment. As for the Second Coming, though, he believes that it won't happen until after a seven-year Tribulation period, which follows the Rapture.

"Jesus's second coming to establish His kingdom on earth, to reign from Jerusalem, to defeat evil—that's known as the Second Coming. That can't happen at any moment," he said. "That can only happen after seven years of what is commonly referred to by Christians as the Tribulation, the seven worst years of evil and natural disasters and war and famine in the history of mankind."[16]

So, in theory, Rosenberg said that the Second Coming is always at least seven years away at any given moment—that is, until the Rapture unfolds, at which point many Bible scholars believe that the seven-year countdown will likely begin.

It's important to go back for a moment to pre-Tribulationists' belief that the Rapture is most likely the next event on the prophetic time-table. Rosenberg said that he believes this is likely the case, though he isn't dogmatic about it.

"The doctrine of imminence doesn't say that no other prophetic event will happen before the Rapture," he explained. "It just says that no other prophetic event absolutely must happen before the Rapture."[17]

That's an important distinction, Rosenberg argued, explaining that the reemergence of Israel precluded the Rapture, though some Bible scholars would have never expected that the Jews would return to their homeland in the centuries leading up to 1948.

"We now have seen the rebirth of the state of Israel and the ingathering of the Jewish people, and it's all happened prior to the Rapture," Rosenberg said. "We also see Matthew 24 coming to pass—wars, rumors of wars, false messiahs, natural disasters, apostasy in the church."[18]

Here, Rosenberg was speaking about Jesus's words in Matthew 24,

in which Christ spoke about the destruction of the temple as well as
the coming signs of the end times. Verses 4 through 8 read:

> Jesus answered them, "Take heed that no one deceives you.
> For many will come in My name, saying, 'I am the Christ,'
> and will deceive many. You will hear of wars and rumors of
> wars. See that you are not troubled. For all these things must
> happen, but the end is not yet. For nation will rise against
> nation, and kingdom against kingdom. There will be famines,
> epidemics, and earthquakes in various places. All these are
> the beginning of sorrows."

Rosenberg said that a series of things are happening now that he
believes were prophesied in that section of Scripture, and yet the
Rapture still hasn't unfolded, corroborating his view that other events
could unfold before the Rapture.

"We live in a state of expectation," Rosenberg said.[19]

Mirroring Rosenberg's views on Israel, others, like Kinley, have also
noted that prophecy is filled with mystery and that the answers and
clues often emerge slowly and over a long period of time.

The *Wake the Bride* author wrote, "Virtually no one could have
envisioned the rebirth of Israel, and the return of the Jews worldwide
to the land God had previously given to them" even a few hundred
years ago. Yet, this is now standing out to many as a realization of
prophecy.[20]

No one knows for sure the future order of eschatological events,
and it's clear that many believers have been surprised by world events
that have seemingly taken the fulfillment of prophecy in unexpected
directions.

While many pre-Tribulation Rapture enthusiasts believe that the
next key event will be the "taking up" of believers, there are many
others who embrace a Rapture event that is situated quite differently
in the prophetic time sequence. In the next chapter we'll explore these
ideas more deeply.

Chapter 4

OTHER IDEAS ABOUT THE RAPTURE

NOT EVERYONE IS convinced that the Rapture is the next major event on God's prophetic timeline. Some—like *Bible Answer Man*'s Hank Hanegraaff—patently reject the notion of a "taking away" of believers.

Hanegraaff's dismissal of the pre-Tribulation Rapture comes along with his push back against many of the other end-times scenarios that have been proposed by dispensationalists. He opts for a much simpler version of eschatological events. When I asked if his perspective is that Jesus simply returns in the Second Coming before the creation of a new heaven and a new earth, Hanegraaff made it clear where he stands.

"That's not my perspective. That's what the Scripture says, and there's no warrant whatsoever—where does anyone find biblical warrant for a pre-Tribulational Rapture?" he rhetorically asked. "You have to impose that on the difficult text."[1]

Hanegraaff specifically pointed to 1 Thessalonians 4:16–17, which he said is the "seminal text for a pre-Tribulational Rapture," to break down exactly how and why he believes those Scriptures—which I extensively highlighted in the previous chapters—are being improperly interpreted.[2]

"If you actually read that passage, you find out that it has nothing to do with a pre-Tribulational rapture," he said. "There's nothing in the passage whatsoever that suggests that Jesus Christ comes back, hovers in midair, and then returns to heaven with a raptured church. That's simply imposed on the biblical text."[3]

A closer reading, Hanegraaff said, shows that 1 Thessalonians 4 is actually a "glorious passage on the hope of resurrection," that should bring great comfort to Christians.[4]

"It's a great and glorious passage on the hope of resurrection. What Paul is saying is we do not grieve like the rest of men who have no hope," he explained. "Why? Because we believe that Jesus died and rose again, and therefore, we believe that God will bring with Jesus those who have fallen asleep in Him."[5] Rather than grieving like the rest of humanity, Hanegraaff said that believers can have confidence in resurrection for lost loved ones, as he said that these verses tell us that restoration will one day come for those in the Lord.

Hanegraaff is just one of the many critics who take aim at the pre-Tribulational Rapture theory, as others, like author Dr. Michael Brown, also remain quite skeptical. While Brown came to faith forty-four years ago in a church that embraced the pre-Tribulational paradigm, he told me that he eventually came to reject it.

"It is not a doctrine taught clearly anytime in church history before the 1800s, and no one would deduce it from Scripture without outside help," he said. "Jesus told us that in this world we would have tribulation [John 16:33], and many passages in the New Testament point to us being here right until the end."[6]

In addition to the pre-Tribulation Rapture, there are at least four other ideas about when and how the "taking up" of believers could potentially unfold.

Let's begin with the post-Tribulation Rapture, which John Piper, a popular pastor and chancellor of Bethlehem College and Seminary in Minneapolis, Minnesota, defined as "the view that the rapture and the glorious second coming are part of one simultaneous event." He continued, "The saints rise to meet the Lord in the air and accompany him back as the rightful king of the earth."[7]

Post-Tribulationists—contrary to their pre-Tribulationist counterparts—believe that Christians alive when the end times ramp up will not be spared from the Tribulation period and will, instead, go through it right along with nonbelievers.

Piper made a case for his belief in a post-Tribulation Rapture in a brief position paper on his website DesiringGod.org, where he dove into the scriptures that are most prevalently linked to Rapture theology.

He started by looking at the language of 1 Thessalonians 4:17, particularly the word *apantesin*, which is the Greek word for "meeting," noting that this same word is also used in Matthew 25:6 and Acts 28:15.

"In both places it refers to a meeting in which people go out to meet a dignitary and then accompany him in to the place from which they came out," he wrote.[8]

Piper argues that the form of "meeting" here is one in which believers meet Jesus in the air and then welcome Him to reign on earth, explaining the idea that Paul did not intend to reference a separate event from the Second Coming.

The pastor went on to ponder why Paul wouldn't have explicitly said in 2 Thessalonians 2 that Christians won't have to worry about the Tribulation if, indeed, they would be spared from those events. Likewise he pointed to Matthew 24, Mark 13, and Luke 21, in which Christ describes the end times, to note that a Rapture separate from the Second Coming is not mentioned. In fact, Piper believes that the chapters essentially make it sound as though believers will be present when the signs that Christ details come to fruition.

And while pre-Tribulationists generally look to Revelation 3:10 as evidence that their theory holds sway, Piper has an interpretation of his own that he believes can actually help to underpin and corroborate a post-Tribulation Rapture.

As highlighted earlier, that verse reads, "Because you have kept My word of patience, I also will keep you from the hour of temptation which shall come upon the entire world, to test those who dwell on the earth." Piper wrote that the part about Christ keeping people from "the hour of temptation" (translated as "the hour of testing" in the NAS) might not indicate a pre-Tribulation Rapture.

"To 'be kept for [sic] the hour of testing' is not necessarily to be taken out of the world during this hour, and thus spared suffering," he wrote. "Compare Gal. 1:4 and Jesus' prayer for his disciples in John 17:15 where to 'keep from' does not mean physical removal. And notice the inevitability of martyrdom in Rev. 6:9–11. The promise is to be guarded from the hour in the sense of being guarded from the demoralizing forces of that hour."[9]

Pre-Tribulation adherents claim, though, that God has a pattern of rescuing those devoted to Him, as Rhodes explained in *The 8 Great Debates of Bible Prophecy*; on the flip side, the Bible also says that believers will experience challenges and "tribulations" in life.[10] That said, Rhodes, like Kinley, rejects a post-Tribulation Rapture and differentiates the forms of Tribulation when it comes to end-times paradigms.

Rhodes said that post-Tribulationists would also point to Revelation 20:4–6 to support their view, holding that believers who die during the Tribulation come back to life just before the Millennium and reign with Jesus. Those verses read:

> I saw thrones, and they sat on them, and the authority to judge was given to them. And I saw the souls of those who had been beheaded for their witness of Jesus and for the word of God. They had not worshipped the beast or his image, and had not received his mark on their foreheads or on their hands. They came to life and reigned with Christ for a thousand years. The rest of the dead did not come to life until the thousand years were ended. This is the first resurrection. Blessed and holy is he who takes part in the first resurrection. Over these the second death has no power, but they shall be priests of God and of Christ and shall reign with Him a thousand years.

In his extensive work *Christian Theology*, theologian Millard J. Erickson reviewed all of the available Rapture theories, concluding that the "posttribulational position emerges as the more probable."[11]

"The pretribulational position involves several distinctions that seem rather artificial and lacking in biblical support," he wrote. "The division of the second coming into two stages, the postulation of three resurrections, and the sharp separation of national Israel and the church are difficult to sustain on biblical grounds."[12]

Those looking for answers on the Rapture are not merely limited to the pre-Tribulation and post-Tribulation paradigms, as there are other less prevalent ideas about the Rapture that have attracted support among smaller Christian cohorts.

The next viewpoint worth exploring is the mid-Tribulation Rapture, which—much like it sounds—proposes that the Rapture will take place in the middle of the seven-year Tribulation period, rather than at the beginning or end.

It's one of the "mediating positions"—alternative Rapture theologies that have not generally attracted widespread adherents. Erickson described the mid-Tribulation Rapture as holding "that the church will go through the less severe part (usually the first half, or three and a half years) of the tribulation, but then will be removed from the world."[13]

Dr. Steve W. Lemke, professor of philosophy and ethics at New Orleans Baptist Theological Seminary, provided a detailed account of the beliefs encapsulated in the mid-Tribulation worldview and concluded that it is "far from the majority among evangelical scholars."[14]

And the theological constructs don't end there, as there is a pre-wrath theory in which the Rapture happens near the end of the Tribulation period.

Possessing some similarities to the mid-Tribulation Rapture theory, a pre-wrath Rapture would essentially be one in which believers are taken through most of the Tribulation, facing both persecution at the hands of fellow humans as well as whatever horrors Satan has in store. That said, Christians are essentially spared from God's wrath, hence the name "pre-wrath." Brown said that he personally believes that Christians will be protected during the Tribulation.

"I do believe that we will be protected from God's wrath—but we don't have to be taken out to be protected—but not from the wrath of Satan and the wrath of man," he said. "It's also clear from the New Testament that we are looking forward to the Lord's appearing—a public, visible event—not to a secret Rapture."[15]

Rhodes explained that pre-wrath proponents have argued that God's wrath doesn't unfold until after the sixth seal in Revelation, as that's when the word *wrath* first appears—an idea that is embraced by Marvin Rosenthal.

Keeping that in mind, those who embrace the pre-wrath theory believe that the Rapture unfolds between the sixth and seventh seals in Revelation. Rosenthal would argue that God's wrath follows and that the term "tribulation" really isn't accurate to describe the entire seven-year period, according to Rhodes.[16]

In contrast, the partial Rapture theory sees "a series of raptures" unfolding, according to Erickson.[17] Those multiple Raptures will take place throughout the Tribulation period, proponents believe, with the first unfolding before the Tribulation. Others who were unprepared for the initial Rapture will follow throughout the seven-year Tribulation, with a Rapture unfolding at the end of the period as well.[18]

"Partial rapturists reason that those Christians who are not as committed as others will lose the privilege of participating in the initial rapture prior to the tribulation period," Rhodes wrote. "This will be the consequence they pay."[19]

Let's circle back now to those who essentially see a conflation between the Rapture and the Second Coming. Dr. Sam Storms, a well-known amillennialist, Christian thinker, and pastor, is among those who fall into this category. Departing from Hitchcock, Hindson, Rosenberg, and others, Storms sees a singular second coming of Christ that incorporates the idea of a Rapture, rather than a separate Rapture event that precedes Christ's second coming.

"Some people would say the next big thing is the so-called Rapture of the church, when Christ returns and withdraws all of people from the earth and leaves behind those who are in unbelief," Storms told me. "And people will talk about what they call the 'Tribulation' and the 'Antichrist' and the rebuilding of the temple in Jerusalem."[20]

Like Hanegraaff, the theologian doesn't believe that there's any one specific political, moral, or social event that must come next before the Second Coming, as Storms contends that Jesus's return is the next big event for believers to be looking out for.

Before that happens, though, Storms does believe that the Bible tells us that there will be intense persecution against Christians.

"I do believe that the New Testament indicates that as we come ever closer to the return of Christ that there will be intensified persecution of the people of God," he said. He didn't purport to know what that would look like, pondering whether it would include laws that force Christians to violate moral convictions, whether tax exemptions would be revoked, or whether more serious penalties would follow.[21]

"I do believe that we have a good bit of evidence that there will be a global persecution of the body of Christ," Storms said, describing it as an effort to both silence and eliminate the collective voice of believers.[22]

While he believes that it will appear as though Christianity has lost its voice and witness, Storms is hoping for a "tremendous awakening" and revival of faith that could come in conjunction with Jesus's second coming.[23]

He reiterated, though, that, aside from persecution, he does "not see anything in particular that must happen first, that must precede the coming of Christ."[24]

Unlike some who flatly reject the presence of the Rapture in the Bible, Storms finds an intriguing middle ground, essentially formulating a paradigm in which the "catching up" of Christians directly relates to Christ's return.

Storms told me that he rejects a pre-Tribulation Rapture, but that he believes that 1 Thessalonians 4 and 1 Corinthians 15 "both indicate that, when Christ returns, He will...catch up to Himself all Christians who are living."[25]

He then proceeded to explain where he departs from the pre-Tribulationist.

"The way I understand 1 Thessalonians 4...is that it's not so that we can then retreat into heaven with Christ while events carry on as they were," Storms said. Instead, he believes that Christians will be "raised and glorified" during the Rapture and will then continue on with Jesus to the earth, complete with their resurrected bodies.[26]

"I think what Paul is saying [in 1 Thessalonians 4] is, 'Yes, Christians will be raptured...but then, as Christ continues His descent to the earth in order to destroy His enemies, the church of Jesus Christ—along with all of the saints who have died before us—together with the angelic hosts will constitute His...parade [and final battle against Satan]," Storms explained. "I think [the Rapture] is the first phase of a singular Second Coming."[27]

Postmillennial theologian Douglas Wilson openly rejects the sort of "secret" Rapture that pre-Tribulationists hold to, but he believes anyone who embraces the notion of a Second Coming must also consider the language that is found in 1 Thessalonians 4:17.

"In Thessalonians it says, 'Then we who are alive will be caught up to meet the Lord in the air,'" Wilson said. "In that sense, every Christian who believes in the Second Coming believes in the Rapture."[28]

He continued, offering a brief recap of what he believes will happen surrounding the Rapture: "The Lord comes; we're caught up, meet Him in the air, and then return with Him here. So, I don't think we're snatched away. I believe that we rise up and greet and meet the Lord and return with Him here."[29]

And that's where Storms, Wilson, and others truly depart from dispensationalists and those who hold to a pre-Tribulation worldview, flatly rejecting a so-called "left-behind scenario" in which there is chaos following a Rapture that leaves the world wondering where millions have disappeared to.

"I think the Rapture is synonymous with the general resurrection of the dead," Wilson said. "I would deny a Rapture in the sense that dispensationalists hold to it, but I don't deny the resurrection of the dead."[30]

Again, the debate will never truly be settled—at least not before the eschatological truths embedded in the Scriptures are fulfilled—but exploring the various worldviews is most certainly important.

The existence of an array of ideas surrounding the pre-, post-, and mid-Trib and pre-wrath perspectives is the result of complex themes and biblical ambiguity. One can only do his or her best to distill, understand, and properly frame the evidence, coming up with competing theories that continue to divide many faith experts.

Next, we'll explore the Tribulation period, which is deeply related to and dependent on the concept of a Rapture.

Chapter 5

THE TRIBULATION

NOW THAT WE'VE tackled the Rapture, it's essential that we dive into the Tribulation period, as it is one of the key end-times fixtures when considering literal approaches to eschatology.

The previous chapters offered an introduction to the premillennial worldview, but a deeper dive into Scripture and the theological realm opens the floodgates to other interpretations, including amillennialism, postmillennialism, and preterism.

For now, let's start by further exploring the premillennial worldview. As I have noted, dispensational premillennialists believe that, after the Rapture—during which they say that believers will be taken up to meet Christ in the clouds—there will be a seven-year period characterized by God's judgment on mankind.

That period of time, known as the Tribulation, is said to be comprised of two main parts: three and a half years of a faux peace that will be ushered in by the Antichrist, followed by three and a half years of chaos and destruction. The latter part is known by some in theological circles as the Great Tribulation.

This breakdown is incredibly important to dispensational premillennialists; some see the Book of Revelation as predominately centering on this seven-year period of time that they believe precedes Christ's return.

"The Book of Revelation is not about the Rapture primarily; it's about the Tribulation," famed *Left Behind* coauthor and premillennialist Tim LaHaye told me. "The seven-year Tribulation that is outlined carefully several times in that book was designed by God to shake this world so dramatically that the unsaved who have not rejected Christ can hear about Him."[1]

Adherents believe that the Tribulation period will, at first, seem like a harmonious time, as the Antichrist will formulate a seven-year peace deal. But dispensational premillennialists believe that something major is slated to unfold halfway through that time period, with the Antichrist beginning to show his true colors, ushering in intense persecution and inflicting acts of unimaginable terror on anyone who decides to become a Christian.

Then they believe that Christ will return and triumph over evil through a Messianic kingdom that He will establish on earth. To understand where, exactly, the idea of a tribulation originates in the Bible, one can look to Revelation 11:1–6, in which John writes:

> I was given a reed like a measuring rod. The angel stood, saying, "Rise and measure the temple of God and the altar, and those who worship in it. But exclude the court which is outside the temple, and do not measure it, for it has been given to the nations. They will trample on the Holy City for forty-two months. And I will give power to my two witnesses, and they will prophesy for one thousand two hundred and sixty days, clothed in sackcloth." These are the two olive trees and the two candlesticks standing before the God of the earth. If anyone desires to harm them, fire proceeds out of their mouth and devours their enemies. If anyone desires to harm them, he must be killed in this way. They have power to shut heaven, that it may not rain during the days of their prophecy. They have power over waters to turn them into blood and to strike the earth with every plague as often as they desire.

There are a number of theories about who these two witnesses are. Some say that they are Moses and Elijah, others posit that they are Enoch and Elijah, and still others proclaim that they are two unknown individuals who will be selected by God.

LaHaye, who tackled the issue in a post on his official website, said that these "two unique witnesses" who will preach for 1,260 days have been identified as "Moses and Elijah" by "most prophecy teachers."[2]

In attempting to back the notion that these witnesses will be Moses and Elijah, LaHaye's website notes that both men were involved in the transfiguration of Christ, and that Malachi—the final book of the Old Testament—proclaims that Elijah will one day return to Israel.[3] Malachi 4:5–6 reads, "See, I will send you Elijah the prophet before the coming of the great and dreaded day of the LORD. He will turn the hearts of the fathers to their children, and the hearts of the children to their fathers, lest I come and strike the earth with a curse."

Regardless of their identities, Revelation 11 goes on to say that "the beast that ascends from the bottomless pit will wage war against them and overcome them and kill them" (v. 7). They will lie in the street while "those from every people and tribe and tongue and nation" will look at their bodies, refusing to bury them (v. 9).

Then the witnesses will stun the world by coming back to life before ascending into heaven before the masses, the Bible explains.

One interesting detail that commentators have noted is the reference to "every people and tribe and tongue and nation" being able to witness the events involving the witnesses. Considering the time frame during which John wrote Revelation, the ability for everyone on the earth to simultaneously see something wasn't logistically possible. But fast-forward two thousand years, and the opportunities are ripe for such an event to have a worldwide audience via the Internet, television, and other emerging modes of technology.

If the language is figurative, of course, this assessment is meandering and fruitless, but if literal, as some argue, then these theories are clearly compelling.

It's also important to note the prevalence of the number 1,260, which is mentioned in Revelation 11 as being the time period during which the witnesses prophesied.

That time period—believed to be forty-two months, or three and a half years—is referenced in Revelation 12:6, which reads, "The woman fled into the wilderness where she has a place prepared by God, that they may nourish her there for one thousand two hundred and sixty days."

In Revelation 13 there's once again a reference to the "beast" widely believed by some to be the Antichrist, who is said to utter "great things and blasphemies" and to exercise authority for forty-two months (v. 5). Verse 6 continues, "He opened his mouth to speak blasphemies against God, to blaspheme His name and His tabernacle and those who dwell in heaven."

Many Bible commentators believe that there's an implicit relationship between the mentions of 1,260 days and 42 months. If one multiplies 42 months by 30 days, the total is 1,260. Following that logic,

42 months and 1,260 days appear to be references to the same time period.[4]

Now, if we dive a bit deeper, forty-two months also equals three and a half years, which, according to premillennialists, is half of the overall seven-year time frame during which they believe that the Tribulation will take place. They contend that the chaos with the witnesses and the other calamities mentioned in Revelation are slated to come during the second three-and-a-half-year period of the Tribulation after the Antichrist's true colors are shown.

"We think we're in chaos today," LaHaye said. "This is nothing like it's going to be during the Tribulation period when God pours out His wrath."[5]

— — — — — — —

If your head is spinning with all these details and theories, it's understandable—and warranted. This involves a multitude of complex material and theories, and it becomes even more multilayered when one starts to look back at the Old Testament to find affirmation for dispensational premillennial end-times theories.

Consider that Bible expert Ed Hindson, who thinks that the Tribulation will likely begin not long after the Rapture, told me that he believes that this seven-year Tribulation period isn't only referenced in Revelation, but that it can also be found in Daniel 9 in the Old Testament.

"It coincides with the seventy 'sevens' in Daniel chapter 9, so it would be a seven-year period," Hindson explained of the Tribulation. "And then references in the Book of Revelation to three and a half years indicate that there is a dramatic shift at the midpoint of that period of time, and that dramatic shift generally involves the execution of the two witnesses and the Antichrist intensifying his persecution against believers."[6]

Of course, the natural question at this point is: What are the seventy "sevens"? According to dispensational premillennialists, the Book of Daniel provides the answers, with adherents meshing those Old Testament scriptures with details that are presented in Revelation to assemble a firmer understanding of the Tribulation.

"We find that the Prophet Daniel was very accurate from chapter 11, verse 36 on to the end," LaHaye explained, calling John and Daniel "the two great prophets."[7]

"You'll find that he is picturing the very things that Revelation talks about, and I don't see a difference when you understand what era the writers were writing."[8]

While some critics of dispensational premillennialism believe that Daniel 9 was exclusively discussing Antiochus Epiphanes, a second-century BC Greek king who presided over Syria, many premillennialists also see a futurist interpretation as being entirely appropriate as well.

It is in verses 23 through 27 that Gabriel delivers a message to Daniel:

> At the beginning of your supplications the command went out, and I have come to tell you, for you are greatly beloved. Therefore understand the matter and consider the vision:
>
> Seventy weeks have been determined for your people and upon your holy city, to finish the transgression, and to make an end of sins, and to make atonement for iniquity, and to bring in everlasting righteousness, and to seal up the vision and prophecy, and to anoint the Most Holy Place.
>
> Know therefore and understand that from the going forth of the command to restore and to rebuild Jerusalem until the Prince Messiah shall be seven weeks, and sixty-two weeks. It shall be built again, with plaza and moat, even in times of trouble. After the sixty-two weeks Messiah shall be cut off and shall have nothing. And the troops of the prince who shall come shall destroy the city and the sanctuary. The end of it shall come with a flood. And until the end of the war desolations are determined. And he shall make a firm covenant with many for one week. But in the middle of the week he shall cause the sacrifice and the offering to cease. And on the wing of abominations shall come one who makes desolate, until the decreed destruction is poured out on the desolator."

There are a variety of perspectives about what, exactly, is happening here. As we will explore in a subsequent chapter, many believe that Daniel 9 is providing prophecy involving the future Antichrist. Thus, one view is that the latter part of the passage deals with the Antichrist's rise to power (hence the reference to the "middle of the week," translated as "middle of the 'seven'" in the NIV, and the related idea that the Tribulation will consist of two different time frames).

Others, though, as Rhodes notes in *The 8 Great Debates of Bible Prophecies*, believe that the entire passage pertains to Jesus's life and death. And still others posit that everything that was prophesied in Daniel 9 already came to pass more than two thousand years ago, with no remaining future projections set to unfold.

These latter individuals would, thus, reject the exercise of connecting the verses in Daniel to Revelation in attempting to project out to currently unfulfilled events and happenings.

Rhodes breaks down each viewpoint in detail in his book. To begin, let's explore those who hold to a futurist viewpoint, contending that scripture in Daniel 9 is referencing something that is yet to unfold.

Those with the future in mind believe that God has set up a prophetic timeline for Israel. Here's how Rhodes explains that dynamic: "The prophetic clock began ticking when the command went out to restore and rebuild Jerusalem following its destruction by Babylon (verse 25). According to this verse, Israel's timetable was divided into 70 groups of seven years—a total of 490 years."[9]

Futurists believe that the first 483 years, which account for the first sixty-nine sets of 7 years, went from the start of the decree until the arrival of the "Anointed One," also known as Jesus Christ, the Messiah, in Jerusalem.

It was at the time of Christ's triumphant return just before the crucifixion that futurists believe that the prophetic timeline paused, with Rhodes writing that futurists believe that this was "483 years to the day after the command to restore and rebuild Jerusalem had been given."[10]

Again, it's all very complicated, but the idea is that the pause at the 483-year (69-weeks-of-years) mark indicates a long gap that will continue until the seventieth and final seven-year "week" in Israel's existence. The idea, as Rhodes wrote, is that Daniel 9:26 details events that will actually unfold during that gap. It reads:

> After the sixty-two weeks Messiah shall be cut off and shall have
> nothing. And the troops of the prince who shall come shall
> destroy the city and the sanctuary. The end of it shall come with
> a flood. And until the end of the war desolations are determined.

This seemingly refers to Christ's death, the destruction of Jerusalem (which unfolded in AD 70), and difficulties for the Jews moving forward, according to Rhodes.

But then there's a reference to a "covenant" that is made for one "seven." If one keeps with the general meaning of a "seven," this period would be seven years—and this is where some see intense connections between Daniel and Revelation, as Daniel 9:27 (NIV) reads:

> He will confirm a covenant with many for one "seven." In the middle of the "seven" he will put an end to sacrifice and offering. And at the temple he will set up an abomination that causes desolation, until the end that is decreed is poured out on him.

It is believed that the final seven-year period in Israel's history will unfold when the covenant—the apparent peace accord facilitated by the Antichrist—is signed.

In contrast, there are those who say that Jesus is the sole centerpiece of the prophecy in Daniel 9. Rather than the Antichrist being the individual who forms the covenant with Israel, they would hold that it is actually Christ who forms the covenant that does away with sacrifices, Rhodes noted.[11]

To affirm this view, they would point to verses such as Matthew 26:28, Romans 15:8, and Galatians 3:17. These scriptures focus on covenants, with the claim that what's happening in Daniel 9 is a prediction of Christ's coming death:

- "For this is My blood of the new covenant, which is shed for many for the remission of sins" (Matt. 26:28).

- "Now I say that Jesus Christ has become a servant to the circumcised on behalf of the truth of God, to confirm the promises made to the patriarchs" (Rom. 15:8).

- "And this I say, that the law, which came four hundred and thirty years later, does not annul the covenant that was ratified by God in Christ, so as to nullify the promise" (Gal. 3:17).

The idea here is that Jesus has solidified the covenant between God and man, but Rhodes argues that a natural reading here indicates that the covenant referenced in the text seems to happen well after Jesus's death as well as the destruction of Jerusalem in AD 70.

That in mind, he believes that it's an entirely different covenant being spoken about—one that could easily comport with what's discussed by John later on in Revelation.

He then provides an outline of what he believes will unfold based on what's presented in Daniel 9 and Revelation: the signing of a covenant, the rebuilding of the Jewish temple, the end of sacrifices, and the Antichrist's ending of the agreement with Israel.[12]

Many premillennialists believe that the "abomination that causes desolation" being referenced indicates that the Antichrist, after ending sacrifices, will essentially make himself a god and command worship of his likeness—something that would require the rebuilding of a third temple, as many believe will eventually come.

— — — — — — —

Bible scholar Dr. Michael Heiser, though, once again encouraged caution, explaining that there is some mystery surrounding the seventieth week that should lead believers to be careful in how they construct their end-times viewpoints.

"Let's take the seventieth week; not only do we not know...we don't have a verse that would actually tell us that the seventieth week is the Tribulation," he said. "If you actually read the passage, seventy weeks are decreed about your people in verse 24. Then a verse later it says, 'There's going to be this anointed prince and there will be seven weeks, then for sixty-two weeks shall it be built again.'"[13]

The mention of one week then emerges again in verse 27, but Heiser raised some important questions: "How do we know that the seventy weeks of verse 24 are to be considered consecutively or even in the one set, when they're divided in the next verse—and then one week is isolated in a verse after that? How do we know that we should even put them together or keep them apart?"[14]

In the end, he concluded that we simply don't know the answers to these questions, which is why there are a number of systems and theories that have emerged surrounding the seventieth week.

"You can make any system look beautiful and coherent if you play with the language and you started at one place so that it works out, and this is what everybody does," he said. "They just pick a system that they think makes the most sense, and they run with it, and they present it as 'the biblical view of the end times.'"[15]

And while premillennialists have laid out very specific ideas about what seems to be happening in Daniel in regard to outlining events that will have a future fulfillment, there are also those who believe that the Great Tribulation already came to pass.

In fact, Dr. Sam Storms told me that he believes that it is "an accomplished fact of past history, that it occurred when Rome destroyed both city and temple and slaughtered or enslaved the Jewish people."[16]

"I don't see a coming, future seventieth week of Daniel, in relation to which we must locate the Rapture," Storms said, referencing how the Rapture ties in with beliefs in the Tribulation. "The Rapture comes at the end, as the first phase of a singular event known as the Parousia, or second coming of Christ."[17]

With all of this in mind, it is clear that the Tribulation, much like the Rapture, is a complicated construct that yields a variety of divergent explanations.

There's no homogeneous understanding of exactly what this time frame will look like, with some seeing the paradigm as unfulfilled and others believing that the Tribulation already took place deep in the past. It's a seemingly never-ending battle.

Next, let's look next at the discussion and debate surrounding the Antichrist.

Chapter 6

THE ANTICHRIST

T HE CONCEPT OF the Antichrist—a diabolical biblical figure who many believe will emerge on the international scene before Christ's second coming—has captivated Christians and ignited fierce debate for more than two millennia.

So how much do we know about this somewhat elusive figure who is not explicitly named in prophetic scriptures but who occupies such a prevalent position in theological circles?

"Well, not as much as we'd like," famed end-times author Joel Rosenberg candidly told me through a chuckle, explaining that end-times experts such as himself wouldn't mind if the Scriptures offered a few more clues and details about the nature and identity of the Antichrist.[1] Rosenberg and his peers—including leading Bible prophecy expert Mark Hitchcock, who describes the Antichrist as the "final Gentile world ruler before Christ comes"—generally point to verses in both the Old and New Testaments to highlight the few details that they believe provide some background on the matter.[2]

From the Book of Daniel to 2 Thessalonians, 1 John, and Revelation, many see the presence of the Antichrist throughout the Scriptures, believing him to be a future figure who will one day gain global political power.

The Apostle Paul, writing in 2 Thessalonians 2:3–4, described a rebellion in which "the man of sin" would be revealed—a man whom he described as being "the son of destruction, who opposes and exalts himself above all that is called God or is worshipped, so that he sits as God in the temple of God, showing himself as God," Paul continued.

In fact, Dr. Michael Brown told me that he believes 2 Thessalonians 2 is "probably the clearest single passage" that corroborates the notion that there will be a definitive Antichrist figure who will rise to global power in the future.[3]

44

Many theologians also cite Revelation 13:5–8 as describing what they believe to be parallel details about the Antichrist, describing the "man of sin" referenced in 2 Thessalonians as "the beast." Those verses in Revelation read:

> He was given a mouth speaking great things and blasphemies. And he was given authority to wage war for forty-two months. He opened his mouth to speak blasphemies against God, to blaspheme His name and His tabernacle and those who dwell in heaven. It was granted to him to wage war with the saints and to overcome them. And authority was given him over every tribe and tongue and nation. All who dwell on the earth will worship him, all whose names have not been written in the Book of Life of the Lamb who was slain from the foundation of the world.

Earlier, in Revelation 13:3, it is prophesied that this same beast will have a "deadly wound" that will be healed and that the entire world will be captivated by this fact—so enamored that many will end up following him.

"He's going to come on the scene with a glib voice and talking wonderful, and butter would melt in his mouth—you know the type," author Tim LaHaye said while describing the Antichrist. "And he's brilliant and attractive, and he cons his way into leadership and controls the whole world, and then he is killed by the uprising when Christ comes."[4]

Bible professor Dr. Gregory Harris wrote about these very issues, explaining that the wound as well as the healing are significant, as they will collectively "cause the world at large to worship the beast, who is considered by most evangelical commentators to be the Antichrist."[5]

Harris's explanation that "most" Evangelicals consider this beast to be the Antichrist gives just a hint to the fact that many, but not all, pastors, theologians, and Bible experts walk away from Scripture with this same view of a singular figure who will fiendishly emerge on the international stage to wreak worldwide havoc.

— — — — — — — —

Part of the reason that a debate continues over what this "beast" really references is potentially due to the dearth of blatant mentions of the word *Antichrist* in the Scriptures. There's also complex language in Revelation that has caused some to look cautiously—and even skeptically—at the prospect of a literal interpretation.

Neither Paul nor John use the term *Antichrist* in either 2 Thessalonians or Revelation, and the word appears in only two New Testament books, which were both authored by John: 1 John and 2 John. Some of those mentions are plural, and seemingly not confined to references about a sole end-times figure.

"As 1 John 2 makes clear, there have been 'antichrist' figures in the world for two millennia, since those who actively deny Jesus are antichrist in their behavior," Dr. Michael Brown said, despite noting his belief in a future Antichrist.[6]

Let's take a brief look at those scriptures. In 1 John 2 the author warns that it is "the last hour" and tells readers that, as they have heard, the "antichrist will come" and that "even now there are many antichrists" (v. 18). The use of the plural form of the word has created some discussion and debate about what, exactly, John means here, as he goes on to define "antichrists." He writes in verse 19: "They went out from us, but they were not of us, for if they had been of us, they would no doubt have remained with us. But they went out, revealing that none of them were of us."

John's definition continues in verses 22 and 23, when he asks, "Who is a liar but the one who denies that Jesus is the Christ?" and responds by noting that, "Whoever denies the Father and the Son is the antichrist. No one who denies the Son has the Father; the one who confesses the Son has the Father."

The author returns to this theme in 1 John 4:1–3 when he writes about false prophets in the world, decrying those who do not acknowledge that Jesus is from God as having the "spirit of the antichrist, which you have heard is coming and is already in the world."

Hank Hanegraaff corroborated Brown's assessment of the term *antichrist* by summarizing John's definition as "anyone who denies that Jesus Christ is coming in the flesh"—a pretty broad statement that would involve a massive array of actors throughout church history and through the modern era.[7]

Ideas about the Antichrist stem not only from the New Testament but also from the Old Testament, with LaHaye offering a recap of what he believes the Antichrist will do in the end times, tying descriptions in Daniel to those expressed in Revelation.

"He's going to offer world government and leadership and peace in our time, and then he's going to get buffed up and the false prophet comes along and makes an idol for him," he said. "And then they demand the same thing that they demanded in the Old Testament of Daniel—that he worship the king."[8]

Daniel reports seeing four beasts in a dream in chapter 7 that represent four kings of the earth; the fourth beast is described as different from the others and has numerous horns on its head.

"The ten horns out of this kingdom are ten kings that shall arise; and another shall rise after them, and he shall be different from the first, and he shall subdue three kings," Daniel wrote of his vision in verse 24, recapping an explanation that he was given for the imagery. "He shall speak words against the Most High and shall wear out the saints of the Most High and plan to change times and law. And they shall be given into his hand until a time and times and half a time," he continued in verse 25.

Rosenberg also points to Daniel 9 when discussing Old Testament references to the Antichrist—a chapter that has been given a great deal of attention considering that dispensational premillennialists see it as key to predicting what's to come.

"It talks about [how] the prince will come from the people who destroyed Jerusalem and the temple," he said, explaining that the temple was destroyed in AD 70 by the Romans.[9] The assumption, then, is that the Antichrist will likely come out of Roman origin, which could mean that he will be of European descent, some argue.

Mark Hitchcock agrees that the Antichrist is likely to come from the old reunited Roman Empire, which he said includes parts of North Africa and the western part of Asia, citing Daniel 9 as containing this prophecy.[10]

As for a specific timeline of events, Rosenberg detailed what he believes will be the general prophetic timeline involving the Antichrist's rise to power, saying that Daniel's description of the Antichrist as a "little horn" might hold some significance when it comes to his power and persona.

"He begins as a little horn—a little amount of strength and a little amount of power," Rosenberg said, imagining the Antichrist to be a smooth and charismatic talker who woos others "with talk of peace."[11]

But despite this façade, he said that the Antichrist will "speak blasphemy" and will describe himself as God. Rosenberg warned that the Antichrist will take over the world and will create a "global tyranny" that is unlike anything that's been seen on the earth before. "He will act as though he himself is God, and he will demand people to worship him," Rosenberg said. "Those who do not worship him will not be able to buy and sell and will eventually be executed."[12]

Hitchcock also believes that the Antichrist will initially gain accolades and subsequent power due to a faux platform of peace in the Middle East. Performing signs and miracles that captivate the masses, the Antichrist, Hitchcock believes, will be "indwelled by Satan."[13]

"He's going to come giving people and telling people what they want to hear," he explained, noting that Daniel 9:27 reads, in part, "And he shall make a firm covenant with many for one week."[14]

Shedding additional light on that covenant agreement, Rosenberg said that he believes that the Antichrist will preside over a peace deal with Israel that will last seven years, explaining that he doesn't know why seven years is the allotted time frame, but that something major happens halfway through that period—a theory that ties into the Tribulation period that we discussed in the previous chapter.

"The Antichrist breaks that deal, he invades the beautiful land Daniel describes that is Israel, and he sets up his throne [there] in the land of Israel and desecrates a temple that has already been rebuilt," Rosenberg continued. "So, we would be expecting to see Jewish people in the land of Israel…preparing and eventually building a third temple."[15]

It should be noted that Babylonian King Nebuchadnezzar II destroyed Jerusalem's first temple in 586 BC, and the Romans destroyed the second temple in AD 70. A third temple has never been built, though many believe—based on interpretations of Scripture— that it will be reconstructed at some point in the future.

It is from this midpoint in the seven years that Hitchcock sees the situation intensifying, as the Antichrist's "mask is going to come off, and he's going to show who he really is."[16]

"From the midpoint of that seven-year Tribulation on he's going to dominate the world religiously, politically, and economically," he continued. "People are going to have to bow the knee to him or starve to death, take his mark upon them, which I take it is basically his name, the numerical value of his name—666."[17]

These scholars believe that Jesus will defeat the Antichrist after the Second Coming, thus ushering in the eventual biblical conclusion of a new heaven and a new earth, as documented at the end of Revelation.

— — — — — — — —

Despite the details about the Antichrist that the Bible does seemingly give, there's still much to ponder about this individual's identity. But is attempting to definitively identify him truly a prudent task?

Over the centuries many have speculated and proposed that the Antichrist could be a host of individuals, including Roman emperor Nero, King George III (during the American Revolution), various Catholic popes throughout history—even President Barack Obama, among other commanders in chief. But the quest to accurately identify the Antichrist has been thus far unsuccessful.[18]

Many Bible scholars warn against attempts to explicitly identify the biblical figure, stating that the Scriptures never implore or instruct Christians to spend their time trying to figure out the Antichrist's identity.

"We are not supposed to be in the business of trying to guess who this person is, because for even a good period of time as he's emerging, he will be considered a little figure, a small side show to larger players," Joel Rosenberg said.[19]

And many others have agreed with this sentiment. Identifying the Antichrist is a "misdirected quest," Reformation Bible College president Dr. Stephen Nichols wrote back in 2001.[20]

"The text never calls upon us to identify the antichrist," he continued. "In fact, some have argued that to impose such a construct as *the* antichrist upon the text is unwarranted."[21]

There's clearly some danger—and likely a fair bit of embarrassment—in purporting to know the identity of the Antichrist, as time and time again individuals throughout church history have simply been flat wrong in making bold proclamations on the matter. Nichols explained:

Those labeling the antichrist as Jewish were equaled, in the early church, by those nominating various Roman emperors for the role. In the later Middle Ages, Muslims vied for the distinction. Some attempts at naming the antichrist provided helpful physical descriptions just in case one may perhaps encounter the antichrist. One anonymous description dating from the third century records, "These are the signs of him: his head is as a fiery flame; his right eye shot with blood, his left eye blueblack, and he hath two pupils. His eyelashes are white; and his lower lip is large; but his right thigh slender; his feet broad; his great toe is bruised and flat."[22]

Rather than determining who the Antichrist is, many faith leaders simply warn believers to be aware of the signs of the times and to properly understand what they believe to be the key events that will take place during the end times.

While the Antichrist is most certainly a part of that paradigm, figuring out his identity—pending you believe that the future diabolical figure will indeed arrive on the scene—is neither needed nor warranted, they argue.

Like the other complex subjects we've covered, the debate over the Antichrist will not easily be resolved; for now we will turn our attention to the beasts mentioned in Revelation.

Chapter 7

THE DEBATE OVER THE NATURE OF THE BEASTS

A S YOU'VE PROBABLY caught on by now, the concept of the Antichrist—like everything else in the Bible prophecy realm—isn't immune to controversy and debate. Now we turn our attention to the two beasts mentioned in Revelation 13.

Some reject the idea of future diabolical "beasts" who wreak havoc in the Middle East, pushing back against the commonly held belief among many Evangelicals that one of them will be the Antichrist.

Dr. Sam Storms, an amillennialist, sees something a bit different unfolding when it comes to John's references in Revelation 13 to a "beast rising out of the sea" and a "beast rising out of the earth," arguing that these verses might not be speaking about forces that are restricted to just one time frame in the historical narrative.

"My understanding of what John is saying when he refers to the beast...and he portrays him in these rather graphic terms and with these images of ferocious animals and the like—I believe what he's describing for us...[is a] transcultural movement, if you will, that is opposed to Christ and His kingdom," Storms told me.[1]

Rather than a single individual, he sees the beast of the sea—which is most commonly associated with the idea of an antichrist—as potentially being a collective reference to numerous diabolical people over time.

"[There have been] many people, at many times, in many ways throughout the course of church history who have conspired collectively to deny the Christian gospel," Storms said.[2]

He went on to cite Roman rulers who sought to exterminate Christians as well as a fourth-century priest by the name of Arius, who was declared a heretic by the Council of Nicaea for refusing to sign a statement of faith that held Jesus as being of the same divine nature of God.[3]

Other related movements that were cited by Storms as denying the gospel include certain sentiments embraced by medieval Roman Catholicism that he said corrupted the gospel, European deism (the belief that God created the world but then disconnected Himself from its affairs), Marxism, Darwinian evolution, the proabortion movement, the radical gay rights movement, and Islamic fundamentalism.

"All of these are in their own ways expressions of this collective image that the Book of Revelation calls 'the beast.' So, again, it can express itself in the form of an individual, a movement, a philosophy, an institution, a nation, or a political movement of some sort," Storms said. He continued, "Anything and everything, individually and corporately, that sets itself up against Jesus is an expression of the concept of the beast."[4]

This notion then flows into interpretations of the Old Testament scriptures in Daniel 7 and Daniel 9 that many pastors and theologians connect with the language and claims made by John in Revelation 13.

While some Christians, as noted in the previous chapter, believe that those Old Testament texts are sure-fire projections into the end times that focus—at least, in part—on a singular future Antichrist, Storms offers up a different option regarding the nature of the beast.

"In Daniel's case, I think that he had in mind, specifically, one particular historical manifestation of the beast, and that was the Syrian ruler Antiochus Epiphanes, who in the middle of the second century BC appeared on the scene and slaughtered the Jews and defiled the temple," Storms explained. Antiochus Epiphanes, he contended, was likely the first manifestation of the anti-kingdom power that is also discussed in Revelation 13.[5]

More specifically Daniel 9:27 speaks of an "abomination that causes desolation" (NIV) that would unfold, with many believing that the verse was a prophecy about Antiochus Epiphanes's invasion of Jerusalem and defiling of the temple.[6] Rhodes wrote in his book *The 8 Great Debates of Bible Prophecy* that, in 168 BC, Antiochus Epiphanes set up an altar to Zeus and sacrificed a pig on it—acts that were seen as abominations that cause desolation. "Antiochus was thus a prototype of the future antichrist," Rhodes wrote.[7]

LaHaye explained that Antiochus Epiphanes was "the worst, most evil king that ever existed"—a description that clearly distinguishes the political leader as possessing an elevated fiendish state. "He did unmis-takable evils to human beings...persecuting them, blinding people, just deliberately torturing their lives, and so on. And he's finally mur-dered by his own family, he was so evil," he continued. "He is a type of the Antichrist in the Tribulation period."[8]

And the horrific descriptors didn't end there. LaHaye also called Antiochus Epiphanes a "symbol of evil," explaining that, in addition to desecrating the temple, he demanded to be worshipped—acts that crossed a line with God and led to his destruction.[9] It's this same ruin that the author believes will befall the Antichrist in the end times.

It's important to note that Jesus Himself references the abomina-tion that causes desolation in Matthew 24:15 as well as Mark 13:14, two centuries after Antiochus Epiphanes's actions. In the former verse Christ said, "So when you see the 'abomination of desolation,' spoken of by Daniel the prophet, standing in the holy place (let the reader understand)." If Daniel's prophecy was intended to have no future prophetic connection and was merely limited to the actions of Antiochus Epiphanes, one wonders why Jesus would later reference it while speaking of a future event that was set to take place well after Antiochus Epiphanes's time.

Here too there are numerous theories and ideas about what connects these prophecies to the New Testament end-times narrative.

A number of arguments and explanations could be made when considering why Christ used the phrase "abomination of desolation," including dual prophecies that are unfolding both in close proximity to the time He was speaking and in the future, a strictly futurist view of the Antichrist, or, as Storms argues, a collective reference to many "beasts" or antichrist figures over thousands of years.

As for what he believes Christ is saying in Matthew 24 and Mark 13, Storms said that it is a likely a prophecy involving Titus Vespasianus Augustus, a Roman general and eventual emperor.[10]

"I think Jesus refers to Titus in the first century...when Titus led the Roman armies and destroyed Jerusalem, and destroyed the temple, and enslaved and slaughtered the Jewish people in AD 70," Storms said.[11]

Hank Hanegraaff also weighed in to share some similar perspective on the matter.

"[Antiochus Epiphanes] succeeded in desecrating the temple, but did not succeed in destroying the temple," he said. "Jesus, in the Olivet Discourse, looks back to that Old Testament antichrist, and He warns about a coming beast. That coming beast is going to not just defile the temple, but it is going to manifestly destroy the temple."[12]

While he likened Antiochus Epiphanes to an "Old Testament antichrist" of sorts and said that there was clearly another antichrist that Jesus was referencing in the Olivet Discourse, Hanegraaff also pointed back to John's definition of an antichrist as anyone who essentially denies "the deity and incarnation of Jesus Christ."[13]

"The notion that there's going to be some Antichrist in the twenty-first century is true and it's false," he said. "It's true in the sense that, as John said, there will be people and institutions that deny the deity of Jesus Christ, the fact that Jesus came in the flesh and the incarnation, that He is really God in human flesh."[14]

Hanegraaff continued, "There's the sense in which you can say, those that deny the deity of Jesus Christ are antichrist, from a biblical perspective."[15]

But he does not embrace the notion that there will be another "beast" as is referenced in Revelation, explaining that there was an "antichrist figure" at the time that was impacting the struggling church.[16] The beast in the text, he said, was representative of the issues—a tribulation of sorts—that the early church was facing at the hands of brutal Roman emperor Nero Caesar.[17]

With this in mind, Hanegraaff said that there's "no warrant for driving the text into the twenty-first century" in the form of a literal future Antichrist figure, as he believes a close reading of the text simply doesn't warrant it.[18]

It's a subject that the theologian has spent a great deal of time speaking and writing on, attempting to push back against the ongoing speculation about the identity of the Antichrist that has raged for centuries. "Rather than joining the sensationalistic game of pin-the-tail-on-the-Antichrist, Christians need only go to Scripture to find the answer," Hanegraaff once addressed the matter.[19]

Hanegraaff said that there is "no basis...whatsoever" for a theology that sees future individuals filling the roles of the beast of the sea and the beast of the earth introduced in Revelation 13; he said that these descriptions are archetypal.[20]

"[John is] drawing on Daniel's apocalyptic description of evil world empires, or powers," he said. "He describes an emperor in his own epic of time, who arrogantly sets himself and his empire against God, a person who persecutes the saints, a person who grossly violates the commandments, through disgusting demonstrations and depravity, not the least of which was his demand to be worshipped as Lord and God."[21]

Hanegraaff said that this wasn't merely restricted to Nero, but that it also applied to Rome as an empire, with its rulers at the time demanding that they be worshipped. When Christians pushed back against such adoration, they suffered greatly.

"You have the New Testament Christians saying, 'No, no, we're not going to call you Lord and Savior. It's not Caesar that's Lord and Savior. It's Christ that is Lord and Savior,'" he explained. "As a result, they're going to suffer greatly, but their vindication is going to be for a thousand years. In other words, they're going to suffer for ten days, to use the language of Revelation, but their vindication is going to be a thousand years. Their suffering is going to be short; their vindication is going to be eternal."[22]

Dr. Shane J. Wood, professor of New Testament studies at Ozark Christian College, also said that he doesn't expect a future Antichrist figure to emerge, though he understands why some people do interpret Scripture in that way.

"What they're really describing is 2 Thessalonians 2, with the man of lawlessness. That's where they really get legs under it," he told me. "From Revelation 13 itself, they wouldn't really have much of an antichrist figure. They figured out ways to jigsaw puzzle it in to fit their theological schema."[23]

Wood argued that Revelation 13—which discusses the beasts— can best be understood by considering the contents of the preceding chapter. It is in Revelation 12 that there is a mention of a red dragon in pursuit of a woman who is having a child, with robust imagery driving the narrative. The relevant verses (1–4) read:

> A great sign appeared in heaven: a woman clothed with the
> sun, with the moon under her feet, and on her head a crown
> of twelve stars. She was with child and cried out in labor and
> in pain to give birth. Then another sign appeared in heaven:

There was a great red dragon with seven heads and ten horns,
and seven diadems on his heads. His tail drew a third of the
stars of heaven, and threw them to the earth. The dragon stood
before the woman who was ready to give birth, to devour her
Child as soon as He was born.

Wood went on to cite verse 5, noting that it proclaims that the
woman gave birth to a male child "who was to rule all nations with an
iron scepter." This figure, he said, is Jesus, though he contended that
there are actually multiple levels worth considering when it comes to
the woman's identity.

"On one level, this is Mary. We're in Bethlehem," he said.[24]

But Wood added that there is also a broader imagery here that
speaks to the cosmic battle between good and evil that has been
raging since the days of Genesis.

"In chapter 12, when it introduces this dragon in his pursuit, in his
zeal, at verse 9, it says, 'That ancient serpent called...Satan, who leads
the whole world astray' [NIV]" Wood explained. "It's this collision, this
cosmological collision between Satan and Christ."[25]

Rather than looking at the text as prophesying a future scenario in
which an antichrist rises and takes power with the help of the second
beast, the scholar reiterated that he believes that the imagery is actually pointing to the "cosmic war that's been raging since Genesis 3."[26]

This, of course, is just another perspective on the matter, with theories and ideas about the identity and nature of the Antichrist running
the gamut. Just consider what Dr. Michael Heiser had to say about the
notion of Old Testament "foreshadowings" of the Antichrist.

"They can be foreshadowings. I think Antiochus does some things in
the intertestamental period that really are very striking when it comes
to some of the talk in Daniel—Daniel 9 and later on in chapters 10 and
11," Heiser explained. "There are some things in there that are pretty
close correlations, but there are also some things that are missing."[27]

He, like many others, referenced the most intriguing fact that could
back a futurist mentality—Jesus's mention of the abomination of desolation—adding that it appears as though there had to be a broader
reason that Christ invoked the language and specifically mentioned
the Prophet Daniel by name.

"I tend to think that the Antichrist material is still valid, or still in effect, and that there will come a person who will play this role in the scheme of the larger eschatological picture," Heiser said. "I don't think we're really given too much information."[28]

Regardless of whether Jesus was referring to a future end-times antichrist or to one of many collective "beasts," Storms said that John's intentions in Revelation are clear, as he "takes all of that imagery, all of that language, and he kind of compresses it into one final portrait of this hideous creature that he describes in Revelation 13."[29]

That hideous creature, Storms believes, encompasses all of the afore-mentioned individuals and movements. That said, he doesn't entirely dismiss the notion of a final antichrist who rises to power during the end times.

"Having said that…will there be one particular individual who emerges in the end times, who will, himself, be the Antichrist—who will, himself, in some way lead or galvanize or organize all of this…into a singular force?" he rhetorically asked. "I'm open to that possibility."[30]

Storms said that it's quite possible that a final antichrist in this vein could be referenced in 2 Thessalonians 2:3–4. "That may be what Paul is talking about in 2 Thessalonians 2 when he talks about the man of sin, the man of lawlessness," the theologian said, though he added the caveat that he's not quite convinced, but still wouldn't be surprised if that's what's going on there in the scriptures.[31]

Another point worth considering is what, exactly, Daniel was seeing when prophesying—and whether he himself knew what was unfolding, including the identity of the individual responsible for the abomination of desolation.

"Remember, he only saw visions that came from God, and I don't think he understood some of the nuances for the end times that we're living in," LaHaye said. "He was more interested in the times in which he lived and then getting the children of Israel right with God and back to rebuilding the temple and so on, and reestablishing their mandate with God."[32]

LaHaye said that he does not believe that the prophet understood the eschatological elements the way that believers do today.

– – – – – – – –

So, let's briefly take a more clinical look at the categories of belief surrounding the Antichrist. Writing in the theological journal *Bibliotheca
Sacra*, Bible professor Dr. Gregory Harris broke down the differing
views on the matter.

Those perspectives include the Nero Redivivus View, the
Reincarnation View, the Nonpersonal View, the Antichrist View, and
the Revived Roman Empire View.[33]

Since our purpose here is to provide the essentials, we won't spend
too much time delving into each one of these, though I will provide
a recap of each to help readers understand the debate as well as the
underlying reason why everyone isn't in agreement on the Antichrist
front.

- The Nero Redivivus View is a historical view that
  holds that John and early church members believed
  that an evil Roman Caesar would come back to life. It
  was mainly believed by some that Nero, a tyrannical
  emperor who persecuted Christians, would return as
  the aforementioned "beast" in Revelation 13. While
  some in the early Christian church held to this theory,
  Harris explained that it's not all that surprising considering that the ruler had so brutally dealt with believers,
  though he cautioned that they were potentially mistaken on the matter.[34]

- Another theory on the "beast" is the so-called
  Reincarnation View, which consists of the notion that
  an individual such as Nero—or someone else—could
  potentially reincarnate, emerge on the scene in another
  form, and forge on with the plans that are detailed in
  Scripture.[35]

- Others look at contents of Revelation and come to adopt
  the third perspective, known as the Nonpersonal View:
  that the text is speaking about spiritual issues involving
  evil forces that led to persecution among early believers,
  Harris explained. Some might contend, though, that

this nonpersonal view is a lens into the evil that will come in the future prior to Christ's return. Either way, Harris questioned these sentiments.

"How would the increase of evil promote worldwide amazement and the worship of the beast and Satan (Rev. 13:3)?" he wrote. "And why would the world come to any conclusion about waging war on impersonal forces?"[36]

- The fourth perspective—the Antichrist View—consists of what was discussed earlier in this chapter: the rise of an antichrist who is injured and healed, and who will come to power and usher in worldwide deceit.

- Rather than taking the form of an individual, the fifth and final view, the Revived Roman Empire View, holds that the "beast" is actually the Roman Empire, which will one day be healed and will again rise to worldwide domination during the Tribulation period. This is based on a reading of Daniel 2 and Daniel 5 that see the use of "king" and "kingdom" being used interchangeably, Harris explained. The wound itself could then be healed of an empire and not merely an individual, as many believe will be the case with the Antichrist.[37]

As you can see, there's much discussion and debate to be had about what's really unfolding in the Scriptures when it comes to the beasts and the nature of the Antichrist. If the fulfillment is literal, there's a future antichrist figure who will take control and plunge the world further toward the end.

If it's not, though, perceptions and proposed theories about the events that will unfold during the end times could end up being quite incorrect. With no worldwide leader who rises to power and persecutes believers, the scenario becomes somewhat less contentious.

— — — — — — — —

We've spent a great deal of time here speaking about the beast out of the sea in Revelation, but what we haven't yet addressed in detail is that John's vision also includes a second beast—the beast out of the earth, a separate entity that is also described as being both diabolical and tyrannical.

To recap what Revelation 13:5–8 says about the first beast: he is said to exercise authority for forty-two months as he utters blasphemies against God and demands that the world worship him after being given authority "over every tribe and tongue and nation."

It is the image of a second beast that simply adds to that horror, as this creature is described as having "two horns like a lamb" but speaking "like a dragon" (v. 11). This latter beast is known as the false prophet.

"The false prophet will appear like a lamb on the outside, but then on the inside of the false prophet...he's going to have a dragon heart," Charlie Restivo, pastor of Calvary Chapel in Westchester, New York, said during a 2014 sermon. "He's going to speak like a dragon."[38]

While similar to the first beast in terms of its authority, this beast will work to ensure that those on earth worship the former, and will perform wonders. Revelation 13:15–17 explains:

> He was allowed to give breath to the image of the beast, that the image of the beast should both speak and cause as many as would not worship the image of the beast to be killed. He causes all, both small and great, both rich and poor, both free and slave, to receive a mark on their right hand or on their forehead, so that no one may buy or sell, except he who has the mark or the name of the beast or the number of his name.

That number, of course, is 666, known traditionally as the mark of the beast. Not much is known about the nature of this number, though many Bible scholars believe that one must receive it during the end of days to engage in basic commerce; those who do take the mark will presumably not be able to enter the kingdom of heaven.

It is absolutely unclear exactly what 666 stands for. We know that it is the "number of a man," though many have wondered if it pertains to letters in a name or some other marker. Without going too deep into the weeds, the use of "666" is believed to be a form of gematria, which is defined by *Merriam-Webster* as follows: "a cryptograph in the form of a word whose letters have the numerical values of a word taken as the hidden meaning."[39] Basically it involves adding up the numbers in a person's name (words have numerical values in this system), though its usage here gives us no definitive clue as to who the Antichrist is or will be.[40]

Ron Rhodes spoke further about this false prophet, telling me that he believes he will play a key role in the end times by attempting to control the world through religion.

"One way to bring unity to people especially on a global level is religion," Rhodes said. "He's going to be used in a terrible way to build a false religion that will serve to bring unity to the world."[41]

Many believe that the false prophet's main goal will be to move people toward worshipping the Antichrist. "There's going to be a false religion for a time, but after that religion has served its purpose...the Antichrist is going to destroy it, because from that point forward he wants to be worshipped," Rhodes explained.[42]

In essence, there's an unholy trinity of sorts that includes Satan, the first beast, and then the second—a twisted and mirrored version of the very Christ-centered Trinity that has brought salvation to humanity.

"This beast rounds out what I believe to be the unholy trinity; Satan has always longed to be like God...like the most high God," Restivo said. "He wants to be in the place of father God."[43]

It is this false prophet who Restivo believes will join the Antichrist, a political leader, by serving as a religious leader. He likened the beast from the sea to the "opposite of the Holy Spirit."[44]

"The false prophet, I want you to notice...comes out of the earth and he had two horns. Now, horns speaks of authority," Restivo said. "But I notice that this one has no crown, and with him not having a crown means that he really doesn't have any political power." He continued, "He's going to be a religious guy, and he's going to be pointing back to the Antichrist."[45]

Again, the notion is that the beasts are connected to and indwelled by Satan, mirroring, in many ways, the relationship between the Father, Son, and Holy Spirit.

Despite the power that the beasts are said to gain in the Scriptures, Revelation details what will befall them, painting a vivid picture in which Jesus Christ returns on a "white horse," proceeding to successfully battle over the forces of evil and subsequently triumph.

John detailed the fate of both beasts in Revelation 19:19–20:

> Then I saw the beast and the kings of the earth with their
> armies gathered to wage war against Him who sat on the
> horse and against His army. But the beast was captured and
> with him the false prophet who worked signs in his presence,
> by which he deceived those who received the mark of the
> beast and those who worshipped his image. These two were
> thrown alive into the lake of fire that burns with brimstone.

Interestingly, when addressing discussion and debate over the nature
of the Antichrist, Dr. Gregory Harris pointed out that he does not
believe that these individuals are "merely personifications of empires,"
as "no empires will be cast into the lake of fire," concluding that these
references in Revelation are likely talking about individuals.[46]

It's important to highlight a divergent view that Dr. Shane Wood
offered on the two beasts of Revelation, noting that he believes there is
an unholy trinity, but that each component references something not
quite so literal.

"What's interesting is if you look at the dragon and then the two
beasts…they make up an unholy trinity in the Book of Revelation.
They are these counterparts," he told me. "You have the dragon, where
a lot of the language used for him is paralleling the Father. You have
the beast from the sea; a lot of the language used to describe him is
parallel to the Son."

As for the second beast of the earth, Wood said that there is language that seems to mirror the Holy Spirit. He explained:

> The whole job of the second beast is to actually breathe life into
> things, to breathe into them life and to bring them to life. Then
> they are going to point, to worship, toward the beast who had
> a wound to the head that raised from dead and to the dragon.
> You have this unholy trinity that is paralleling the Trinity.
>
> Then it's from that construction that you see why it is that
> Rome is functioning the way they are functioning. Rome is
> basically in bed or in league with this unholy trinity. Then
> really the rest of Revelation is a tale of two cities or a tale
> of two brides. You have the city of Rome and you have the

New Jerusalem. You have the prostitutes in Revelation 17 and you have the bride in Revelation 19. They're both the physical manifestations of the trinities they belong to.[47]

Now, let's look at the millennial debate.

Chapter 8

THE GREAT MILLENNIAL DEBATE

ONCE YOU GET past the great debates over the timing—and mere existence in Scripture—of the Rapture, Tribulation period, and Antichrist, you move on to the next major point of contention: the millennial kingdom.

Premillennialists generally believe that Revelation contains information that was both pertinent to John's contemporaries as well as to future generations. This, of course, would include the view that the book provides explicit details about Christ's impending return and the new heaven and earth to come.

The latter part of Revelation takes readers through a complex and vibrant narrative, with many biblical experts believing that Revelation 19 explicitly describes how Jesus will one day triumphantly return from heaven with a "sharp sword" coming out of His mouth to achieve final victory.

The text proclaims that Christ, accompanied by armies, will defeat the "beast and the kings of the earth with their armies." Both the Antichrist and the false prophet are present in chapter 19.

Despite the Antichrist and false prophet having amassed world power, the biblical story doesn't end well for either of these evil forces, as verse 20 tells us that they "were thrown alive into the lake of fire that burns with brimstone."

What directly follows in Revelation 20 is an introduction of the millennial kingdom, with the chapter opening by describing yet another scene filled with complex imagery in which an angel comes down from heaven to seize the "dragon," also known as Satan, binding him for "a thousand years."

This act will purportedly prevent the devil from further deceit until that thousand-year period concludes, and it is followed by the release of Satan for a brief time, according to verse 3. That's just a brief recap of what's presented in the text.

It is the reference to Christ's one-thousand-year rule before Satan's release, which is mentioned in Revelation 20:7–8—verses that recount the devil's exit from prison and his effort to "deceive the nations which are in the four corners of the earth, Gog and Magog, to gather them for battle"—that has sparked fierce eschatological debate.

One of the central questions that has emerged is whether readers are intended to take the millennial period literally or figuratively. With no clear consensus, theologians continue to battle over whether Christ will physically reign on the earth during a set, thousand-year time period, whether He's already been doing so from heaven following His death and resurrection, or whether there is no literal real-world application at all to these scriptures.

With that in mind, let's explore the array of biblical interpretations among Christian leaders when it comes to Jesus's thousand-year reign. Christians generally fall into one of the following categories: premillennialism, amillennialism, postmillennialism, or preterism.

Postmillennial theologian and pastor Douglas Wilson explained the differences between the main three millennial worldviews as follows: "Premillennialists believe that the Lord comes, then the millennium. Amillennialists believe [there is] no literal millennium, no earthly millennium. Postmillennialists believe there is an earthly millennium, but that Jesus comes at the conclusion of it, at the end of it."[1]

Despite his own proclivities, Wilson provided a very rough estimate of where he believes most conservative Evangelicals in North America stand on the millennium, assuming 75 percent are premillennialists, 20 percent are amillennialists, and just 5 percent are postmillennialists.

He called the presence of the premillennial worldview "very, very strong," predicting that it holds a dominant view among American Evangelicals.[2] It is, most certainly, the view that dominates the perspectives of some of the most well-known eschatology commentators, as observed in the interviews for this book.

Others have crafted different ways of viewing what will happen following Christ's return in Revelation. But what is the impetus for each of these views? Let's take a closer look at the latter chapters of Revelation, which contain the scriptures that are at the heart of the overarching debate, beginning with Revelation 20:4:

I saw thrones, and they sat on them, and the authority to judge was given to them. And I saw the souls of those who had been beheaded for their witness of Jesus and for the word of God. They had not worshipped the beast or his image, and had not received his mark on their foreheads or on their hands. They came to life and reigned with Christ for a thousand years.

Verse 6 says that those who share in this "first resurrection" will be "priests of God and of Christ and shall reign with Him a thousand years." In fact, the term "thousand years" actually appears six times in Revelation 20:2–7—a fact that individuals who believe in a literal reign often cite.

What do these references actually mean? Many dispensational premillennialists, who generally embrace a literal interpretation of Revelation and believe that the book was written in AD 95, argue that Jesus will establish a kingdom on the earth following His return, and they believe that it will last one thousand years.

Evangelical expert Joel Rosenberg is among those who argue in favor of a Messianic kingdom that lasts ten literal centuries.

"[Christ] needs to come before that to the earth to set up that one-thousand-year kingdom," Rosenberg said. "That makes me a premillennial believer. He comes before the millennial kingdom."[3]

The prophecy expert was candid, though, in noting that he believes that one would probably find that a majority of Christians likely don't necessarily take a premillennial end-times stance, instead seeing Revelation 20 as more symbolic than literal.

His view on the matter does not necessarily conflict with Wilson's eschatological estimate in that Wilson was specifically speaking about Evangelicals and not Christians more generally. "My perception is that if you take Catholicism, mainline Protestantism, sort of independent evangelicalism, and then all the rest, you'd end up with an amillennial or a postmillennial majority," he said. "Most denominations don't teach that there will be a thousand-year reign."[4]

As with many end-times subjects, the battle is really rooted in one's view of just how literal the Scriptures should be taken.

Evangelical scholar Dr. John Noē once wrote that premillennialism is "known for its insistence that the words of prophecy be interpreted 'literally whenever this does not lead to absurdity,'" which essentially forms the underpinning of all associated end-times views, not simply opinions about the Millennium.[5]

It is through this lens that Noë explained that a futuristic view on both Old and New Testament texts is taken, though he separated out a subgroup known as historic premillennialists—individuals who he said combine both preterist (past) and futurist views when it comes to eschatology.[6] We will spend some time looking at the preterist worldview in a subsequent chapter.

Thus, it should be noted that premillennialists are divided into two key camps: dispensationalist premillennialists and historic premillennialists.

In describing the key difference between the two related systems in his book *The 8 Great Debates of Bible Prophecy*, Rhodes wrote, "Dispensational premillennialism...distinguishes between the church and Israel and holds that in the millennium, God will fulfill the unconditional promises He made to Israel."[7]

In contrast, he said that historic premillennialism "does not insist on the distinction between the church and Israel (the church is viewed as spiritual Israel), nor does it demand a consistently literal interpretive method."[8]

Theologian William Lane Craig has further differentiated historic premillennialism from its dispensational counterpart by noting that it is "a millennial view that doesn't involve rapture theology—just classic millennial theology."[9]

That said, Dr. Sam Storms explained that, when it comes to the Millennium debate, many of those who embrace historic or nondispensational premillennialism "would agree that there's going to be this thousand-year rule of Christ on the earth between the Second Coming and the eternal state."[10]

But he said that these individuals wouldn't see the primary purpose as being bent on reestablishing Israel as a theocratic nation, considering the view that the modern-day church is essentially spiritual Israel.

Premillennialists look to Jesus's words to John in Revelation 1:19 to find what they believe to be an outline for the book in its entirety—one that they say shows that the twenty-two chapters that comprise Revelation are to be grouped together and divided for different purposes. That verse reads, "Write the things which you have seen, and the things which are, and the things which will take place after this."

With that in mind, Noē explained that premillennialists generally see Revelation 1 as being focused on the past glorification of Christ, Revelation 2 through 3 as focusing on seven present churches at the time of its writing, and Revelation 4 through 22 focusing on end-times prophecy.[11]

Pastor Greg Laurie, who embraces a literal Millennium period, laid out his case for what he believes will unfold during the end times: "I believe that Christ will come back at the end of the battle of Armageddon in the Second Coming and that He will establish His kingdom," he said. "But it doesn't end with the Millennium."[12]

Speaking of the latter chapters of Revelation detailed at the start of this chapter, Laurie said that he believes that there are some misconceptions about Revelation 21:2, the verse that describes "the Holy City, the New Jerusalem, coming down out of heaven from God, prepared as a bride adorned for her husband."

"Effectively at that point, heaven and earth become one," Laurie said. "We need to understand that right now heaven is a real place for real people, but sometimes Christians will say, 'One day I will die and go to heaven and stay there forever.' That's not really true."[13]

The pastor said that, though Christians will die and go to heaven, the latter portion of Revelation makes it clear that heaven will eventually come to earth, calling that event the "ultimate conclusion" to the end-times paradigm.

Laurie also pointed to Jesus's words in the Beatitudes (Matt. 5), which discuss God's favorable view of the "peacemakers," with the scriptures saying that the "meek...shall inherit the earth."

"In the Lord's Prayer, He taught us to pray, 'Thy kingdom come. Thy will be done on earth as it is in heaven' [DRA]."[14]

Laurie continued, "I believe that in the Millennium reign—the Millennium reign of Christ—we'll be in glorified bodies, but they will be real bodies in a real place, and we'll be doing real things."[15]

Pastor John Hagee, senior pastor of Cornerstone Church in San Antonio, Texas, and founder of Christians United for Israel, corroborated these views, telling me that fifty-eight years of studying

Scripture has solidified his premillennial worldview—a perspective that he called the "only rational Bible position."[16]

"That position is that God would call the Jewish exiles from the nations of the world to form the state of Israel before the Rapture of the church," he said. "We believe the state of Israel, reborn May 15, 1948, is that state and will be the place to which Messiah will come to rule the world from the city of Jerusalem for one thousand years in the golden age of peace called the millennial reign."[17]

— — — — — — — —

Of course, premillennialists are only the first brand we'll look at while exploring the Millennium. Next comes the amillennial view, which rejects the notion that the thousand-year period is literal, instead believing that the text is symbolic when it references that time frame.[18]

Adherents see Jesus as presiding over the current church age; thus the millennial kingdom that is referenced in Revelation is, in the minds of amillennialists, unfolding as we speak, with Christ ruling from heaven.

Storms told me in an interview for this book that he believes that the differences between historic premillennialism and the amillennialism that he embraces are minimal.

"It's really only one difference, and that is: Will there be—following the second coming of Jesus but before the creation of the new heaven and earth—a thousand-year reign of Jesus on the earth called the Millennium?" Storms said.[19]

While many premillennialists would answer affirmatively, he said that amillennialists would reject such a notion. That said, Storms explained that the differences become greater when specifically comparing dispensational premillennialism to amillennialism, as the views of the former are "significantly and substantially different from amillennialism."[20]

"That version of premillennialism believes that when Christ rules on this earth for one thousand years...that He will reestablish His authority and His kingdom centered in Jerusalem—and that the Jewish people will have unique privileges and promises fulfilled in and for them that are [not available to believing Gentiles]."[21]

Storms said that he holds a strong disagreement with such a view, believing that the one thousand years referenced in Revelation 20 is symbolic rather than literal, and that this is a reflection of "every other number in the Book of Revelation."[22]

"I think a careful reading of Revelation 20 indicates that the so-called one-thousand-year reign is not one thousand years that you can mark on a calendar," Storms said, instead calling it a "reference to completeness" which he believes can be likened to Christ's current rule in heaven. "Christ has been seated at the right hand of the Father and…He rules and reigns throughout this present church age."[23]

Storms also penned a blog post back in 2007 defending his eschatological view in an effort to help clear up any confusion and affirm that amillennialists actually do embrace a millennium view. He wrote:

> Contrary to what the name (Amillennialism) implies, AMs do believe in a millennium. The millennium, however, is now: the present age of the church between the first and second comings of Christ in its entirety is the millennium. Therefore, while the AM does deny the Premillennial belief in a personal, literal reign of Christ upon the earth for 1,000 years following His second coming, he affirms that there is a millennium and that Christ rules.[24]

It's clear that amillennialists don't flatly reject the notion of a millennium; they simply don't embrace a literal reign of Christ on earth, arguing that Revelation 20 is the only place in which the theology of a literal one-thousand-year reign can be gleaned. Considering the complex and symbolic nature of Revelation, they take a more spiritual view of what such a reign would look like.

Commenting on the amillennial perspective, William Lane Craig said that it's more about not seeing a viable reason for the presence of a literal reign.

"The amillennialist would say the millennium serves no purpose. Why do such a thing as to have this strange earthly kingdom?" Craig wrote. "Why not simply, upon people being raised from the dead and judged, go into the eternal state of heaven or hell?"[25]

Specifically commenting on arguments made by Storms, Craig explored some of the key details that have led some theologians to reject premillennialism. Among those issues is sin, seeing as Christ's earthly reign following His return would mean that sinful individuals would be living alongside resurrected Christians—something that amillennialists believe is impossible as it would mean that Christ would be reigning during a time in which sin was still running rampant on the earth.

"They have a body that Paul described as immortal, incorruptible, powerful, and glorious. They are now free of sin. Sin has been done away with. These are glorified saints," Craig wrote of the amillennialist perspective. "Yet we are to imagine them living in a society with mortal, sinful, corruptible people and that this is the kind of interrelationship that they would have? It just seems inconceivable that you would have that sort of mixture."[26]

Amillennialists, on the other hand, do believe that good and evil will coexist in the world until Christ's second coming, with the latter being defeated upon His return.

It should be noted that there are other differences, including the fact that amillennialists do not "identify this period of tribulation with Daniel's 70th Week, as does the dispensational premillennialist, nor [do they] define its purpose as having anything to do with the restoration of national theocratic Israel," though some do believe in mass Jewish salvation during the end times, according to Storms.[27]

Sharing some areas of agreement with premillennialists, amillennialists also hold that there will be intense tribulation, apostasy, and quite possibly an antichrist during the end times; the nature of these elements simply differ a bit.

━ ━ ━ ━ ━ ━ ━

Next come the postmillennialists, who, like their amillennialist opponents, generally don't believe that the thousand-year period is literal.

They see most of Revelation up through chapter 19 as having already been fulfilled in AD 70, with differing views among adherents when it comes to remaining chapters 20 through 22.[28]

"The postmillennialists are those who believe that Jesus is coming again at the conclusion of the Millennium," pastor Douglas Wilson explained. "That means that the Millennium is brought about, not by the Lord's physical presence, but through missionary work, preaching the gospel, and so on."[29]

Putting this into perspective, Ron Rhodes explained that there's an idea among postmillennialists that "for an extended time—roughly, called one thousand years—the church will Christianize the world."[30]

The driving notion is that the world will get "better and better, so that when Christ comes again, the world will be ready for Him," Rhodes explained.[31]

Under a postmillennial worldview, adherents believe that Jesus won't return until after the Millennium age—a time during which the Christian faith flourishes. Theologian Kenneth L. Gentry described the dynamic as a "progressive cultural victory and expansive influence of Christianity in history."[32]

This is the key area in which amillennialists and postmillennialists differ, as the former reject the notion that Christianity will gain major prevalence throughout the earth, with Storm writing that "it is here, and for all practical purposes only here, that [Amillennialism] differs from Postmillennialism."[33]

Postmillennialists see the millennium as a time in which the gospel will spread globally and have "triumph"—a power so profound that it results in the "subduing of the forces of unbelief and sin," Craig explained.[34]

Adherents find this belief inherent in Scripture, as Jesus called believers in Matthew 28:18–20 to fulfill the Great Commission—Christ's call to "help take His message of love and forgiveness to every person in every community, in every city, in every country of the world and make disciples of all nations," as recapped by the late Bill Bright, cofounder of Campus Crusade for Christ (now known as Cru).[35]

It is in Matthew 28 that Jesus calls His disciples to travel the nations, baptizing, teaching, and making disciples of the masses. With that in mind, Craig noted that postmillennialists will look to verses such as the parable of the mustard seed and the yeast in Matthew 13:31–32 to corroborate their belief that the kingdom of God will progress.[36]

Those verses read: "He told them another parable, saying, 'The kingdom of heaven is like a grain of mustard seed which a man took and sowed in his field. This indeed is the least of all seeds, but when it has grown, it is the greatest among herbs and is a tree, so that the birds of the air come and lodge in its branches."

In the end, this, among other references, would likely be used to advance the notion of Christian triumph, though those ideas don't come without fervent pushback from individuals who reject the postmillennial worldview.

Premillennialists would generally find these ideals somewhat problematic, considering that there's a belief that they see a world in which there will be intense struggles and problems before the end—not necessarily triumph.

Observing the postmillennial view from a thirty-thousand-foot view, premillennialists, among others, would wonder if and when, considering the rise of the horrifically violent Islamic State, among other emerging problems across the globe, domestic and international affairs will ever take a turn for the better. After all, a spiritual improvement, it would seem, would be a requirement for the fruition of the postmillennial worldview.

When I asked Douglas Wilson, a postmillennialist, to respond to the critique that the world is actually worsening at a time when postmillennialists are expecting it to improve, the theologian said that he believes some critics are likely "standing too close to the picture." These individuals, he said, can only see the "brush strokes."[37]

"You need to stand back across the museum gallery and look at the whole picture at once," Wilson said of contemporary affairs. The theologian explained that it's all about how one examines the historical narrative. "If you're looking at human history in five-year increments, it does appear to be getting worse and worse, depending on who just got elected." But when you expand that lens to look at five-hundred-year increments, he said the paradigm changes. "Basically, if you look too closely, you're staring at the brush strokes and not at the picture," Wilson said.[38]

If given the chance to try and persuade dispensationalist premillennialists, Wilson—who is also a partial preterist—said that he would try and persuade them that he's "not a liberal," as he knows that his critics would surely dismiss some of his beliefs on the end times as being out of line with Scripture.[39]

"If I say that the Matthew 24 business or the Book of Revelation was fulfilled in the first century... it looks to them like I'm explaining away the Bible, or, as they would describe it, I'm spiritualizing the Bible," Wilson said.[40]

In the end, he said, "Virtually all current contemporary postmillennialists are partial preterists."[41]

As for his personal beliefs about the end times, Wilson said that, though he believes that many of the verses ascribed to the end times have already come to pass—including much of Revelation—he thinks that the latter portions of the book are still yet to come.

"I believe that the overwhelming majority of the book—with the exception of the last part, where the New Jerusalem is fully manifested...I believe that is happening now and will continue to happen—but, the seven-headed beast, and the seven heads, or seven hills, and seven kings, all of that, I believe happened, was fulfilled, in the first century."[42]

As for the evolution of the postmillennial view, Wilson said that there's been a shift in ideology over the past two hundred years, as many in the nineteenth century seemingly sided with premillennialists on one key fact: the literal length of the Millennium.

Postmillennialists believed that the time frame would be one thousand years, but that it was "the last one thousand years of the church age."[43]

Thus, early postmillennialists didn't believe in Christ's literal earthly kingdom, but they did embrace the notion that the Millennium would be the final one thousand years of the church's existence. But Wilson said that this view has largely disappeared in the modern era.

"Most contemporary postmillennialists believe that the Millennium is not a literal one thousand years, but that it's coextensive with the church age," he explained.[44]

— — — — — — —

It was perhaps most refreshing while writing this book to hear what William Lane Craig had to say about the Millennium. While many biblical experts have their rigidly set and strict ideas about what they believe is happening in Revelation 20, he took a much more subdued approach, admitting to me that he's simply "uncertain."

"I really am quite uncertain about how to interpret this," he said.

"It's the only place in the New Testament where the idea of a millennium is predicted...[it is] difficult to know if it is meant to be taken literally."[45]

— — — — — — — —

Others like Hanegraaff—who shares some similar beliefs to partial preterists (like Wilson) who see much of Revelation as having already been fulfilled—believe that the context of Revelation is important to understanding exactly what's happening in the text.

Explaining the book as seven letters to seven churches, he said that John's purpose was to encourage the churches that were in the midst of the Caesar cult to "be faithful and fruitful."[46]

"They're going to suffer terribly for a short time, but their vindication is going to be an eternal vindication...a thousand years has to do with a metaphor," he said. "The reason that I'm quite certain about that is the Bible uses metaphors throughout the biblical text, but here you have apocalyptic language."[47]

He argued that language shouldn't be taken in this case in a "wooden, literal sense," saying that he is certain that this is the case, citing other biblical examples of the use of "one thousand" in Scripture to drive home his point.[48]

"If you look through the Scripture, whenever thousand is used as a whole number, it's always used in a metaphorical way. You have a highly figurative passage," Hanegraaff said. "You can have an angel coming down...having the key to the abyss, and holding in his hand a great chain. He sees the dragon, that the ancient serpent is the devil, and binds him for a thousand years."[49]

He said that this is "figurative apocalyptic language," wondering how an angel—a non-corporeal being—could hold a chain, for example.[50] As for Hanegraaff's claim about instances of the Bible's metaphorical use of one thousand, he cited these verses:

- "Know therefore that the LORD your God, He is God, the faithful God, who keeps covenant and mercy with them who love Him and keep His commandments to a thousand generations" (Deut. 7:9).

- "For every wild animal of the forest is Mine, and the cattle on a thousand hills" (Ps. 50:10).

- "For a day in Your courts is better than a thousand else-where" (Ps. 84:10).

His point was that taking the millennial kingdom in a literal sense is problematic since it's the only instance in Scripture that he believes that the number is viewed literally.

"The only place that you find a thousand years mentioned, and now we're going to read it in a wooden, literal sense? We're going to posit that Jesus comes back, and then there's going to be a semi-golden age?" Hanegraaff rhetorically asked. "This is, quite frankly, madness, particularly when you think about the fact that Jesus is the substance that fulfills all the types and shadows."[51]

— — — — — — — —

All of the debate over the premillennial, amillennial, and postmillennial worldviews aside, I'll briefly touch on what happens in the biblical text after references to the debated one-thousand-year reign in Revelation 20:4–6.

It's a complicated and multifaceted mixture of verses, but let's dive into a quick review: Satan is released from prison and heads out to deceive the nations in the four corners of the earth, gathering them for battle. (We'll get into the Gog and Magog debate in subsequent chapters as well.)

When they surround the "beloved city," fire comes from heaven and they are defeated, before joining the beast and false prophet in the "lake of fire and brimstone" (vv. 9–10).

From there the dead are judged, the institution of death abolished, the creation of a new heaven and a new earth accomplished, and the making of everything new comes to fruition in Revelation 21, with the description of the restoration of Eden following in chapter 22.

On a final note in this chapter, let's briefly circle back to the potential reasons why Satan is released following the one-thousand-year period, as Revelation 20:3 reads, "After that he must be set free for a little while."

Naturally this has created a fair number of questions, mainly: Why does Satan need to be released after the one thousand years are over?

There is clearly ambiguity when it comes to the purpose for this release. There are also questions surrounding what will be happening on earth during Jesus's reign. If humans alive at the time continue to have babies, will they be born sinful? If so, how does this play out in practice?

We can't dive into these themes in-depth in this book, but it is worth noting that they are some of the other areas of contention for which a consensus will likely not be reached in the near-term.

Chapter 9

UNDERSTANDING SCRIPTURE
AND ESCHATOLOGY

I T'S CLEARLY STATED right there in the Bible!"
That's the tone that many strike when debating Scripture, but a
deeper wade into the discussion over biblical narratives makes it
clear that there are many theological ideas, theories, and paradigms
that are anything but plain, simple, or settled.

Just consider how many Christian denominations we have these
days. And ponder, for a moment, the vast disagreements over the
Rapture, Millennium, Tribulation, and other eschatological issues that
we've spent a great deal of time exploring thus far in this book.

Prophecy is, perhaps, among the most heated biblical subjects, as
finding harmony between the many camps is a difficult task, to say
the least.

We've already discussed the fact that interpretive methodology is
key, but there are some fancier words that theology types will invoke
when discussing the science of biblical interpretation: hermeneutics
and exegesis. There are concepts that we should properly understand
if we really want to know what's at the center of the end-times debate.

Hermeneutics involves the study of methods and principles of interpretation of the Bible, and exegesis refers to an explanation or interpretation of a biblical text.

In a 2014 article on Lifeway.com, Wayne McDill explained that the
purpose of hermeneutics is to use certain principles so that the "text
will disclose its meaning to the interpreter."[1] Boiling the definition
down, hermeneutics is the variety of ways in which individuals read
the Bible in an effort to discern meaning.[2]

To determine the intended lessons and meanings of Scripture,
McDill encouraged pastors and readers to determine the genre of
the text, explore the context of the text, read for obvious meaning,

examine the language, explore through the lens of how God deals with man, and examine the theological themes within.[3]

In the end, different hermeneutical approaches include various lenses through which Scripture is read. Perhaps Dr. Ellen White best explained this feature of hermeneutics in a 2011 article for *Bible History Daily*. She explained that the existence of differing goals among interpreters has led to a plethora of hermeneutics, going on to provide some key examples to help illustrate that different methods can yield various types of interpretations.

"For example, if you want to understand how Moses's life in the wilderness differed from daily life in the ancient Levant, you would use an archaeological/anthropological hermeneutic," White wrote. "However, if you want to understand the gender politics between Miriam and Moses in the wilderness, you would use a feminist or womanist approach to the text."[4]

GotQuestions.org offered the following illustration to help readers best understand how to approach the different genres for optimal understanding: "A proverb should be understood and applied differently from a law."[5]

When it comes to an explanation or interpretation of text, there are four major types of hermeneutical methods worth briefly exploring: literal, moral, allegorical, and anagogical.[6]

- The literal calls on Bible readers to do exactly as it sounds: interpret the meaning of Scripture as it is written by looking at what it's saying and the grammar as well as the historical narrative.[7] Famed end-times author Tim LaHaye, who takes the Scriptures literally, shared with me advice that he learned from Dr. David Cooper, a theologian who once said in reference to the Bible, "Take every word at its literal meaning unless the facts and the context indicate otherwise."[8] It's a line that LaHaye, who penned the monumentally popular Left Behind book series, used to affirm his belief that "all Scripture should be taken literally."[9]

- Then there's the moral approach, which entails looking at biblical texts in a way that seeks to derive lessons on

ethics—a process that could involve the third major
form of hermeneutics: allegory.[10]

- The allegorical approach relies upon examining hidden
  meanings and grander narratives than what is literally
  being written in the text.

- The fourth and final major form of hermeneutics is anagogical, which "seeks to explain biblical events or matters of this world so that they relate to the life to come,"
  according to *Encyclopaedia Britannica*.[11]

The interpretive rules and regulations don't end there, either. More
specifically, when it comes to how to decipher the gospel, the law, and
God's plan of redemption for human beings, there are three main paradigms through which to view the Bible: dispensationalism, covenant
theology, and new covenant theology.[12]

Dispensationalism is a theological system that involves a strictly
consistent literal methodology of examining Scripture.[13] Ron Rhodes
expanded upon this definition in his book *The 8 Great Debates of Bible
Prophecy*, writing that the approach also involves "a clear distinction
between Israel and the church" and "the glory of God as God's ultimate purpose for the world."[14]

Those who embrace dispensationalism believe that there are two
separate prophetic destinies outlined in the Bible: one for Israel, which
will take place on earth, and the other for the church as a whole, which
involves the heavenly realm.[15]

In addition to embracing the distinct relationship and prophecy
involving Israel and the entirety of the Christian church, dispensationalism involves God "structuring His relationship with mankind
through several stages of revelation" based on "dispensations," Matt
Perman explained in an article on the subject.[16]

Keeping in mind that the general definition of dispensation is "a
system of revealed commands and promises regulating human
affairs,"[17] those who embrace dispensationalism generally see seven
distinct dispensations throughout the biblical narrative. Outlined by
Rhodes in *The 8 Great Debates of Bible Prophecy*, they include:[18]

- **Innocence:** Found in Genesis 1:28–3:6, this involved Adam and Eve and ended with their decision to sin and violate God's rule.

- **Conscience:** Extending from Genesis 3:7–8:14, Rhodes describes this as beginning with the Fall and extending through the flood in Noah's time.

- **Human government:** Involving the events in Genesis 8:15–11:9, this dispensation involves the creation of human government in an effort to stave off evils.

- **Promise:** This involves the promises God made to Abraham involving his descendants, as recounted in Genesis 11:10 through Exodus 18:27.

- **Law:** Involving a sweeping array of scripture from Exodus 19 through John 14:30, this involves God's delivering of the law to Israel, which was set in place until Jesus's arrival to fulfill what had been promised.

- **Grace:** Encompassing scripture outlined from Acts 2:1 through Revelation 19:21, this involves life on earth before the new heaven and new earth.

- **Kingdom:** Involving text in Revelation 20, this involves the millennial kingdom, which premillennial dispensationalists believe will be a literal ruling of Christ on earth following His return for a period of one thousand years.

All of this to say, a literal approach to Scripture is clearly the hallmark of the dispensationalist perspective. Perman detailed an important note about the role of Israel not only in dispensationalists' biblical narrative but also in their view about how God's relationship with humanity will eventually play out.

Adherents see God's promises for Israel in the Old Testament as having a future far beyond the time in which they were written. Rather than being fulfilled in the future formation and growth of the Christian umbrella, dispensationalists believe that Israel will be restored as a nation to the land on which the nation once stood. This, of course, made the 1948 re-creation of the state of Israel so notable for dispensationalists, as we'll address in later chapters. Critics, though, would counter that the Old Testament prophecies were more geared toward alluding to a world that would be inherited by the entirety of Christianity, not that Israel itself would be re-created in that process, as Perman explained.[19]

Noted Christian author Jeff Kinley said that there are some misconceptions about the definition of "dispensationalism" among some individuals who do not subscribe to the theology, saying that he's often met with the following question: "Oh, so you believe in different ways to be saved throughout history, eh?" Such a dynamic, he said, couldn't be further from the truth.[20]

"My understanding of what people call 'dispensationalism'…is this: since God's revelation of Himself to mankind was, by necessity, gradual and progressive, man's knowledge of his relationship with God (including everything…truth about sin, salvation, God, and heaven) was, therefore, limited," Kinley said.[21]

To put this in simpler terms, the author said that dispensationalists would believe that biblical figures such as Noah actually knew less about the coming Christ and God's plan for redemption than Abraham did, with Isaiah having less knowledge than Paul, who came along later on to compose much of the New Testament.

As time went on, dispensationalists believe that these messages became clearer, with Kinley explaining that it simply "makes logical and theological sense" for God not to "require Old Testament believers to possess and exercise a full and complete understanding when placing faith in Him and His provision for sin and salvation."[22] After all, biblical figures living in Old Testament times likely did not yet have the knowledge to fully comprehend all of the ins and outs of God's salvation plan.

"As the light and content of God's revelation grew over time, His followers understood more specifics about exactly how He would accomplish their redemption," Kinley said. "But no matter what 'dispensation' they found themselves in, the basis for salvation was always the same, even though the content of their faith was incomplete."[23] That future plan for salvation obviously involved Jesus Christ, with practices such as the Jewish sacrificial system, among others, pointing toward what was to come.

Moving outside of the classical dispensationalist realm, there are two other related worldviews that are essential to briefly explore: revised dispensationalism and progressive dispensationalism. The former takes a literal approach to Old Testament covenants with Israel but holds that there is simply one new covenant that applies to both Israel and the church, according to Rhodes. That covenant presently applies to the church and will later apply to national Israel, seeing Israel and the church as a collective "one people of God," he explained.[24]

As for progressive dispensationalists, they see the dispensations as being related and successive rather than disconnected events, cumulatively culminating in God's redemptive plan.[25]

Under progressive dispensationalism, adherents are open to some figurative interpretation of certain verses and themes, leading them to advocate for a slight departure from what traditional and classical dispensationalists argue.

Here's how Dr. Darrell Bock, a professor of New Testament studies at Dallas Theological Seminary and one of the individuals responsible for the formation of the progressive dispensational worldview, differentiated between the three brands of dispensationalism in an interview for this book.

"The earliest version of dispensationalism argued for a complete distinction between the church and Israel. They didn't cross in any way or any shape or form," he said. "Then, revised come along and said, 'Well, there is some overlap; there is some association in the covenants, with association in the covenants in terms of fulfillment.'"[26]

Bock went on to explain that the third form of dispensationalism—progressive—holds that "all the covenant promises of God, in one way or another, have some form of initial fulfillment in the church."[27]

"So it has to do with the level of continuity in the program between Israel and the church," he said. "While all dispensationalists maintain an ultimate distinctive between Israel and the church, the two are not to be mixed in such a way that the church replaces Israel in the program of God."[28]

Thus, the debate between traditionalists and progressives gets into the weeds a bit, but is, at least in part, based on an understanding of God's promise to David in the Old Testament. God outlined the Davidic covenant to the Prophet Nathan in 2 Samuel 7, proclaiming that David's kingdom would be established "forever." Here's how verses 11 through 16 read:

> The LORD declares to you that He will instead bring about a house for you. When your days are complete and you lie down with your fathers, I will raise up after you an offspring from your body, and I will establish his rule. He will build a house for My name, and I will establish his royal throne forever. I will be a father to him, and he will be a son to Me. When he goes astray, I will correct him with the rod of men and afflictions of the sons of men. My commitment will not abandon him, as I removed it from Saul, whom I deposed before you. Your house and dominion will endure before Me forever, and your throne will be established by the LORD forever.

It is the establishment of this throne that serves as a key difference between traditional dispensationalists and their progressive counterparts, as the latter believe that Jesus is, at this time, sitting on the Davidic throne and ruling over humanity. Traditionalists, though, would counter that, though Jesus is ruling, He's not necessarily on David's throne.[29] Both traditional and progressive dispensationalists would embrace the notion that Israel has a place in the future, according to Bible professor H. Wayne House.[30]

— — — — — — — —

Moving on from the dispensational debate, the second interpretive framework for exploring the biblical narrative is covenant theology, in which strict literalism on the prophecy front is pushed to the side.

Consider that adherents would see Old Testament covenants with Israel being fulfilled by the church in the New Testament, rather than a literal refounding of the Jewish state. In the end, Christianity and the church are seen as the new Israel, but in a spiritual sense rather than a literal one.[31] Instead of formulating a series of dispensations, the hermeneutical approach involved in covenant theology, according to Rhodes, is "built on two primary features—the covenant of works and the covenant of grace."[32]

The idea rests on the notion that God created a covenant with Adam that was based on works—one in which humanity's first man would be able to relate to the Lord and seek eternal life by abiding by the Almighty. But covenant theology holds that Adam's failure led God to create a new covenant in which grace was the new gold standard for humanity's ability to achieve eternal life. Here's how Perman explained it:

> The covenant of works, instituted in the Garden of Eden, was the promise that perfect obedience would be rewarded with eternal life. Adam was created sinless but with the capability of falling into sin. Had he remained faithful in the time of temptation in the Garden (the "probationary period"), he would have been made incapable of sinning and secured in an eternal and unbreakable right standing with God. But Adam sinned and broke the covenant, and thereby subjected himself and all his descendants to the penalty for covenant-breaking, condemnation.[33]

From there, such a prospect was achieved through an acceptance of the new covenant of grace through Christ.[34] Adherents of covenant theology believe that God structured His relationship with mankind through covenants and not dispensations.

Perman wrote that these covenants are "not new tests of man's faithfulness to each new stage of revelation" as dispensations are, but are, instead, "rather differing administrations of the single, overarching covenant of grace."[35]

Interestingly Kinley said that, when assessing covenant theology, he actually sees at least two "dispensations" or sorts, comprised of the old and then the new covenants. If holding the definition of "dispensation" as "a system of revealed commands and promises regulating human affairs," this idea holds merit.[36]

— — — — — — —

Of course, the debate over how to interpret Scripture and God's relationship with human beings doesn't end with dispensationalism and covenant theology, as there's also a construct known as new covenant theology, which Bible professor and expert Dr. Larry Pettegrew described as residing somewhere "between covenant theology and progressive dispensationalism."[37]

Consider that the new covenant—which is detailed in the Old

Testament by the Prophet Jeremiah in Jeremiah 31:31–34—is believed to have been established in the life and death of Jesus Christ. Those verses read:

> Surely, the days are coming, says the LORD, when I will make a new covenant with the house of Israel and with the house of Judah. It will not be according to the covenant that I made with their fathers in the day that I took them by the hand to bring them out of the land of Egypt, because they broke My covenant, although I was a husband to them, says the LORD. But this shall be the covenant that I will make with the house of Israel after those days, says the LORD: I will put My law within them and write it in their hearts; and I will be their God, and they shall be My people. They shall teach no more every man his neighbor and every man his brother, saying, "Know the LORD," for they all shall know Me, from the least of them to the greatest of them, says the LORD, for I will forgive their iniquity, and I will remember their sin no more.

This new covenant is referenced throughout the New Testament in Luke, 1 and 2 Corinthians, and Hebrews, tying Christ to the fulfillment of this Old Testament redemptive promise. See some of these verses below:

- "In like manner, He took the cup after supper, saying, 'This cup is the new covenant in My blood which is shed for you'" (Luke 22:20).

- "In the same manner He took the cup after He had supper, saying, 'This cup is the new covenant in My blood. Do this, as often as you drink it, in remembrance of Me'" (1 Cor. 11:25).

- "Who has made us able ministers of the new covenant, not of the letter but of the Spirit. For the letter kills, but the Spirit gives life" (2 Cor. 3:6).

- "For this reason He is the Mediator of a new covenant, since a death has occurred for the redemption of the sins that were committed under the first covenant, so that those who are called might receive the promise of eternal inheritance" (Heb. 9:15).

With that in mind, Pettegrew maintains that new covenant theology differs somewhat from covenant theology when it comes to addressing this pledge. He posits that new covenant theology "proclaims that the entire Mosaic Covenant has passed away as a law code, and that Christians are supposed to live under the New Covenant."[38]

The difference, Pettegrew maintains, is that many covenant theologians believe that the new covenant is simply an update of the old, with parts of the Mosaic covenant continuing on when it comes to Christian ethics.

Perman further explains that covenant theology breaks Old Testament Mosaic Law into three groups: civil laws that regulated Israel's government, ceremonial laws, and moral laws. While the first two are no longer operational following Jesus's death, he said that covenant theologians still hold to moral laws. New covenant adherents, in contrast, wouldn't accept such a division of laws, arguing that canceling any part of the law would render all of it no longer applicable; the law of Christ would thus be seen as paramount by these individuals, thus canceling out Mosaic code.[39]

This, in supporters' views, is a way of handling the complexities surrounding the attempt to discern which Old Testament laws should apply to believers today, as it places the full authority of moral guidance upon Jesus's teachings and the contents of other New Testament scripture.

It is this distinction, though, that Kinley, for one, flatly rejects.

"I don't see the legitimacy in new covenant theology in dismissing the moral law of the Old Testament," he said. "I agree that Christ fulfilled all of the Mosaic Law, and that as believers we are under no obligation to fulfill the Law. Faith in Christ satisfies the requirements of the Law. Period."[40] But Kinley said that he personally views the moral laws in the Old Testament as showcasing God's eternal character and, thus, transcending time, making those provisions applicable, pertinent, and appropriate to consider throughout the ages.

This carries through to some of the contentious ethics issues that continue to be at the forefront of discussion and debate today, he argued. "In other words, had Paul not declared the mind of God regarding homosexuality, we would still understand it to be morally offensive and deficient from Old Testament passages that spoke to that moral issue," he said.[41]

———————

I've explored these ideas to help the reader understand that there's far more at play than a series of debates over various eschatological elements. There are overarching lenses through which the Bible is viewed—a diversity of interpretive frameworks that lead believers in divergent directions when it comes to a variety of biblical issues, including prophecy.

Of course, one must approach all of this with a fair level of cautiousness. Speaking of the aforementioned debate, Kinley said that one's view of dispensationalism or eschatology more broadly isn't a "test for Christian fellowship," and that he believes that the events prophesied in Revelation will become clearer as time goes on.

"I do anticipate that global coming events will make it clearer that the Revelation scenario is not only literally viable, but perhaps a lot closer to us in time than anyone realizes," he said. "For that reason, as we continue seeing the foreshadowing of end-times prophecy, I anticipate some will rethink their views on eschatology."[42]

Much of the contemporary end-times debate obviously centers on the Book of Revelation, though there are countless portions of the Old and New Testament that are pieced together by many Bible experts to create a proposed timeline of eschatological events.

Interpretation is key, of course, and understanding is reliant upon the way in which one views God's relationship with humanity and, in turn, the way in which an individual sees that relationship being illustrated and documented in Scripture.

Some faith leaders may gloss over prophecy, but Tim LaHaye told me that it's important to note the seemingly undeniable prevalence of eschatology in Scripture when considering how much attention it truly deserves.

"You know, 28 percent of the Bible, Old and New Testament, was prophetic at the time it was written, so obviously—if God would have almost 30 percent of His holy scriptures being prophecy of things to come—it must have been important to God," he explained.[43]

Chapter 10

UNDERSTANDING REVELATION

NOW THAT WE'VE briefly discussed hermeneutics and the various views on God's redemption plan, it's essential to briefly explore the different ways in which the Book of Revelation—often seen as the most complex and debated book of the Bible—can be understood.

Dr. Darrell Bock maintains that there are two key reasons why Revelation is a difficult book to pin down: complexities surrounding the apocalyptic genre that the text encompasses and the struggles among some to embrace the idea that most of the book focuses on an end-times paradigm that is filled with events that have yet to come to fruition.

"The genre itself is indirect in the way that it communicates things," he said. "It's a genre that's intentionally trying to conceal what it is saying, so that if anything is said that's particularly revolutionary, the church doesn't get into trouble, and so it does it through symbolism."[1]

Many view Revelation as a mixture of three different genres: apocalyptic, prophetic, and epistolary literature.[2]

— — — — — — — —

It's the related struggle with the eschatological view of the text that also derails some, Bock explained. "People wrestle with the idea of a book that's strictly about the future or mostly strictly about the future and what that relevance is for people who are literally centuries removed from what is described in the book," he said. "And so another option that oftentimes is not appreciated is the idea that the history in the short term actually pictures... what the end is going to be like."[3]

In essence, Bock believes that there's a fascinating mix unfolding in which there's a short-term message that comes along with predictive elements of what's to come later on in the future. "I think that combination makes more sense of what's going on in the book than other ways of reading it," he said. "But a lot of people want to read Revelation flat; they want it only to apply to one period of time."[4]

Bock warned, "The moment you do that, you could create problems for yourself."[5]

Dr. Michael Brown agrees that contemporary Christians should see Revelation as being relevant to them as well as to first-century Christians.

"Christians should view the Book of Revelation as relevant to them today, as part of God's Word, but especially relevant for John's initial target audience," he said. Additionally, Brown said that there's a future audience worth considering in assessing the book—"believers living in the final generation, when history will reach its climax."[6] But he also had a warning for Christians that mirrored and seemingly corroborated Bock's concerns.

"What often happens, however, is that each generation thinks it's the last generation, thereby over-applying Revelation to its own day," Brown said. "It's also important to remember that this is apocalyptic literature, describing world events in cosmic terms."[7]

Explaining the book's context, Pastor Greg Laurie noted that he believes that Revelation comes with an internal outline proclaiming that the book involves things that are "past, present, and future."[8]

Laurie specifically referenced Revelation 1:19, which reads, "Write the things which you have seen, and the things which are, and the things which will take place after this," seeing it as a layout of the subsequent twenty-one chapters.[9] This, of course, is only one way of looking at the Bible's final book.

— — — — — — —

When it comes to eschatology, interpretation is everything. With that in mind, there are four general lenses through which Revelation can be viewed: the idealist, historicist, futurist, and preterist lenses.

According to theologian Douglas Wilson, the idealist view is one in which the text of Revelation really has no definitive meaning and is just "a vivid way of picturing the battle between good and evil."[10]

It distinguishes itself from the other approaches in that it doesn't seek to find specific individuals, groups, or events within the text of

Revelation. It sees these elements as being written to potentially represent struggles that will unfold between Jesus's first and second comings, without getting more specific in the process.[11]

The historicist view sees Revelation as being fulfilled throughout church history. It is what Dr. Cornelis P. Venema, professor of doctrinal studies at Mid-America Reformed Seminary, called "a visionary symbolization of the sequence of events that will occur throughout the course of the history of the church."[12]

The view essentially sees the book as detailing a timeline of actual events, people, and groups that will collectively help usher in "God's redemptive purposes," according to Venema, who wrote in a primer for Ligonier Ministries that historicist interpretations have, in the past, seen the Catholic Church or the pope as being Babylon in Revelation 17; the rise of Islam was also seen during the medieval church as the beast from the sea in Revelation 13.[13]

"[The] historicist view... sees the Book of Revelation as being fulfilled down through church history," Wilson further explained.[14]

The third lens is the futurist view, which sees Revelation as mostly being unfulfilled to date, believing that the events detailed in chapters 4 through 22 will unfold before Christ's return and during the end of days.[15]

This is where most premillennial dispensationalists would fall, believing that the majority of the events in the book have not yet happened—a view that is expressed by many of the theologians and Bible experts who were interviewed for this book, including LaHaye, Rosenberg, and Laurie, among others.

"Really, I think many of the things that John was speaking about in the Book of Revelation were in the way distant future," Laurie told me, citing his view. "I think that he is pointing to the future and giving that outline in the beginning of the book—rather I should say Jesus gave us that outline in the beginning of the book to John, telling us how to interpret it."[16]

The fourth lens, preterism, involves the belief that John was, indeed, prophesying in Revelation, but that the book is describing events that were already fulfilled two thousand years ago.[17]

"'Preterist' is the Latin word for 'past,'" Wilson explained. "The preterist view says that the Book of Revelation was future when John wrote the prophecy, but it was fulfilled in the first century largely, and it's in our past."[18]

There are different degrees to which preterism is embraced, which we will explore in depth in the next chapter.

There's also a fifth "eclectic" approach that merges each of the four to combine their strengths, while pushing associated weaknesses of each to the side.[19]

This has been a relatively quick summary of the various views on Revelation, which clearly consist of diverse ideas that can be difficult to pin down. Wilson gave me a quick recap that is helpful for summarizing what I've laid out in this chapter:

> Here I am in 2015. I look back, and if I see most of the Book of Revelation fulfilled in the first century—which I do—then I'm a preterist. If I think that it's going to be fulfilled in the next forty years, I'm a futurist. If I think that it was fulfilled throughout the two thousand years of church history, I'm a historicist. If I think it's just a big allegory, then I'm an idealist.[20]

— — — — — — —

Naturally one's worldview impacts everything that a person believes to be true about the elements of eschatology that are found in both the Old and the New Testaments.

Hank Hanegraaff, who shares some views with partial preterists, broke down his personal take on Revelation, calling it the "revelation of Jesus Christ," and pointing to the first chapter to detail how he believes the book should be read.

"You see that in the very first part of the Book of Revelation, which God gave to show His servants what must soon take place," he said. "In fact, Jesus then says in the introduction of the book, 'The time is near.'"[21]

Here, Hanegraaff focuses on Revelation 1:3, which reads, "Blessed is he who reads and those who hear the words of this prophecy and keep those things which are written in it, for the time is near."

With the more near-term time frame in mind, Hanegraaff argues that Jesus isn't "linguistically challenged in the least," and that the

Christian Savior would have said that the book's fulfillment would be thousands of years away, if that were the case, rather than alluding to a scenario that was near. "Soon and near means soon and near," Hanegraaff said. "And it's an unconscionable abuse of language to suggest that that means a time far off, or two thousand years away."[22]

And while many modern-day Evangelicals view the Bible book as a road map of mostly unfulfilled prophecy, when asked what in Revelation has yet to be fulfilled, Dr. Shane J. Wood, a New Testament professor, simply narrowed it down, in his view, to the second coming of Christ.

Wood, who said that Revelation is cyclical in nature, joked that, if he really wanted to torture his students, he'd make them formulate an outline of the scriptures within it, explaining that they are "not linear."

"That's what's frustrating to us. As Western minds, we're looking for Roman numeral one, capital A. We're looking for a linear outline that we could follow," Wood said. "That's not even the way a Jewish mind primarily function[ed]. I'm not saying they have no linear thought, but they are very cyclical on their thinking."[23]

Chapter 11

PRETERISTS

ESPITE THEIR DIFFERENCES, premillennialists, amillennialists, and postmillennialists each see at least some portions of Revelation as offering projections into future events that have not yet been fulfilled, but another group of biblical theorists takes an entirely divergent view on the fulfillment of eschatology.

Full, or extreme, preterists—whose name is derived from the Latin word *praeteritus*, which essentially means the "past"—believe that John was, indeed, prophesying in Revelation, but that the book describes events that were already fulfilled two thousand years ago.[1]

Or, more specifically, as theology writer and preterist Riley O'Brien Powell explains, many adherents see "all of Bible prophecy as having been fulfilled in the ministry of Jesus, through his first century advents, and in the ongoing progress of God's people in the world."[2]

Full preterists—who are just one cohort out of a wider group of preterists—would generally argue that there are no remaining future proclamations or prophecies embedded in the biblical text, departing entirely from the vast majority of Christians who embrace the premillennial, amillennial, or postmillennial viewpoints that take starkly different stances on the matter.[3]

As is typically the case when it comes to prophecy, preterists—like their peers in other end-times groups—are anything but homogeneous, with Bible expert Dr. Richard L. Mayhue breaking their diverse perspectives into three main groups: mild preterism, moderate preterism, and extreme preterism.[4]

Those on the "mild" side believe that the Tribulation unfolded during the first three centuries of the Christian church based on judgments against the Jews in AD 70 and Rome in AD 313 (the Edict of Milan was crafted that year, paving the way to the permanent tolerance of Christians in Rome), though mild preterists still believe that a second coming will one day come to fruition.[5]

Moderates believe that most Bible prophecies were already fulfilled in AD 70 when the temple and Jerusalem were destroyed. They believe, though, that Jesus's second coming is impending and that a new heaven and earth will follow.[6]

Finally, Mayhue described what he said are full, or extreme, preterists—individuals who believe that all prophecy—including Jesus's second coming in Revelation—has already come to pass and is essentially fulfilled. If there's some form of an end times to come such as what many others believe is explicitly predicted in Revelation 19 through 22, full preterists simply don't see it as being outlined in the Bible.[7]

— — — — — — — —

To evaluate preterist ideas, one must be aware of the dates. Mayhue, who is a critic of preterism, argues that an analysis of the dates surrounding the writing of Revelation, Matthew 24:34, Matthew 10:23, and Matthew 16:28 all provide "time indicators by which preterism...lives or dies."[8]

Unlike premillennialists who believe that John wrote Revelation around AD 90, preterists generally maintain that the book was penned before AD 70, most likely between AD 63 and 68 during Roman emperor Nero's reign, essentially seeing it as another version of Jesus's Olivet Discourse.[9]

It was in that sermon on the Mount of Olives that Christ predicted the destruction of the temple and spoke—according to many Bible scholars—of the end times that would one day come to fruition.

The preterist belief that Revelation was written before AD 70 is predicated upon the fact that it was during that year that the Romans torched the Jewish temple in the midst of the first Jewish-Roman War.[10] Arguably, it was a time during which great calamity befell the region. If it were written later, as many believe, then the notion that Jesus returned in AD 70 would clearly be called into question; that's why an earlier date is embraced by preterists, as it coincides with their framework.

In Matthew 24:2 Jesus told His disciples of the temple: "Do you not see all these things? Truly I say to you, not one stone shall be left here upon another that shall not be thrown down."

Preterists see a connection between Jesus's prediction that the temple would be destroyed and the timelines laid out in Revelation, as Dr. John Noē explained:

> Preterists further point out that Revelation's 3½-year period ("42 months," "1,260 days," and "time, times, half time"; Rev 11:2, 3; 12:6, 14; 13:5) corresponds with the exact time frame of the worst tribulation in Jewish history, the AD 66–70 Jewish-Roman War. It culminated in the destruction of Jerusalem and the Temple and forever ended biblical Judaism and the old covenant, animal sacrifice system—just as Christ had perfectly predicted (Matthew 23–24).[11]

While preterists believe that this has already happened, others—including premillennialists, as discussed in previous chapters—see the 1,260-day time block as being currently unfulfilled, believing that it will take place sometime during the future end times. Premillennialists also believe that the Antichrist will reign for forty-two months (which equals 1,260 days) during the final three and a half years of the seven-year Tribulation period, which we covered in a previous chapter.

Detailing her own preterist view on eschatology, Powell wrote that she believes "God no longer lived in the temple made with hands" after the Roman assault on Jerusalem and the destruction of the temple. "God lived in a temple of people now—his Kingdom of people on earth," she wrote. "So Jesus was coming back to establish the 'heaven and earth' of the New Covenant world.... Jesus was coming to establish the new 'heaven and earth' and to speed the passing of the 'heaven and earth' of the Old Covenant world."[12]

While Dr. Shane J. Wood said that he believes that AD 70 was a "big deal," he believes that full preterists are overemphasizing it in their theology.

"It was a big deal, because of what it actually solidified that Jesus said. Jesus makes two major predictions in His life," he told me. "Those two predictions are, number one, 'The temple will be destroyed' and number two, 'I will come again.'" Wood continued, "The temple being destroyed is very significant because it actually validates His claim He will come again."[13]

In the end, he said that some preterists are making the events of that time "a little more significant than…what we have evidence for."[14]

— — — — — — — —

When it comes to defending the heart of their eschatological views, preterists also look to Jesus's words in Matthew 24:34—statements that He uttered after both predicting the fall of the temple as well as the signs of the end times: "Truly I say to you, this generation will not pass away until all these things take place."[15]

As Dr. Stanley Toussaint notes, it is the use of the word *generation* that preterists would point to, as it is used in other places in the Gospels to describe the current and present generation of individuals living at the time of each occurrence in Scripture.[16] Thus, if verses like Mark 8:12, Luke 7:31, Matthew 11:16, and others use the word in that form, preterists believe that Jesus was talking of events that would come before the close of the current generation that He was speaking to.

To summarize: rather than a projection into a future end-times scenario, preterists maintain that Jesus's shared eschatological signs that are detailed in Matthew 24 have already come to pass, according to Toussaint. "Because verse 34 says, 'This generation will not pass away until all these things take place,' they hold that the predictions in verses 4–14 regarding famines, earthquakes, false messiahs, wars, and so forth were all fulfilled in the days just before A.D. 70,'" he wrote.[17]

— — — — — — — —

Contrary to the preterist view, dispensationalists, though, see the reference to "this generation" as being tied to the future generation of Jewish individuals who will be living during Christ's return.[18] Mayhue said that "generation" can be interpreted in a "pejorative" sense, referring to sinful people who have rejected Christ, or that it can be meant temporally to reference a span of people starting with Jesus's contemporaries and extending into the future generation that will be alive during His second coming.[19]

As for preterists who believe that Matthew 24:4–33 (as well as Mark 13:5–29 and Luke 21:8–31) were already fulfilled, Toussaint said that such a belief requires the overlooking of several verses, including scripture about Jesus's return.[20]

In the end, Toussaint said that Matthew 24:34 is a difficult verse to contend with, regardless of one's eschatological stance, as questions and debate abound surrounding what, exactly, "all these things" encompasses in the verse when Jesus says, "Truly I say to you, this generation will not pass away until all these things take place."

It should be noted that it is in the Olivet Discourse that many preterists believe that Jesus rejected Israel, considering that He said the following in Matthew 23:38: "Look, your house is left to you desolate." It is in the next chapter with the prediction of the destruction of the temple that they believe that the desolation was complete.[21]

Many preterists would argue that there were rumors of war, famines, earthquakes, false prophets, and other signs before AD 70, maintaining that the abomination of desolation mentioned by Jesus in Matthew 24:15 could have referred to the occupation of murderous zealots, the Romans torching the temple, or other events that either came before or during the fall of Jerusalem that year, according to Toussaint.

Of course, many Bible scholars would reject this sentiment and, instead, see the abomination that causes desolation—which is also referenced in Daniel, Matthew, and Mark—as a prophecy pertaining to the future Antichrist who they believe will one day rise to power.

As previously stated, one of the key issues here is the use of "you" in the Olivet Discourse in Matthew 24, as Toussaint summarizes. Some certainly view this as speaking of a future generation, while others believe that it is a direct address to the generation alive during the time that Jesus spoke the words.

Toussaint adds an important point that he believes might help with some of the context surrounding Christ's use of "you":

> The second-person plural may be employed of those who are not contemporaries. Illustrations of this are found in the immediate context. In Matthew 23:35 the Lord Jesus, referring to the death of Zechariah, used the words "whom you murdered." Obviously Zechariah was killed centuries before Christ. And Jesus said, "You will not see Me until you say, 'Blessed is He who comes in the name of the Lord!'" (v. 39 [NAS]). This speaks of a future

generation of Israel that will yet make that grand confession. The pronoun "you" may look backward or forward.[22]

When examining Jesus's own words, preterists would look to additional verses as well, including Matthew 16:28 and Matthew 10:23, to corroborate the belief that Christ had indicated that His return would be in the immediate and not deep in the future.

Powell maintains that Jesus was clear and direct, while also using parables to instruct His followers that He would be returning to "his first generation of believers" and not in some future generation.[23]

Consider that Christ said the following in Matthew 16:28: "Truly I say to you, there are some standing here who shall not taste death before they see the Son of Man coming in His kingdom." The idea here is that Christ was specifically proclaiming that He would come back "in His kingdom" before those before Him perished.

Some might push back against the idea of a centuries-old second coming of Christ, wondering why the world didn't see Jesus appear in bodily form in the clouds.

Preterist leader Dr. Don Preston told me in an interview for this book, though, that he believes that people have mistaken expectations about what would be observed during Christ's return.

"Failure to understand Hebraic thought and Hebraic apocalyptic language has resulted in the expectation of the coming of Jesus as a 5' 5" Jewish man riding out of heaven on a literal cloud," he said. "In the [Old Testament] YHVH (God) was said to ride on the clouds when He came in judgment of nations. Yet, He never came literally, visibly or bodily."[24]

To corroborate this point, Preston cited Isaiah 19:1, which reads: "See, the LORD is riding on a swift cloud and shall come into Egypt; and the idols of Egypt shall tremble at His presence, and the heart of Egypt shall melt in its midst."[25]

Furthermore, Preston said that Jesus had said that He would be coming "in the glory of the Father," which he takes to mean that Christ would come in the way that the Father had. "Since the Father had never come literally, visibly, bodily—and yet, He had been said to come on the clouds, this should control our understanding of Christ's coming on the clouds," he continued, later adding "Jesus's coming is never posited as His revelation as man, but as King of kings and Lord of lords. To reveal Him as God—not man."[26]

This is a perspective that is shared by Powell as well. She wrote:

> The presence of God, in the paradoxical form of Roman armies, trampled the city of Jerusalem for 42 months, or 3 1/2 years—just as prophesied, "...it is given to the nations, and they will trample the Holy City for 42 months" (Revelation 11:2). Afterwards, even the Jewish historian, Josephus, recognized that this was a Divine intervention—a Coming of God—breaking into and changing history forever.[27]

Upon closer examination, some say that a rationale for a return of Christ in AD 70 based on Jesus's seemingly more immediate words might not be so cut and dry. Toussaint noted that Matthew 16:28 mirrors Mark 9:1 and Luke 9:27—and that there's something worth mentioning about each of these verses: they are followed by Christ's transfiguration—an account that was also recapped in 2 Peter 1:16–18.

It is in Matthew 17 that the Bible recounts how Peter, James, and John joined Jesus on a mountain, where He "was transfigured before them." The description that follows includes some remarkable imagery, including Jesus's face shining like the sun and His clothes becoming "white as the light."

Then the three saw Moses and Elijah talking with Christ. (Remember, this is one of the reasons that some experts, including Tim LaHaye, believe that it is possible that the two witnesses in Revelation 11 could be Moses and Elijah.)

While preterists cite Jesus telling His disciples that some of them would "not taste death" before seeing Him "coming in His kingdom" to corroborate a belief that Christ already returned in AD 70, critics of this worldview see something else entirely.

For those who flatly oppose full preterism, they believe that the Transfiguration that follows Matthew 16:28, Mark 9:1, and Luke 9:27 is key to understanding what, exactly, Jesus was saying when He discussed coming into His kingdom.

"It is not without significance that all three Synoptics follow this prediction with the account of the Transfiguration; there must be some connection in the minds of the Gospel writers between the Lord's words and the Transfiguration," Toussaint wrote.[28]

Preterists also point to Matthew 10:23, which states, "When they persecute you in this city, escape into another. For truly I say to you, you will not have gone through the cities of Israel before the Son of Man comes." Critics push back against this interpretation in the same way.

As Mayhue noted, "A futuristic interpretation of 'coming' in Matt 10:23 is contextually, grammatically, hermeneutically, and theologically more reasonable than the other views."[29]

- - - - - - -

It's worth looking at the concluding chapters of Revelation as well. While some might see the latter chapters as problematic to a preterist worldview, that simply depends on which preterist one is speaking to.

Full preterists have been able to remedy their belief in all end-times prophecies being fulfilled in the first century with the portions of Revelation that many believe will lead to an entirely new heaven and earth.

As Noē noted, preterists also hold that the "Babylon" mentioned in Revelation 18 is actually Jerusalem rather than a symbol of some other city in the future, such as Rome or New York City. This too comports with the notion that John prophesies events in Revelation that would unfold not long after the book was composed in the first century.[30]

Hank Hanegraaff wrote an article back in 2011 describing how "puzzled" he is over the debate surrounding which nation Babylon refers to in Revelation 17 and 18. Hanegraaff, whose own ideas have some commonalities with partial preterism—though he doesn't embrace that label—has said that "hundreds" of Bible experts have simply been wrong on the matter.

"On the one hand, hundreds of prophecy experts misidentify the great prostitute as the contemporary Roman Catholic Church. On the other, hundreds of commentators identify the great harlot as ancient (or revived) imperial Rome," he wrote. "The application of the historical principle of biblical interpretation, however, demonstrates that, either way, this is a clear case of mistaken identity."[31]

Hanegraaff—who believes that Christ's second coming is somewhere in the future and does not agree with the full preterist idea that it unfolded during the early days of Christianity—sees parallels between Old Testament references to Israel and the descriptions in Revelation.

"Verse by verse, the painful picture of a people who prostitute themselves with pagan deities emerges (see, e.g., Jeremiah 2:20–24; 3:2–3; Ezekiel 23:9–20). The prostituted bride had little interest in seeking intimacy with God in his temple," he continued. "Instead, she craved intimacy with foreign gods on the threshing floors of perverse temples (Hosea 9:1)."[32]

In the article Hanegraaff also noted the parallels between Ezekiel 16 and Revelation 17, recapping that in both chapters the prostitute commits adultery with kings of the earth. In the former, Jerusalem is discussed as being beautiful, but prostituting herself and being guilty of wickedness. And in the latter, similar language is used.

Powell agrees that "the unfaithful Israel was often described as a prostitute or an unfaithful wife" in the Old Testament, citing Jeremiah 2:2; 3:14; 3:20; Isaiah 54:5; 1:21; and Ezekiel 6:9, among other verses.[33]

She also referenced the clothing in Revelation 17:3–5, with verse 4 reading: "The woman was arrayed in purple and scarlet, and adorned with gold and precious stones and pearls." Powell tied this back to the priestly garments in Exodus 28:5–6—which reads, "They shall take the gold, the blue, the purple, and the scarlet, and fine linen. They shall make the ephod of gold, of blue, and of purple, of scarlet, and fine twined linen, the work of a skilled workman"—in an effort to tie Israel to Babylon.[34]

Preterists' wildly diverse views on Revelation 21–22, which speaks of the new heaven and new earth, obviously depend on whether they subscribe to a mild, moderate, or extreme preterist worldview.

Hanegraaff told me in a past interview for TheBlaze that he embraces the future second coming of Jesus, despite disagreeing on many of the eschatological theories posed by dispensationalists, among others. Noting that "paradise lost becomes paradise restored," he highlighted that those who want a relationship with Christ will have it, while those who have denied the Savior will not enjoy this benefit.[35]

"Well, the Bible says…that Jesus is going to appear a second time," he said. "Those who have lived on the planet…Jesus said, do not be amazed by this…there will be the ultimate judgment that takes place, which those who have a relationship with God in this time-space continuum are given that relationship in eternity, and those who did not want a relationship will have that validated in eternity as well."[36]

Unlike Hanegraaff, who believes that Christ is still due to return to set up a new heaven and a new earth, full preterists believe that the new heaven and earth are the "present world," with Powell writing in a Q&A section on her website that "what makes the Heavens and Earth 'new' is not an act of God physically re-creating them, but a renewing and reconciliation of all things in Christ, through his sacrifice, resurrection and return in AD 70."[37]

Thus, at least some full preterists would believe that Christ's return already renewed the heaven and earth in compliance with what is outlined in the latter portion of Revelation.

"It is assumed—with no proof and contrary to all preterist writers—that we deny the Second Coming. No, we affirm it," Preston told me. "We simply keep it in its proper chronological context."[38]

Preston went on to explain some of the "misconceptions and misrepresentations" that he believes surround the preterist worldview.

"It is assumed—falsely—that we deny the physical resurrection of Jesus," he said. "It has been claimed—falsely—that if preterism is true, that there is no life after death." Preston called both of these claims from critics "false to the core," adding that he has heard some critics say that there is no point in living ethically if, as preterists claim, prophecy has already been fulfilled. This too he pushed back against.[39]

"The realization that we live in the presence of a loving, holy, righteous God demands that we conform to His image—'Be ye holy, because I am holy,'" he said.[40]

Partial preterist Douglas Wilson, though, had some cautions about full preterism, explaining that he can't quite get on board with the notion that "every last prophecy in the Bible was fulfilled in our past."[41]

"The problem with that is that, if you look at the Apostles' Creed, where it says, 'Jesus Christ will come to judge the quick and the dead,' there's only been one creedal statement that the universal church has agreed on with regard to eschatology," Wilson said. "And it's that line, and it amounts to 'Hyper-preterism is wrong.'"[42]

A line in the Apostles' Creed—a statement of Christian belief that dates back to at least AD 390—reads, "He shall come to judge the living and the dead." It becomes clear with that statement that the early Christian church believed that Jesus's return was impending and not something of the past.

"The hyper-preterists have to say that there's nothing to look forward to, there is no resurrection of the dead in our future, there is no end of the world, and this is as good as it's going to get, which I think is a radical downgrade from what the New Testament promises," Wilson said.[43]

The theologian said that he has no problem believing that many texts that are traditionally applied to end-times theology by others are actually referring to past events that unfolded in AD 70, but he simply doesn't agree with extreme preterists when it comes to the Second Coming.

"I also believe that there are some texts prophesying the general resurrection of the dead, and Romans 8, where the whole creation is groaning as in the pangs of childbirth," Wilson said. "I believe that those things are yet to be fulfilled, so I'm a partial preterist."[44]

Preterism provides yet another divergent viewpoint on the end times, opening up additional debate about the finer details.

Chapter 12

THE END TIMES ARE UPON US, ACCORDING TO SOME

ARE THE BIBLICAL end times upon us? Perhaps there's no question more simultaneously loaded, disputed, and discussed in modern-day theology than that. While Jesus proclaimed in Matthew 24:36 that "no one knows" the day or the hour, that hasn't stopped some prophecy enthusiasts from issuing some problematic proclamations.

Believers have always wondered whether their era will be at least the start of—or part of—what the Bible describes as the "end of the age"—a time period that the disciples linked to Jesus's second coming in Matthew 24:3.

Today, speculation about the end times most certainly isn't simmering, as domestic and international events continue to fuel questions and chatter of what's to come. American culture is changing at a rapid rate, with many wondering whether shifting tides mean that Jesus's return is drawing ever nearer.

And considering the horror and terror that has been ramping up in the Middle East—the geographical centerpiece on eschatological events—it's unsurprising that many are pondering whether we're beginning to witness the start of the chaos that precedes the end unfolding right before our eyes.

Harvest Crusade founder Greg Laurie has devoted many sermons to the end times, helping believers understand the events that he thinks will one day unfold. He's had no problem openly proclaiming that he believes we're currently living in the last days, tying contemporary world events to prophecy.

Laurie told me that he's heard some people propose that "World War III" is upon us, as the West is embroiled in an ongoing fight against radical Islam, though he said that the battle against extremism has been ongoing for quite some time, reaching a fever pitch with the September 11, 2001, attacks.

The "conflict between the world views of Islam and Christianity [goes] back a lot further than 9/11," Laurie said, adding that it remains to be seen whether these events are part of a more immediate scenario that will led to the end times or if they are part of the final eschatological paradigm.[1]

Despite his uncertainty about how, or even if, the current chaos and in the Middle East fits into the eschatological archetype, Laurie did detail what he believes will happen during the end times by looking at the challenges that we face today in the Middle East.

"This is a conflict of ideas and a conflict of civilization, so in a way it is a third 'World War,' not on the scale of World War I or World War II yet," he said. "But there is going to be a final conflict—and when it happens, the battle of Armageddon, or I could even say the battles, plural, of Armageddon—I don't know if that will be World War IV, World War V, or what number we would give it." Laurie added, "But I know this much: they will be the final conflicts of mankind before the return of Jesus Christ."[2]

So, while the troubling events being perpetuated by the Islamic State might not mean that an immediate eschatological battle is before us, many end-times experts, including Laurie, believe that we're likely marching in that direction.

— — — — — — — —

Of course, one could argue that every second of every day brings the world closer to the biblical end of days, though the central point of contention is how much closer society is actually drawing to Christ's final return and the preceding events that many theologians insist will unfold.

Is it tomorrow? Will it come in a week? A month? Five hundred years? No one really knows, and guessing the precise time and date stamps isn't really prudent—but that doesn't mean believers should ignore the signs.

"As we look to the end times, I always picture it as sort of road signs in the distance," Christian author Jeff Kinley once told me. "You know that they're there but you can't read them. It's unwise to make predictions about that."[3]

The uncertainty is what makes the end-times debate so simultaneously difficult and complex, especially when considering that there are divergent well-crafted end-times scenarios that involve starkly divergent interpretations of Scripture.

Despite the specific timing of the end not being spelled out in Scripture, many experts believe that there are some biblical clues worth examining that tell us, to a degree, what the world will be like prior to Christ's return.

Jesus proclaims in Matthew 24 that the "gospel of the kingdom will be preached throughout the world as a testimony to all nations" (v. 14) prior to the end. That said, Christ also spoke of an increase in wickedness in the end days, leading Dr. Ed Hindson to propose that there will be a great moral crisis during the end times.

"There are clear statements that there will be a growth of evil and moral breakdown and potential reaction against the things of Christ toward the time of the end," he said.[4] Hindson described this dynamic as unfolding on two parallel tracks. On one hand, there will be a great spiritual growth of the Evangelical movement, while at the same time the secular movement will become "more and more 'antireligious.'"[5]

"There will probably be more social, moral, ethical conflicts in the public square between those two positions," Hindson said. "Sixty years ago you would not be having this discussion at this level."[6]

He pointed to the elimination of religious and Christian influence in the public school system to note that there has been a collective sixty years of secularism being taught in America—"generation after generation"—and said that this repetitive behavior has influenced the masses. "They don't think biblically, so we should not expect them to react biblically," he said.[7]

In this same vein Kinley has also said that Christians shouldn't be surprised if their ideas and views begin to become less prevalent and accepted in American society, particularly as culture continues to evolve in a more progressive manner. "We're not mainstream anymore," he told me in a 2014 interview for TheBlaze. "We're more marginal than mainstream."[8]

With ever-changing social views on key moral issues, there's a key question worth asking: Is mankind evolving into a more peaceful, tolerant, and prosperous people, or are we on a path toward ever-increasing moral depravity?

Answering that depends on one's social, political, and theological views, though Kinley falls into the latter camp, as he sees human beings continuously and perilously cutting God out of society.

"I look around my world and I think, 'Wow, we've written God out of our own story here,'" Kinley said, describing the travesty that he sees unfolding. "We're content in living in our own lives."9

The author, who believes Noah, the flood, and the ark literally unfolded as the Bible recounts, investigated these themes in his book *As It Was in the Days of Noah*, drawing parallels between contemporary culture and the "pandemic godlessness of the earth" during Noah's life.10

It's a comparison that some might dismiss, but one that Jesus invoked in the Olivet Discourse in Matthew 24. Here's what Christ had to say in verses 36 through 41—a section of Scripture from which Kinley clearly derived the title of his book:

> Concerning that day and hour no one knows, not even the angels of heaven, but My Father only. As were the days of Noah, so will be the coming of the Son of Man. For as in the days before the flood, they were eating and drinking, marrying and giving in marriage, until the day Noah entered the ark, and did not know until the flood came and took them all away, so will be the coming of the Son of Man. Two will be in the field; one will be taken, and the other left. Two women will be grinding at the mill; one will be taken, and the other left.

Comparing human behavior during Noah's time to the modern era, Kinley said that the differences aren't too profound. While people had forgotten God during Noah's time, he said that he now sees a similar "pandemic unrestrained immorality" and "a falling away of the purity of faith" in contemporary society. "As we ramp up to the end times, there's going to be, as Romans 1 describes, a simmering hostility against God, against biblical morality," Kinley said, going on to decry what he views as a "sliding scale of morality."11

He believes that human beings are creating new ways of doing things based on shifting standards. If those signs are not enough, he also pointed to Israel's reemergence after nearly two thousand years of absence from the international scene to try and convince naysayers and believers alike that prophecy has been unfolding.

"Ezekiel 37:12 says that Israel's going to be re-gathered to the holy land. There are more Jews moving in every day than there have been in 20 centuries," he said. "All the prophecies that we talk about…none of those things can happen unless Israel is a nation again."[12]

This is a point that end-times expert Joel Rosenberg also elaborated when he told me that the central and most prominent prophecy throughout the Old Testament, in his view, is the "rebirth of the state of Israel as a geopolitical entity in the exact land where David was king and where Solomon was king and so forth."[13] Rosenberg maintains that the Old Testament prophets speak about the Jews returning from exile and going back to the Holy Land to rebuild and bloom.

This growth and repopulation of the area is something that Ron Rhodes also spoke to, noting that Israel's reemergence is "the most significant thing that has happened that has laid the groundwork for everything else to happen." It is perhaps most notable, he argued, because it has "never happened before in human history" that Jews from every nation on the globe have streamed back into the homeland, as he believes Ezekiel predicts in the Old Testament text.[14]

While many biblical scholars previously assumed that these prophecies would simply be symbolic prior to the re-creation of Israel on May 14, 1948, Rosenberg said that the literal formation of the country profoundly changed their thinking. "These are very specific concrete prophecies all throughout the Old Testament books," he said. "On May 14, 1948, the prophecies began to become true."[15]

Hindson too agrees and wonders whether Israel's reemergence in the Holy Land is a key event that could signal that the end times are drawing nearer.

"Virtually all future prophecies assume Israel will be back in the land in the last days," he said. "The fact that they finally returned after nearly 1,900 years ought to get our attention that at least the stage is set for whatever God intends for the future."[16]

Hindson continued, mirroring Rosenberg's claims, "The Old Testament prophets themselves were convinced that Israel would potentially face a major invasion in the last days and have to depend on the Messiah to come and rescue them."[17]

He cited other elements from Scripture that led him to believe that the end times could be more rapidly approaching, citing "rumors of war," the global economy, the presence of weapons of mass destruction, and moral decay. Hindson said that these signs constitute "flashing warning lights" that cannot be ignored, providing a lens into what's to come.[18]

"You've got a crisis in the Middle East. Constant rumors of war…and that tension could potentially lead to the kinds of wars that the Bible discusses in the end times," Hindson said. "The fact that a global economy already exists indicates to me the potential at least for someone—or a group of people—taking over."[19]

While it's impossible to know if the end times are definitively upon us, many clearly believe that current events are mirroring some of the signs embedded in eschatological scriptures. Now let's turn our attention to the geography of these events.

— — — — — — —

Many premillennialists see the Middle East as ground zero when it comes to the key events and wars that they believe will unfold during the end times.

"The crosshairs of the target are right on Israel…the general geography is the Middle East," Hindson told me. "End-times wars, as they're depicted in the Bible geographically, are always set in the Middle East."[20]

And he isn't alone. Kinley is careful not to name specific dates, timelines, and figures, though he unabashedly believes that the current world dynamic—especially considering events in the Middle East—is providing some signs that humanity is forging ever closer to what he and other Christians believe will be a biblical end.

"It looks like things are really shaping up for a showdown in the Middle East," Kinley told me. "I mean, think about it; if someone came in right now and brought peace to that region, that area, to that conflict, we would hail them as a world leader."[21]

Considering the biblical narrative, Hindson said that it is essential for people to pay attention to what's going on in region. With the rise of the Islamic State and the ongoing tensions between Israel and its neighbors, it's hard to avoid doing so.[22]

Chaos and uncertainly are running rampant in the Middle East, dominating the headlines on a daily basis. The question on many people's minds is: What's next?

It's a curiosity that has end-times experts increasingly in-tune with the sociopolitical narrative, as they believe that the news of the day is in many ways reflective of the prophecies that many Christians have become certain are coming into play.

"Everybody really senses that this is a powder keg—that something is really getting ready to happen there with Russia moving in," Kinley said, noting that there are theories surrounding how the Islamic State, Syria, and Russia all play into a potential biblical end-times paradigm. "So it's a real dark moment in history—it's a volatile movement in our existence."[23]

Despite being cautious on the predictive front, Kinley said that there are signs unfolding around the globe that lead him to believe that the situation is moving in that direction.

"It's really unknown as to how these things are really going to play out, but I do think that these things are like chess pieces being placed into their exact locations to prepare for what I think will be a future conflict in that area," he said.[24]

Next, let's explore the divergent views on what could come down the pipeline when it comes to eschatological fulfillment.

Chapter 13

GOG, MAGOG, AND THE REESTABLISHMENT OF ISRAEL

O NE OF THE more elusive prophecy debates surrounds the words *Gog* and *Magog*. Though they are given very few mentions in the Scriptures, they are believed by some to be titles for important key players in end-times eschatology. The terms, which appear together in Ezekiel 38:2 and Revelation 20:8, have sparked a great deal of theological discussion and debate throughout the ages; contemporary faith leaders and theologians have divergent views about what, exactly, Gog and Magog refer to.

Joel Rosenberg is among those who have spent a great deal of time exploring the issue, publishing a series of blog posts in 2011 that provided a detailed analysis, beginning by explaining that Ezekiel, a Hebrew prophet, wrote the book that bears his name more than twenty-five hundred years ago.

Rosenberg explained that "the Lord gave him [Ezekiel] a vision of events that would take place in the future"—mainly in the "last days." He also broke down his belief that Ezekiel chapters 36 and 37 prophesy the rebirth of Israel, which Rosenberg believes came to fruition with the re-creation of the state in 1948.[1]

— — — — — — —

Before getting further into the Gog and Magog discussion, it's wise to take a deeper look at some of the verses embedded in that Old Testament prophecy that express hope for the nation of Israel.

Ezekiel 36:7–8 reads, "Therefore, thus says the Lord GOD: I have lifted up My hand that surely the nations who are about you shall themselves bear their invectives. But you, O mountains of Israel, you shall shoot forth your branches and yield your fruit for My people

Israel. For they shall come soon." The chapter goes on to prophesy that Israel will be given favor by God and that many people will once again live in the Jewish state, with ruins being rebuilt and with a fruitful future that would be more robust and successful than at any time in Israel's past history.

Verse 11 reads, "And I will multiply man and beast upon you. And they shall increase and bring forth fruit. And I will settle you as you were before and do better to you than at the beginning. Thus you shall know that I am the LORD." Verse 12 continues, "Indeed, I will cause men to walk upon you, My people Israel, and they shall possess you, and you shall be their inheritance, and you shall no longer bereave them of children."

The chapter also describes God's past judgment of the people of Israel, explaining how the Lord dispersed and scattered Jews among all other nations. But, according to the text, God's promise is then to gather them back together from all over the world and bring them back to their land—a pledge that is repeated throughout the chapter.

In chapter 37 Ezekiel descriptively recounts seeing a valley of dry bones, with the Lord telling him to prophesy that they should come back to life. After Ezekiel complied, he said that he heard a rattling noise and the "bones came together, bone to its bone" with tendons, flesh, and skin taking form.

With the bones representative of Israel, the final vision for the Jewish state in chapters 36 and 37, according to Ezekiel, is an Israel in which formerly barren and desolate land is rejuvenated and reinhabited—a future event that God promises will show the rest of the world that it was He who took action to bring Israel back to fruition and glory.

It's not only in Ezekiel 36 and 37, though, that some see Old Testament prophecy predicting a future worldwide regathering of Jews in the Promised Land. Here are some of the other verses that are seen as predictive of the same event:[2]

- "In that day the Lord shall set His hand again the second time to recover the remnant of His people, who shall be left, from Assyria, from Egypt, from Pathros, from Cush, from Elam, from Shinar, from Hamath, and from the islands of the sea. He shall set up a banner for the nations, and shall assemble the outcasts of Israel, and gather together the dispersed of Judah from the four corners of the earth" (Isa. 11:11–12).

- "Surely, the days are coming, says the LORD, when the city will be built to the LORD from the Tower of Hananel to the Corner Gate. The measuring line shall stretch out straight to the hill Gareb, and shall then turn to Goah. The whole valley of the dead bodies and of the ashes, and all the fields to the Kidron Valley, to the corner of the Horse Gate toward the east, will be holy to the LORD. It will not be plucked up nor thrown down any more forever" (Jer. 31:38–40).

- "Therefore say, Thus says the Lord GOD: I will gather you from the peoples and assemble you out of the countries where you have been scattered, and I will give you the land of Israel" (Ezek. 11:17).

- "Afterward the children of Israel will return and seek the LORD their God and David their king. They will come in fear to the LORD and to His goodness in the latter days" (Hosea 3:5).

- "I will whistle to them and gather them in, for I have ransomed them; they will be numerous as they were numerous before. When I scatter them among the nations, they will remember Me in the distant lands; they will live with their children and then return. I will bring them home from the land of Egypt, and gather them from Assyria. I will bring them into the land of Gilead and Lebanon, until there is no room for them" (Zech. 10:8–10).

There's obviously a great deal of debate surrounding whether modern-day Israel is the fulfillment of the prophecies detailed in the aforementioned verses.

While many believe that these scriptures projected that the modern-day state of Israel would come to fruition, others see these Old Testament proclamations as pertaining to the aftermath of the

Babylonian captivity during which the Jews were forcefully taken by King Nebuchadnezzar II and held in Babylonia after being expelled from Judah following its conquest around 597 BC. The Jews were later permitted to head back to their land in 538 BC after Cyrus the Great, a Persian leader who conquered Babylonia, granted them permission.[3]

Like much else in the prophetic realm, there's debate over what, exactly, these verses are referencing—and whether today's Israel is prophetic in nature, or a mere consequence of political events.

Kinley told me that he is less than satisfied with the idea that the return from the Babylonian captivity satisfies the aforementioned prophecies, calling it a "partial return"—a migration from Babylon to Judea and not a massive return of Israelites "from the four corners of the earth," as stated in Isaiah 11:11–12.[4]

In addition to likening the return from Babylonia to a relatively small return, Kinley also said that the aforementioned prophetic verses in Zechariah were written *after* Judah's return from Babylon. If this is the case, that clearly opens the door to some other questions about the purpose of the verses and whether they could have possibly been fulfilled with the captivity and return.

In breaking this issue down, Kinley specifically points to Ezekiel 37:25–28, which states that the Jews "dwell in the land that I have given to Jacob My servant, in which your fathers lived," adding, "And they shall dwell in it, they and their sons and their son's sons forever. And My servant David shall be their prince forever."

Here's the sticking point for Kinley: if, indeed, these verses were already fulfilled centuries ago as some modern-day scholars believe, then there is a slight problem with the text. As noted, Ezekiel 37 pledges that the Jews will be in the land "forever." As any historian knows, they were later expelled and dispersed throughout the world in AD 70.[5]

Despite having a small presence in the area after that time, the Jews remained out of the land for the next twenty centuries, not returning there again as a physical state on the map until 1948. If "forever" is to be believed as the operative term, then Kinley, among others, looks at the text as not being fulfilled until the twentieth-century return to the land. And if that prophecy about the return to the land was truly only fulfilled so recently in the twentieth century, then there are clearly additional questions surrounding whether the texts referring to Gog and Magog in Ezekiel 38 and 39 are still yet to be fulfilled.[6]

Furthermore, Kinley contends that it's important for readers to pay attention to the mention of "David My servant" in Ezekiel 37:24–25, as this section, again, makes a "forever" promise regarding the Jews in the land. Those scriptures read:

> David My servant shall be king over them. And they all shall have one shepherd. They shall also walk in My judgments, and observe My statutes and do them. They shall dwell in the land that I have given to Jacob My servant, in which your fathers lived. And they shall dwell in it, they and their sons and their son's sons forever.

Verse 26 goes on to discuss a "covenant of peace" that will be everlasting. Kinley collectively commented on these scriptures, explaining that he believes that these mentions of "David" have nothing to do with the Old Testament Israeli king and everything to do with Jesus.

"Obviously not the King David from 1 Samuel since that David had been dead for hundred[s] of years," Kinley said. "This could only mean Him who would occupy David's throne at a future time and in eternity."[7]

Interestingly, when the angel Gabriel appeared to Mary in Luke 1:26–38 and told her that she would be with child, he mentioned David in his description of the Savior to come.

"He will be great, and will be called the Son of the Highest," Gabriel said. "And the Lord God will give Him the throne of His father David, and He will reign over the house of Jacob forever. And of His kingdom there will be no end" (vv. 32–33).

Kinley argues that Ezekiel harmonizes with Revelation quite well, with modern-day events proving that these scriptures are coming to fruition before our eyes.

"I believe Israel's return to the land began in the late 1800s, gathering gradual steam until finally blasting off in 1948 with the official rebirth of Israel as a recognized nation and homeland," Kinley said. "Every time a Jew relocates to Israel today, we witness Ezekiel's prophecy being fulfilled."[8]

These ideas aren't exclusive to Evangelical Christians, as some Jews are—like their Christian counterparts—still awaiting certain events that are mentioned in Ezekiel to unfold.

Rabbi Aryeh Spero, a Jewish theologian and author, also sees the 1948 re-creation of Israel as a fulfillment of prophecy, saying that the destruction that the prophet spoke of happened two thousand years ago, but that other pieces of the puzzle didn't come to fruition until much later.

"[Ezekiel] talks about the destruction of Jerusalem, which was all part of the destruction of the temple, and he talks about the desolation of the land," he said. "Then he speaks about the day that will come when the land will be reborn, where the lands that were fallow will be replenished and the people will return to the cities, and there'll be joy."[9]

Spero, like Kinley and many others, believes that Israel's reemergence in 1948 sparked a mass return of Jews—one that seemingly meshes with the situation being spoken of in the Old Testament, specifically in Ezekiel. "[There] was always a Jewish presence in Israel, but there wasn't a mass migration back, and the Jews didn't have sovereignty," he said.[10]

Spero also flatly rejected the idea that the verses are speaking about the Babylonian exile, saying, "There was nothing in return after the Babylonian exile that could compare to what is happening now in Israel."[11]

In addition to Israeli sovereignty—something that was unimaginable to many before 1948—Spero described the fruitfulness of the land as well as the great cities that have emerged. There are things that he believes simply did not happen after the return from the Babylonian exile.

"When they returned from Babylon, there never was real Jewish sovereignty. There wasn't even a Jewish army," he said. "You had in the time of the Maccabees a guerrilla band that was able to just beat for a while the Syrian Greeks, but you didn't have sovereignty."[12]

It wasn't until 1948 that Spero said that the land was "really being replenished on a scale that it never was after the Babylonian exile."[13]

But not everyone is so convinced that contemporary Israel is a definitive fulfillment of Old Testament scripture.

Despite viewing the founding of the modern state of Israel as "significant," Heiser said that he doesn't see any specific Old Testament verses that it directly fulfills. Of the verses that many might cite in Ezekiel, Jeremiah, Isaiah, and other Old Testament books, Heiser said that some might ask why these texts can't be simply referring to the return from exile.

"Why do we have to look at the fulfiller, that verse or those verses as being something in the remote distant future for a biblical writer? Why couldn't that be fulfilled by the return from exile?" he rhetorically asked. "It's a very simple question, but again, some of these prophecy pundits that are real popular [have] never even asked the question."[14]

Heiser said that too many prophecy experts have not looked at the context of certain Old Testament verses, instead looking toward the twentieth or twenty-first century.

"They immediately think of their own context and the future, and that's why it looks so clear to them, because they're filtering it through their own time period," he said. "When it's a very logical question to ask. How do we know that this wasn't speaking of the return under Ezra, and under Nehemiah, under Zerubbabel? How do we know that? The answer is, we don't."[15]

There's also a middle-ground approach to these scriptures, as Heiser proceeded to ponder whether the return from exile was complete in the minds of the prophets when those verses were written about the regathering of Israel or whether the return from exile was "an echo of something yet to come."[16]

"In other words, was it a warm-up?" he said, pondering whether there was a double meaning of sorts taking place in the biblical narrative.[17]

Specifically citing Ezekiel 36 and 37, he said that the revival of Israel is clearly defined as being the return of all twelve tribes.

"Even in Jesus's day, Israel was still in exile. Only two tribes had ever returned to their homeland: Judah and Benjamin," Heiser continued. "When Jesus starts talking about return, and restoration, and salvation, and the kingdom of God coming back and all this stuff, here's the question that drives that: If Jesus was thinking, 'The exile is not complete, but I'm here to complete it, the return is not complete, but I am the key figure that's going to result in the return of this.'"[18]

Heiser said that he believes no one knows the answer to this question of whether Jesus was speaking about a literal return of the ten missing tribes or whether He was talking about the spiritual children of Abraham (i.e., the church). "Which marks the fulfillment of restoration?" he asked. "Is it the church, or is it the ten ethnic tribes? Again, nobody asked that question, but it's a very important one." The Bible scholar's point was that there are still many curiosities worth asking—questions that he believes that some in the prophecy realm simply haven't adequately entertained.[19]

— — — — — — —

Now, let's delve deeper into what comes next in the opening of Ezekiel 38—the aforementioned mention of "Gog of the land of Magog"—yet another theme that opens up a floodgate of debate.

Like much else in the prophecy realm, definitive details are hard to come by, but by analyzing information, many biblical experts believe that they have an idea about what Ezekiel is speaking about—a future end-times event that experts like Rosenberg believe could involve some major key players on the international stage.

In the opening of chapter 38 Ezekiel proclaims that the Lord came to him and told him to prophesy against "Gog of the land of Magog, the prince of Rosh, Meshek and Tubal" (v. 2).

God then, through Ezekiel, makes no bones about the fact that He opposes Gog, pointedly saying that He will "put hooks into your jaws, and I will bring you out with your whole army" (v. 4), detailing an apparent military attack that involves other nations as well. Verses 8–9 continue:

> After many days you shall be called. In the latter years you shall come into the land that is restored from the sword, whose inhabitants have been gathered out of many peoples, against the mountains of Israel which had been always a waste. But its people were brought out of the nations, and they, all of them, are dwelling safely. You shall ascend and come like a storm; you shall be like a cloud to cover the land, you and all your troops, and many peoples with you.

God went on to describe this military strike as a diabolical move rooted in evil, as Gog invades and plunders Israel—acts that the text proclaims will ignite God's "fury," leading to punishment for Gog and those who came alongside to try and wage the attack.

To get a glimpse into just how terrifyingly grim the end game will be for Gog and his compatriots, consider the chilling words written in Ezekiel 39:4: "You shall fall upon the mountains of Israel, you and all your troops and the peoples who are with you. I will give you to the ravenous birds of every sort, and to the beasts of the field to be devoured."

It is a moment in which God supernaturally intervenes, "raining fire and brimstone down on the enemy forces and utterly destroying them," Rosenberg writes, describing the battle that he believes has yet to unfold.[20]

The end-times expert takes the events in these chapters to signify an eschatological attack that he believes will come before Jesus's second coming, with Israel's reformation in chapters 36 and 37 unfolding before the battle in chapters 38 and 39.

"Ezekiel chapters 36 and 37 set the stage for the 'War of Gog and Magog' by describing that Israel will be reborn as a country in the last days, the Jewish people will come back to the Holy Land from exile all over the world, the Jewish people will rebuild the ancient ruins and make the deserts bloom again," Rosenberg wrote. "These things have all happened, and this suggests we are getting closer to the fulfillment of the next set of prophecies."[21]

Through a carefully crafted exegesis Rosenberg argues that the "Gog" seen in the Scriptures isn't a person's name but is, instead, a title such as czar, commander, and king—and based on what Ezekiel shares about the individual's plan of attack on Israel, Rosenberg describes him as a tyrant.

That clearly does not drive the reader toward a definitive explanation of who this person is, and the mention of Magog as being the land from which he hails also raises a number of important curiosities. But Rosenberg believes that there are "clues" within the text that can help point the reader to the nation being referenced.[22]

At the heart of the discussion surrounding Magog is the mention in chapter 38 of Gog coming from the "north parts," though Rosenberg cited writings from first-century Jewish historian Flavius Josephus to dive a bit deeper, specifically referencing the book *The Antiquities of the Jews*. It is in that book that Josephus apparently wrote that the people of Magog are those known as the Scythians—"a people group that migrated from the Middle East northward and settled north of the Black Sea and the Caspian Sea in the region we know today as Russia and the former Soviet Republics," according to Rosenberg.[23]

These scriptures and details lead Rosenberg, among many others, to conclude that a Russian leader will possibly join other nations against Israel sometime during the end times. Those other nations, according to Ezekiel 38:5–6, are Persia, Cush, Put, Gomer, and Beth Togarmah.

Many end-times experts have noted that Persia is modern-day Iran, as Persia was Iran's official name until 1935. Rosenberg explains some of the other listed countries as well, claiming that Cush is likely modern-day Sudan, with the nation of Put once residing in what is now Libya and Algeria. As for Gomer, he said that it is likely modern-day Turkey, with Beth Togarmah being a bit more difficult to pin down in terms of linking it to modern states, which likely reside in Central Asia.[24]

Speaking of the same text, Rhodes offered up his interpretation with a similar breakdown, claiming that the coalition would include Persia, Libya, the "'Stan' nations" in Central and South Asia, and Turkey. "The text is clear and there's never been an attack like that before," Rhodes said, going on to add that the nations mentioned in Ezekiel 38 are currently "forming alliances with each other."[25]

Rhodes also pointed toward the virulent rhetoric that has come from some leaders, particularly those in Iran, who regularly call for wiping Israel off of the map. "Everything is lining up as that text indicated," Rhodes said.[26]

Interestingly, though, Rosenberg specifically noted that some historic enemies of Israel such as Egypt, Iraq, Syria, and Lebanon are seemingly not mentioned in the biblical text; thus it is unclear if they would have a potential role in such an event.[27]

Hindson corroborated some of the finer details, explaining that Gog and Magog could quite possibly be references to modern-day Russia, with Iran also coming into the mix. He also mentioned Cush as possibly being Sudan or another nearby nation. In the end, many

Bible experts are quite tuned in to the relationship between Russia and Iran, saying that it could be prophetic in nature. "Every time Russia and Iran get together now for any kind of political, military-related talks or exercises, that ought to get our attention," Hindson said.[28]

It should be noted that there are some compelling arguments that underpin claims from Rosenberg and others who share this worldview, specifically when exploring what unites some of the countries that Ezekiel mentions.

Proponents would argue that the formation of the Islamic faith in the seventh century—nearly a millennium after Ezekiel penned his prophetic work—is a notable event that could have profound implications when it comes to the end times.

In the case of many of the nations that Ezekiel detailed (Russia aside), experts claim that the vast majority are Muslim-majority countries and are, thus, united by the faith; they were, however, not religiously homogeneous during Ezekiel's time.[29] "The one thing that unites them is Islam," Rhodes said. "And Islam didn't even exist twenty-six hundred years ago when Ezekiel wrote these prophecies."[30]

Hindson too noted that "many of the nations that surround Israel today that have a decidedly Islamic focus" could be involved in the Ezekiel coalition, expressing his belief that the "instability of ISIS" could "set the stage for two things happening": a potential Islamic-led attack on Israel as well as a power player like Russia jumping into the mix.[31]

Despite Rosenberg's belief that Ezekiel 36 and 37 have been fulfilled with the re-creation of Israel, in his 2011 blog series, titled "What Is the War of Gog and Magog?", he cautioned that this does not mean that chapters 38 and 39 will unfold in the immediate, though he believes that the world should be ready for such an occurrence.

Getting a bit more specific, Rhodes speculated that the Ezekiel invasion into Israel would likely take place either at the very beginning of the Tribulation period or three and a half years before it begins, as Ezekiel 39:9–10 discusses the Israelis burning weapons for a seven-year period after God destroys the invaders.

"The problem there is that right in the middle of the seven-year Tribulation, Israel has to get out of Jerusalem, because that's when the Antichrist sets up his headquarters there and puts an image of himself inside the temple," Rhodes said.[32]

Ezekiel 39:9–10 reads:

> Those who dwell in the cities of Israel shall go and make fires
> with the weapons and burn them, both the shields and the
> bucklers, the bows and the arrows, and the war clubs and the
> spears, and they shall burn them with fire for seven years.
> They shall take no wood out of the field, or cut down any out
> of the forests, for they shall make fires with the weapons. And
> they shall despoil those who despoiled them, and plunder
> those who plundered them, says the Lord GOD.

In the end, Rosenberg believes that the entire world, as the Bible says,
will be able to see these prophetic events unfold, leading many Muslims
and Jews toward Christ; he goes as far as to say that he believes these
events could usher in "the end of radical Islam" as well.[33]

In Ezekiel 39:29 the prophet concludes, "Nor will I hide My face
from them anymore. For I will have poured out My Spirit on the
house of Israel, says the Lord GOD."

— — — — — — — —

It should be noted that Gog and Magog again make an appearance
in Revelation 20:8, though the mention is brief and fleeting, coming
amid a discussion about Satan's eventual defeat.

Considering that the mention emerges near the end of the Bible
in a section that deals with latter end-times events, there are surely
questions about what this language in Revelation is referring to. Is
it the same event as depicted in Ezekiel? Is it a similar event to Gog
and Magog of the Old Testament? Or is it merely a symbolic mention? These are some of the central questions emerging from the text.
Revelation 20:7–10 reads:

> When the thousand years are ended, Satan will be set free
> from his prison and will go out to deceive the nations which
> are in the four corners of the earth, Gog and Magog, to gather
> them for battle. Their number is like the sand of the sea. They
> traveled the breadth of the earth and surrounded the camp of
> the saints and the beloved city. But fire came down from God
> out of heaven and devoured them. The devil, who deceived

them, was cast into the lake of fire and brimstone where the beast and the false prophet were. They will be tormented day and night forever and ever.

Rosenberg once again exercised caution in tackling these considerations in a Q&A posted to his website, explaining that we cannot be entirely sure whether the war of Gog and Magog will unfold before or after the Rapture, as many Evangelicals have divergent views on the matter.[34]

As for the placement of Gog and Magog in Revelation, Rosenberg offered his detailed view that the events in Ezekiel are actually quite different from what's mentioned in Revelation: "Revelation 20:7–10 does speak of another War of Gog and Magog that occurs at the end of time, after all these other events," he wrote. "But this is a second war, not the war referred to by Ezekiel 38–39."[35]

Citing the linear timelines that he believes are mentioned in Ezekiel and Revelation, he explained, in detail, why he thinks that they are actually different battles entirely, with the first "occurring relatively soon" after the regathering of the Jews and the rebirth of Israel, with the second coming much later after Jesus's millennial kingdom. Rosenberg based these ideas on descriptions presented in the text, including the aforementioned restricted coalition that goes after Israel in Ezekiel and the broader coalition that is seemingly mentioned in Revelation. He believes that the end of the world immediately follows the latter battle.

On this basis, many eschatological experts believe that there are at least two separate battles pertaining to the end times, but some also see a third one unfolding in Revelation 19 in what is commonly known as Armageddon.

Kinley is among those who embrace the three-battle paradigm, explaining that he believes that the "Gog of the land of Magog" in Ezekiel is a battle that will likely unfold during the first half of the Tribulation. The battle of Armageddon, he said, will unfold just before Jesus's second coming, and the battle of Gog and Magog will take place at the end of Christ's millennial reign.[36]

Among those who embrace a premillennial worldview, this would mean that there would be about one thousand years between the first two battles—which will unfold before Christ's one-thousand-year millennial reign—and the final battle of Gog and Magog. Additionally, the Ezekiel battle involves forces from the north, while the latter comes from all directions, or, as the Bible proclaims, from "the four corners of the earth."

Kinley also believes that the target of the Ezekiel battle appears to be Jewish in context, but that the Revelation 20 battle mentions those from the four corners surrounding "the camp of the saints," which seemingly refers to all believers in the millennial kingdom.[37]

As for Armageddon in Revelation 19 and the Gog and Magog battle in Revelation 20, Kinley noted that there's a difference in the way in which Christ is presented. In the former, Jesus emerges on a white horse from heaven, while chapter 20 mentions Jesus sitting on "a great white throne."[38]

Other faith leaders also see differences between the three scriptural mentions. Citing Ezekiel 37, 38, and 39, Pastor Greg Laurie said that he believes that the attack of Gog and Magog mentioned in the Old Testament is "not the battle of Armageddon."[39]

"One of the reasons I believe that is because it says they burned the weapons for seven years," Laurie said. "That is a link to the entire Tribulation period."[40]

The preacher said that he believes that the next battle to unfold won't be Armageddon, as he doesn't see that happening in Scripture until the "end of the Tribulation period," meaning that it is, at a minimum, seven years away, if not more, as he believes that the Tribulation period has not yet begun. "But the battle of Ezekiel 38 is something that can happen at any time, and as we look at home, volatile things are now in the Middle East," Laurie said.[41]

He was careful, though, to explain that, despite embracing the aforementioned chronological timeline, the "Bible is not crystal clear" on the timing of these events, leaving some clear wiggle room and uncertainty on the chronology front.[42]

— — — — — — — —

Some theologians, though, reject the notion that there are three different events taking place—and that these battles will be literal in nature.

Amillennialist Dr. Sam Storms presented a very different interpretation of what's going on with the Gog and Magog verses in an explanatory article on his website, pointing out what he believes are parallels between the battle of Armageddon in Revelation 16:12–16, Revelation 19:17–21, and Revelation 20:7–10.

"It seems that John is providing parallel accounts of the same con-flagration (Armageddon) rather than presenting two entirely different battles separated by 1,000 years of human history," he wrote. "This deserves some attention."[43]

Storms points back to Ezekiel 39:17–20 in an attempt to prove that there's evidence corroborating the notion that "the battle of Armageddon in Revelation 19 and the battle of Gog-Magog in Revelation 20 are one and the same."[44]

He explained that there is a mention of birds assembling to con-sume the flesh of those responsible for the assault against Israel that is detailed in the Old Testament prophecy. Then he mentioned the text in Revelation 19:17–18, which reads:

> And I saw an angel standing in the sun, and he cried with a loud voice to all the birds flying in the midst of heaven, "Come and gather for the supper of the great God, to eat the flesh of kings, the flesh of commanders, the flesh of strong men, the flesh of horses and their riders, and the flesh of all men, both free and slave, both small and great!"

Storms concluded, "It would appear that Armageddon and Gog-Magog are the same event, not two entirely different battles separated by a 1,000 year interregnum."[45]

But the difference between Storms and theologians who were previously mentioned doesn't end there. It's the collection of verses in chapters 16, 19, and 20 that leads Storms, among other amillennialists, to see something symbolic and cohesive—a situation that is quite different from the literal battles that Rosenberg and other premillennialists believe will unfold.

"To put it simply, Armageddon is prophetic symbolism for the whole world in its collective defeat and judgment by Christ at his second coming," Storms wrote. "The imagery of war, of kings and nations doing battle on an all-too-familiar battlefield (Megiddo), is used as a metaphor of the consummate, cosmic, and decisive defeat by Christ of all his enemies (Satan, beast, false prophet, and all who bear the mark of the beast) on that final day."[46]

Kinley, who again sees three separate events unfolding in Scripture, admits that there are some similarities between the battles referenced in Ezekiel and Revelation—including the mentions of birds eating away at flesh—though he sees the "Gog and Magog" language in Revelation chapter 20 as being more of a generic reference than a specific mention of the same events unfolding in Ezekiel.

He likened using "Gog" in Revelation 20 to saying that Saddam Hussein was another Adolf Hitler of sorts or that the diabolical coalition is an "axis of evil"—language used for the sake of making viable character comparisons. The "Gog and Magog" would then essentially be "round two" of what already unfolded in the Ezekiel verses and could even include the same nations, Kinley argued.[47]

Despite some of the same key players taking part in the three battles, Kinley affirmed that he believes that these are distinctive events.

It is clear that the battle over the meanings of Gog and Magog is nowhere near over, as prophecy experts continue to debate over whether the events in Ezekiel have already come to fruition, or whether there is still much to unfold, including battles involving some of today's most volatile nations.

The broader issue, of course, is whether—and, if so, where—modern-day Israel fits into that paradigm. We will explore that topic in the subsequent chapter.

Chapter 14

ISRAEL'S ROLE IN THE END TIMES

ANYONE PAYING EVEN a second's worth of attention to the news cycle knows that Middle East affairs continue to dominate discussion within the sociopolitical landscape, but it's on the theological front, as well, that the region is also a dominant focal point. Israel, in particular, serves as the impetus for a great deal of discussion, as understanding the Jewish people is clearly core to comprehending the themes and central lessons embedded in the Old and New Testaments.

It's also quite clear that one's views on the meaning of prophetic texts in both Testaments are directly tied to how he or she will understand the current state of Israel, both theologically and politically speaking, as well as many of the events that are continuously unfolding in the Middle East more generally.

As we've explored thus far, Israel's emergence back on the international stage in 1948 continues to be quite stunning and is seen as a fulfillment of prophecy by premillennial dispensationalists, among others.

If we're taking an honest look at the reformation of Israel, even an objective observer must concede that it is, at the least, quite curious and captivating to consider that a nation that had been absent from the international stage for centuries found itself officially reclaiming its historical place on May 14, 1948. The situation becomes even more mystifying when considering the tragic events surrounding the Holocaust—the murder of around 6 million Jews—that led up to the mass return to the homeland.

Rosenberg told me that, for centuries before the 1948 re-creation of Israel, there was a "longing deep in the Jewish soul" for a return to the Promised Land to rebuild, but that, as time went on in the centuries following the destruction of the temple in AD 70, Jews subsequently spread to various nations throughout the world, making such a prospect seem implausible. "Over time, the Jewish people suffered so much pain and heartache and it seemed so impossible to ever see these prophecies come true," he said.[1]

But then, centuries later, the horrors of the Holocaust led many Jewish people to immigrate back to the region, joining smaller groups of Jews who had previously moved back in an effort to once again realize a Jewish homeland.[2] It's an event that Rosenberg believes to be truly remarkable.

"For nineteen hundred years, it didn't happen. Think about that… maybe you could not be discouraged as a people for the first five hundred years, but like six hundred, seven hundred, nine hundred, one thousand years go by, and nothing happens," Rosenberg said. "That's why the church abandoned these prophecies."[3]

When it comes to eschatology, Israel clearly plays a key role in how many Christians view God's relationship to mankind as well as the scriptural narrative at large.

— — — — — — — —

One of the biggest debates surrounding the Jewish state centers on a key question, as Rhodes wrote in *The 8 Great Debates of Bible Prophecy*: "Will God's promises to Israel in the Old Testament covenants be fulfilled literally by Israel or figuratively by the church?"[4]

It's essentially a debate over whether God still has promises for the state of Israel and the Jewish people, or whether the Christian church has essentially inherited those promises without such a prospect separately unfolding.

Those who embrace the latter idea believe in something that some critics call "replacement theology"—also known as supersessionism. Critics say that this is, in practice, exactly what it sounds like: the church takes the place of ethnic Israel and, thus, becomes the recipient of God's promises in the Old Testament.

Rhodes, who flatly rejects replacement theology, pointed in his book to pastors like Kenneth Gentry who Rhodes said would cite verses like Galatians 6:16 in which Paul referred to the church as the "Israel of God" as well as "the circumcision" in Philippians 3:3 to back the replacement paradigm.[5]

Douglas Wilson, a postmillennial theologian, said that he embraces supersessionism and delivered a pointed definition in an effort to explain some of the central beliefs associated with this perspective: "The supersessionist position is that the Christian church is Israel now, that God only has one people," he said. "The Jews were that people in the Old Testament, and the Christian church is the new Israel now."[6]

Wilson added, "That would mean a supersessionist could not be a Zionist."[7] As you may or may not know, a Zionist is a person who supports the creation and building of a Jewish homeland in Israel; those supporting the modern-day state would fall under that category, believing that its founding is a fulfillment of prophecy.

As a supersessionist, Wilson said that he believes that all of the promises that God made in the Old Testament to Israel were fulfilled in Christ and are now "available and offered to the Christian church today."[8]

Now, that's where the discussion gets a bit dicey in terms of the overarching eschatological debate. Replacement theologians would likely dismiss any notion of Israel's current existence being a definitive part of biblical prophecy, seeing Old Testament projections involving land being given to the Jews as having already been fulfilled in the distant past, according to Rhodes.[9]

Those who embrace the replacement paradigm—and they include some Catholics and Protestants, alike—believe that the church should be the sole focus, with many seeing modern-day Israel as a merely political institution.

Considering how many centuries it took before Israel found itself back on the map, it isn't surprising that scores of believers throughout church history have come to view the Christian church as the sole continuation and central body.

One of the more intriguing pieces of the debate centers on the fact that some critics reject the term "replacement theology." Hank Hanegraaff is among those who patently reject the term "replacement theology," claiming that it is a descriptor that was created by dispensationalists in an effort to negatively frame their critics.

"It's just a moniker that is designed to be an insult," Hanegraaff said. "In fact, it is the ultimate pejorative leveled at those who deny the heart of dispensationalism, or the notion that God has two distinct people, one of whom will be raptured before God continue[s] His plan with the other."[10]

The theologian then dismissed some of the ideas embraced by dispensationalists as "embarrassing" and mere "sensationalism," saying that dispensationalists use the "replacement" label in an attempt to shut down anyone who disagrees with their worldview by framing those critics as "peddler[s] of godless heresy."[11]

Hanegraaff also argued that the use of "replacement theology" as a term is in itself "very inaccurate," adding that the individuals that it attempts to frame "neither believe that the church has replaced Israel, nor the other way around."[12]

"Instead, they hold that all clothed in Christ constitute one congruent, chosen covenant community, beautifully connected by the cross," he said. "There is neither Jew nor Greek, slave nor free, male nor female—you are all one in Christ, according to the apostle Paul. If you belong to Christ you are then Abraham's seed and heirs according to the promise."[13]

And he wasn't done there, saying that those who embrace dispensationalism are actually the ones who are guilty of a replacement theology of sorts, further breaking down some of the issues that he sees with their worldview.

"Use of the term replacement I think is highly ironic, because the very people who wheeled the term as an insult, themselves, believe the mistaken notion that Israel...will soon replace a raptured church during seven horrific years of tribulation," he said.[14]

Hanegraaff spoke about these dynamics further in an interview for this book, tying many of the beliefs embedded in the dispensational worldview to John Nelson Darby, a nineteenth-century Bible teacher.

No stranger to pushing back against dispensational theory, Hanegraaff explained that the idea is rooted in the notion that God has two distinct groups of people and that they have "two distinct plans and two distinct destinies." His central argument is that this has never been the traditional understanding of Scripture.[15]

"Prior to that, the historic Christian church had never even considered such a thing. There was the notion of premillennialism, but there was not the notion of the secret Rapture," he said. "That idea actually is a function of John Nelson Darby believing in the two people of God theory, as though God is some kind of a racist, or a land broker."[16]

Hanegraaff then laid out evidence for his perspective, proceeding to invoke the Old Testament, saying that when the "children of Israel" left Egypt in the Exodus, it wasn't an ethnic group and was, instead, a "mixed multitude."[17]

"When the children of Israel start looking at entering into the Promised Land, you meet Rahab and her household," he added. "She too, though a Canaanite, sees that Yahweh is the real God, and so she puts her allegiance with Yahweh, the God of Israel. And then you find her in the lineage of Jesus Christ."[18]

Hanegraaff continued, "You have Ruth, who was a Moabite, the archenemy of Israel. She's in the lineage of Jesus Christ too, because she sees all the types and shadows in the Old Testament, pointing forward to a Savior, so she believes in Yahweh, the God of Israel, [and] becomes a friend of God."[19]

He reflected on a similar paradigm that he believes unfolded in Esther 8 after Esther saved the Jews from Haman, saying that there were many individuals from different nations who became Jews.

Verse 17 reads: "In each and every province as well as in each and every city, wherever the king's edict and his decree reached, the Jews had joy and gladness, a feast, and a holiday. Furthermore, many of the people of the land professed to be Jews because the dread of the Jews fell on them."

It is here that Hanegraaff sees a parallel scenario.

"It says on that day, many different people from many different nations became Jews. How did they do that? Did they change their birth mother?" he said. "No. They believed in Yahweh, the God of Israel, and therefore they were brought into all the types and shadows, the civil and ceremonial laws, the temple priests and sacrifices, et cetera, pointing forward to Jesus Christ."[20]

In the end, Hanegraaff said that "God never had two people" and that he believes that there's a "horrifying theology" coming from many church leaders when it comes to biblical end-times paradigms.[21]

"The takeaway from all of that is that the notion of John Nelson Darby...that God has two people...He has to Rapture the one, so

He can go back to work with the other. It's simply nonsense," he said. "There's no biblical basis for it whatsoever."[22]

R. Scott Clark, a Bible expert who has taught church history, also tackled this subject on his website, pushing back against those who use the term "replacement theology." Clark explained that Reformed theology contends that the Mosaic covenant "was never intended to be permanent."[23]

"With respect to salvation, Reformed covenant theology does not juxtapose Israel and the church.... The church has always been the Israel of God," he wrote. "Reformed covenant theology distinguishes the old and new covenants (2 Cor. 3; Heb. 7–10).... The church was temporarily administered through a typological, national people," but the church has existed since Genesis and it continues to exist today.[24]

Rather than the New Testament church replacing the Jews, Clark said that God "grafted" the Gentiles into the "people of God"— something he likened to adding rather than replacing.[25]

Clearly, the argument is complex and multifaceted, with one side using a label—"replacement theology"—that the other side rejects.

This debate aside, Pastor Douglas Wilson doesn't ignore the potential for a prophetic future for Israel in light of the nation's return to the land of its forefathers, though there's a caveat when it comes to his views on Jewish people.

"I believe that there is a prophetic future for ethnic Israel still, but I don't believe that ethnic Israel is currently the anointed people of God," he said. "I'm pro-Israel, non-Zionist."[26]

He also drew a distinction when it comes to an event happening for God's purpose versus an event unfolding with a definitively prophetic purpose.

"I'm a Calvinist, so I believe that everything that happens is God-ordained," he said. "I believe that God caused Israel to come back together in the land for a purpose, and I believe that that purpose relates to Romans 11, but I don't believe that their return to the land was a fulfillment of prophecy."[27]

— — — — — — — —

This debate is clearly a fierce one, with the emergence of modern-day Israel reigning wonder and curiosity about the potential role that the political state will play in the theological end game. Some will dismiss such a connection, though others—as evidenced from the arguments in this book—are prepared to see many of the events surrounding the end times take form in Israel and the Middle East.

"I think the final conflict will occur over Zion, over Jerusalem, over that territory, and for that reason—for that fundamental reason—I do look at the founding of the state of Israel as being significant," Dr. Michael Heiser told me. "I don't view it as a fulfillment of prophecy. I view it as related to things to come, so it's related to prophecy."[28]

Heiser said that Revelation very clearly has Israel as a national entity that plays a role in the end times, and he expects world events to unfold as such. "I don't think there's any doubt that Israel as a land and Jerusalem as a city has a very central role to play in the day of the Lord and the Second Coming and events like that," he said.[29]

Other theologians with a futurist mentality, though, dive a bit deeper in seeing the prophetic significance of Israel, laying out very clear parameters for the nations, events and key players that they believe will be central to the end times. These individuals believe, contrary to what Hanegraaff said, that "the church is the church and Israel is Israel," as Rhodes simply put it.[30]

Laurie, who noted that he and Hanegraaff are friends, pushed back against the theologian's views on the matter, appealing to the Bible to also corroborate his outlook on God's relationship with mankind.

"I don't think it's an issue of race here as much as it's an issue of God chooses who He chooses and does what He does," Laurie said. "This is called the sovereignty of God. God says in Deuteronomy 7:7, speaking of Israel, 'The Lord did not set his affection on you and choose you because you were more numerous than other people[s], for you were the fewest of all people[s]' (NIV), but then He goes on to say He chose them because He loved them."[31]

Laurie called it an "undeniable fact" that the Jews are God's chosen people, expressing his belief that God's promise to Abraham in Genesis is still in effect and is relevant even today.

"You can look back historically on those nations that have made it their business to try to eradicate the Jewish people going back as far as Spain and the more modern days, go back even further, go back to Babylon, go back to Egypt, and then quasi-modern day Spain and

Germany and others," he said. "They were diminished dramatically as nations, and so I think that God loves the Jewish people, and I believe that the Jewish people being gathered into their homeland against all odds and the aftermath of the Holocaust is an undeniable, modern-day miracle."[32]

It was with that latter regathering that Laurie believes "the prophetic clock started to tick."[33]

And author Tim LaHaye had pointedly stronger words for anyone who might embrace the notion that the church replaced Israel, and that there's no future fulfillment of prophecy involving the modern Jewish state.

"I think that's a lie of the devil," he told me. "The church is not Israel and Israel is not the church."[34]

Rather than one continuum in which Israel morphed and dissolved into the church, these individuals see a theology in which each body is distinct from the other, with the modern-day Jewish state slated to still fulfill Old Testament prophecy.[35]

They would argue that Paul's writings actually looked at Israel and the church as distinct and separate, with Rhodes citing 1 Corinthians 10:32, which reads, "Give no offense, neither to the Jews, nor to the Gentiles, nor to the church of God," and mentioning Paul's writings in Romans 9–11.[36]

Kinley also looked to these chapters to explain why he believes that Israel and the church are distinct. While he said that Jews and Gentiles are saved through Christ in the very same way, he said that the Bible clearly segments national Israel from Gentile Christians: "There are future promises yet to be fulfilled to that nation," Kinley said. "For me, covenant theology—the part of it that thoroughly equates the church as the 'new Israel'—hits a brick wall in 1948 when Israel becomes a nation after twenty centuries of being scattered."[37]

In fact, he feels so strongly about national Israel's prophetic role in the end times that he believes that "almost all the prophecies we see in Revelation are irrelevant unless Israel is back in the land once again," arguing that seeing Ezekiel 37 come to life in the reemergence of modern-day Israel actually helps understand the future fulfillment of Revelation 5 through 19.[38]

"I cannot fathom how this modern-day prophetic fulfillment—a 'super sign' of the end times—can be ignored," Kinley told me.[39]

Like Rhodes, he looks to Romans 9 through 11 to understand the segmenting of Israel and Gentile Christians, explaining that the current age—which began with Paul and extends to the present time—features "a partial hardening...on Israel, causing her to be placed on the back burner until the 'fullness of the Gentiles' is complete."[40]

Kinley believes that this completeness will come at the Rapture, at which point God's attention will once again turn to Israel and He will "collectively call her back to Himself."[41]

"So while individual Jews are currently being saved, God's relationship with the nation Israel will be revisited more fully during the Tribulation period," Kinley said.[42]

It was here that Kinley was careful to note that, while he believes that God will turn attention to Israel during the Tribulation, he does not believe that the Lord is currently inactive in dealing with the modern Jewish state. Kinley cited Israel's reemergence, Jews heading back to the land, and preparations based on the hope of a future third temple as evidence of God's hand at work within Israel.

"I do see Him putting the pieces in place for the last days' scenario," he said.[43]

Similar to Kinley's arguments, Rhodes also pushed back against replacement theologians' views on the land, citing later prophecies in Isaiah, Jeremiah, and Ezekiel that spoke to Israel holding on to the land well after Joshua 21:43–45—verses that are commonly cited by those who believe that the church replaced Israel.[44]

Written centuries before Ezekiel, these scriptures seemingly indicate that God's land promises to Israel had all been fulfilled with the writing of Joshua in chapter 21, verses 43–45. They read:

> The LORD gave Israel all the land that He swore to give to their fathers. They took possession of it and lived in it. The LORD gave them rest all around, according to all that He swore to their fathers. Not a man among their enemies stood before them, and the LORD delivered all their enemies into their hands. Not a single word of all the good things that the LORD had spoken to the children of Israel failed. They all came to pass.

However, Rhodes maintained in his book that "every Old Testament prophet except Jonah speaks of a permanent return to the land of Israel by the Jews."[45] LaHaye agrees, believing that "Israel is fulfilling prophecy."[46]

"It helps us to understand that God keeps His word by the way [in] which He's kept Israel alive," he said. "When you think [about it], the children of Israel have been persecuted more than any nation in the history of the world."[47]

LaHaye also pointed to the astounding notion that the Jews remain after many centuries, despite the essential disappearance of other ethnic groups mentioned in Old Testament scriptures. "Where are all the Hittites, and all the Amorites, and all the many people referred to in the Bible?" he rhetorically asked.[48]

Pastor John Hagee too made similar comments about the reemergence of the state of Israel, adding that it is "the only nation in the world created by a sovereign act of God in a blood covenant recorded in Genesis 17:6–8 with Abraham, Isaac, and Jacob and their descendants forever."[49] Verse 8 proclaims that the "land of Canaan" would be given by God to Abraham and his descendants "for an everlasting possession."

"The significance of modern-day Israel in Scripture is that all believers are directed by the Word of God to bless the Jewish people (Genesis 12:3); to pray for the peace of Jerusalem (Psalm 122:6), and to remember that all nations of the world will be judged by how they treat the nation of Israel (Joel 3:1–3)," Hagee said.[50]

Making his way through the Egyptian, Persian, Greek, Roman, Ottoman, and British Empires, Hagee noted that the first five are "gone," while the latter has been "reduced from a global empire to one small island." He said, "World history can be explained in one sentence: The nations that blessed Israel were prosperous of God; the nations that cursed Israel perished."[51]

— — — — — — —

People on both sides of the Israel debate look to Romans 11 as an important chapter in the prophecy debate. The Apostle Paul speaks in the text about Jews and Gentiles, with verse 26 reading, in part, "And so all Israel will be saved."

GotQuestions.org, a website founded by S. Michael Houdmann, notes that a central debate arises surrounding the question of whether "Israel" is referring to the literal nation or whether it is, instead, a discussion about the church after its emergence and growth.[52]

The Bible resource, which with 12 million monthly visitors and 275,000 newsletter subscribers has great influence, explains that those who take a literal approach believe that the Jews who are physical descendants of Abraham will be restored to God, saying that Christ's millennial kingdom will unfold after Israel's spiritual restoration.[53]

Supercessionists, though, will settle on the church being the actual replacement for Israel; the covenants are then fulfilled in a strictly physical sense, and not through a physical fulfillment of Israel, according to GotQuestions.org.[54]

"I do believe that ethnic Israel has a role to play in the evangelization of the world," Wilson said, though, as stated, it's evident that futurists would take that rhetoric further in practice.[55]

Kinley, for instance, sees a much deeper role for Israel to play in the end times.

"One role Israel plays today is somewhat of a 'prophetic countdown calendar,'" he said. "And while there are no specific dates on that calendar, events in Israel do serve as additional storm clouds gathering as the world ramps up to Revelation."[56]

Kinley also took some time to explain that, in the Old Testament, Israel's role was to live in a covenant relationship with God, "steward His revelation, and be a conduit through which the Messiah would come for all nations."[57]

He believes that modern-day Israel will continue to be a "lightning rod in the last days," as the nation will increasingly come into the crosshairs of anger from nations around the globe. "Hatred for her will grow as she defiantly defends herself in a world experiencing a resurgence of anti-Semitism not seen since [World War II] Germany," he said.[58]

As for the continued rise of the Islamic State, ongoing terror attacks, and other increasing concerns for the Jewish state, Kinley said that these acts have actually had a stunning impact, bringing more Jewish people to flee to safety in Israel.

"Though Satan means it for evil, God is using it, not only for good, but also to fulfill prophecy in these last days. That's how sovereign He is," he said. "And yet He has done it before as global sympathy toward Jews following [World War II] played a part in the Jewish state of Israel being reborn in 1948."[59]

With his eyes set on Revelation, Kinley said that both Israel and the land in which it resides will most certainly be the focus of end-times events. "As [the] Antichrist's political and military power grows, his wrath and hatred for God, Jews, and Christians will reach a climax during the last half of the seven-year Tribulation."[60]

Some pre-Tribulationalists like LaHaye also see a political necessity in America's continued support for Israel. The author explained why he teamed up with fellow prophecy expert Dr. Ed Hindson to pen *Target Israel*, a book that provides context for Israel's role during the end times: "I'm trying to get the church...to put pressure on their congressmen and senators, not to let Obama...throw Israel under the bus," LaHaye said.[61]

Detailing his belief that American exceptionalism is predicated upon two things—that the nation was founded on Judeo-biblical principles and has been "better to the Jew than any nation in all of history"—he strongly argued for continued US support of the Jewish state.

LaHaye openly expressed fear over what could happen if America abandons Israel, warning that "we'll lose the blessing of God" if that eventually comes to pass. "What the people don't understand is our greatest future line of defense is to protect Israel," he said.[62]

It's clear that the debate over Israel's role in prophecy is anything but settled, with experts landing on a variety of conclusions regarding what role, if any, the modern-day state will have in the unfolding of God's end-times plans. Interpretations of the textual references to Gog and Magog are very clearly directly tied to how one feels about the Jewish state; likewise, one's views on the Jewish state clearly play a key role in the eschatological timeline that he or she embraces.

As the battle rages on, it is clear that people like Rosenberg, Kinley, Rhodes, and LaHaye will likely continue looking at contemporary events to try and find fulfillments of Scripture, both old and new.

Chapter 15

SYRIA'S CURRENT UNRAVELING AND ITS TIE TO BIBLICAL PROPHECY

I S THE WORLD also about to see biblical prophecy come to fruition in Syria? Among others, Joel Rosenberg has questioned whether events inside the war-torn country in recent years are also related to prophecy, especially in light of what's found in Old Testament scriptures like Isaiah 17 and Jeremiah 49.

"We're watching Damascus unravel...is that the prelude to the completion of those prophesies?" he rhetorically asked. "We don't know, but Damascus is the oldest continuously inhabited city on the planet...so the fact that it is coming apart is quite extraordinary."[1]

Following Russia's air strikes targeting rebels in Syria in October 2015, questions began reemerging in Evangelical circles about whether events surrounding the country's ongoing civil war, which began in 2011, were tied in any way to biblical prophecy.[2]

Rosenberg published a blog post in the wake of the air strikes claiming that Russian president Vladimir Putin is "working hand-in-glove with Iran's government" in formulating operations in Syria.[3] It came the same week as reports that Iran was waging a ground attack, while Russia was carrying out assaults from the air.[4]

Rosenberg, as he did in interviews for this book and past exchanges with TheBlaze on this same subject, specifically referenced the Old Testament in addressing the matter, invoking many of the themes that we dissected in previous chapters.

"The Hebrew prophet Ezekiel wrote 2,500 years ago that in the 'last days' of history, Russia and Iran will form a military alliance to attack Israel from the north," Rosenberg wrote. "Bible scholars refer to this eschatological conflict, described in Ezekiel 38–39, as the 'War of Gog & Magog.'" He added, "Are these sudden and dramatic moves by Moscow and Tehran... simply coincidental, or [do they] have prophetic implications?"[5]

Rosenberg's question is at the center of the very debate surrounding Iran, Syria, and Russia and their perceived involvement in the end times—one that has attracted a great deal of attention both in Christian circles and in media over the years.

The military alliance between Russia and Iran was also discussed by Laurie, who said that the "entrance of Russia... as an ally of Syria and Iran, and this alliance between Russia and Iran is a special interest in the Bible."[6]

He called the current alignments between Russia and Iran particularly notable, though he said that it is important to differentiate between the details he's certain of and those that he cannot definitively speak to.

"I'm very careful when I teach Bible prophecy to not paint myself into a corner and say things that I can't be certain of," Laurie told me. "Do I know with 100 percent certainty that Gog is Russia? No, I do not."[7]

But, despite not being able to say with complete and utter confidence the identities of Gog and Magog, there are some elements surrounding Ezekiel that Laurie said he is most confident about. "Do I know that a force called Gog and Magog will march against Israel? Yes, I do. That's the way I teach it," he said. "I offer my views, but I always give myself a little wiggle room, because clearly people have thought other things in the past and have been wrong, so we want to be very careful to not say this is absolutely the interpretation unless the Bible is completely clear on the topic."[8]

Back in 2013 I first began dissecting this subject in a series for TheBlaze, speaking with experts about what role, if any, they believe Syria will play in eschatological scenarios. I noted at the time that there's one particular Bible passage that's rekindling the entire discussion surrounding how Syria might fit into end-times theology: Isaiah 17:1–3.[9]

It reads, "See, Damascus will cease from being a city; it shall be a ruinous heap. The cities of Aroer are forsaken; they shall be for flocks, which shall lie down, and no one shall make them afraid. The fortress also shall cease from Ephraim, and the kingdom from Damascus, and the remnant of Aram; they shall be as the glory of the sons of Israel, says the LORD of Hosts."

The Syria example is perhaps a perfect paradigm to see how those with different theological viewpoints approach the same texts in very different ways. Consider that the first portion about a "ruinous heap" has some wondering if the present Syria crisis was prophesied in the Bible, but some scholars have countered that Damascus was already destroyed and that this verse refers to an attack by the Assyrians that unfolded in 732 BC.[10]

Specifically noting Isaiah 17:1–3 and Jeremiah 49:23–27, Rosenberg explained in a separate 2013 blog piece that—despite some experts referencing the Assyrian attack—Damascus's destruction has not yet happened. Jeremiah 49:23–27 pledges judgment upon Damascus, proclaiming that it has "become helpless" and that a fire will be kindled in its walls.

"These prophecies have not yet been fulfilled. Damascus is one of the oldest continuously inhabited cities on earth. It has been attacked, besieged, and conquered," Rosenberg wrote. "But Damascus has never been completely destroyed and left uninhabited."[11]

The prophecy expert went on to explain that Isaiah 17 and Jeremiah 49 speak to prophetic judgments that he believes God will dole out on Israel's neighbors and enemies before and during the Tribulation period.[12]

While Rosenberg was definitive in this sense, he did note that the Bible is not specific, in his view, about how the city will be destroyed or what that event will look like. Additionally he noted that the implications of this destruction are not known either, as the Holy Book does not go into substantial detail on the matter.[13]

During a phone interview with TheBlaze in 2013, Rosenberg also explained Syria's significance in the Bible, again bringing up both Isaiah 17 and Jeremiah 49. Claiming that these predictions get "very little attention," he explained that they each speak about the future of Damascus: "The Bible indicates clearly that Damascus will be utterly and completely destroyed at some point in the future—it will be a great cataclysmal [event] and it will be part of God's judgment," Rosenberg said.[14]

He added that he doesn't see "clean hands in the fight" in Syria and wonders if it's possible "that the judgment of Damascus is not only coming" but if it could be coming within our lifetime.[15]

— — — — — — — —

Not everyone is on board with the claim that the Old Testament could be describing future—or even current—events that will befall Syria.

Hank Hanegraaff also spoke about supposed biblical prophecies associated with the end times back in 2013 on his radio show. A caller asked about claims that the Book of Isaiah details coming destruction for Damascus, the capital of Syria, a claim to which Hanegraaff pushed back.

"So, what you're saying is they're tying in the passages in Isaiah to what is currently happening in Syria...and this is just a classic example of newspaper eschatology and shame on the pastors that are doing this, because it either is a case of them not knowing the Word of God, which seems unlikely to me, or simply wanting to invite sensationalism and sophistry," he responded. "If you look at what the Bible actually says, it is very clear that the fulfillment comes in the biblical text as well."[16] And Hanegraaff wasn't done there.

"This whole notion is fulfilled in biblical history when the king of the Assyria captured and destroyed Damascus...if you look at Isaiah chapter 7, there's a permutation of this as well...you see the fulfillment in the very next chapter, Isaiah chapter 8," he continued.[17]

Hanegraaff went on to say that some pastors' decisions to transport pieces of prophecy to the twenty-first century are irresponsible. He called the action "embarrassing" and said that those pastors and Bible experts who embrace the idea are "dragging Christ's name through the mud."[18]

He simply doesn't believe that, on these matters, the Bible's writers were looking so fervently into the future, and he contends that they were speaking about prophecy that would unfold in the immediate and that has already come to pass.[19]

"I think the point we have to probably recognize is that all of the Bible was written for us, but none of it was written to us," he contended. "This book of Revelation was written to seven churches."[20]

Hanegraaff said that end-times prophecy has been touted for centuries, but none of it ever comes to pass. Rather than reading the

Scriptures for what they are, he believes that some theologians are "reading into the Scriptures their own eschatological views."[21]

Dr. Candida Moss, a professor of New Testament and early Christianity at the University of Notre Dame, also penned a 2013 article attempting to debunk claims that Damascus may play a role in end times. She said that the city has already been repeatedly conquered.

"Isaiah lived and wrote in the eighth century BCE [BC] and scholars think that the original prophecy referred to the conquest of Damascus by the Assyrians in 732 BCE [BC]," she wrote. "But that's not the only time Damascus has seen conflict."[22]

Moss went on to list those who had conquered Damascus, including Babylonian king Nebuchadnezzar and Alexander the Great. She also explained that, in the seventh century, Damascus was in the middle of a Muslim siege led by General Khalid ibn al-Walid. Later the Turco-Mongol armies of Timur conquered it around the turn of the fifteenth century, killing the entire population and apparently erecting a tower built with severed heads.[23]

In the end, the debate is fascinating, as both sides—comprised of individuals who believe in Christ and who contend that Jesus will one day return—couldn't disagree more about the alleged signs and symbols present within the Bible's complex text.

Chapter 16

THE BLOOD MOONS BATTLE

CRITICS CHARGE THAT the blood moon phenomenon isn't overtly spelled out in the Bible and that the celestial event is relatively common and benign, but others are intrigued, believing that a specific pattern and frequency of the blood moons could have prophetic significance. The theological proposal, which was discovered and crafted in 2008 by Mark Biltz, founder of El Shaddai Ministries, has attracted both widespread support and debate since its inception.

The blood moons theory is based on the idea that a tetrad—a rare series of four total lunar eclipses—occurring only on Jewish holidays over a two-year period—could indicate that something profound is about to happen involving the state of Israel.

Astronomers and blood-moon enthusiasts alike note that a tetrad includes four total lunar eclipses with no partial lunar eclipses between them; six lunar, or full moons, separate each, according to EarthSky.[1] Total lunar eclipses are known as blood moons, as they are named for the reddish color that results when the earth comes between the sun and moon.[2]

While a blood moon isn't an uncommon occurrence, it's when four of them fall consecutively on Passover and Sukkot—also known as Feast of Tabernacles—that prophetic minds take notice, believing that the tetrad could be a sign of a major, impending event that will impact Israel.

"God is trying to tell us something!" Texas pastor John Hagee, an advocate of the theory and the author of the 2013 book *Four Blood Moons: Something Is About to Change*, said in a press release leading up to the fourth and final blood moon in a tetrad that ended on September 28, 2015.[3] The other dates in the tetrad were April 15, 2014; October 8, 2014; and April 4, 2015.[4] This fourth blood moon was part of the final tetrad of this kind in the twenty-first century. As for Hagee, he, among others, contends that purported messages from God are coming through those tetrads.

"It is rare that Scripture, science, and history align with each other, yet the last three series of Four Blood Moons have done exactly that," reads a description of Hagee's *Four Blood Moons* book. "Just as in biblical times, God is controlling the sun, the moon, and the stars to send our generation a signal that something big is about to happen."[5]

Biltz, who told me that he founded the blood moons phenomenon after examining NASA data and observing the aforementioned pattern, pushed back against claims that his ideas constitute a "theory," and, instead, used the Bible to try and frame the blood moons phenomenon as an undeniable reality.

"In Genesis 1, God literally—in verse 14—says He created the sun and the moon for signs, signals, so that's not a theory, unless you don't believe in the Bible, I guess," he said in an interview for this book. "But for anyone who believes in the Bible is the fact that that's why He created the sun and the moon. The very first reason he says for signs or signals."[6]

Biltz continued, "Then when it says seasons, days, and years, that doesn't mean winter, spring, summer, fall; it means for the biblical Jewish calendar that they used."[7]

Genesis 1:14 reads, "And God said, 'Let there be lights in the expanse of the heavens to separate the day from the night, and let them be signs to indicate seasons, and days, and years.'"

Additionally, Biltz points to Luke 21:25 to corroborate the notion that the moon and sun will provide signs of what's to come. That verse reads, "There will be signs in the sun and the moon and the stars; and on the earth distress of nations, with perplexity, the sea and the waves roaring."

Biltz, who said that his blood moons construct has been spread and further popularized by Hagee, explained that he first discovered it in March of 2008 after he observed a total lunar eclipse over the Temple Mount. The celestial event struck his interest, leading him to explore NASA data to see if he could find anything of substance.

"I went to their ten-year table, and I saw that there were these four total lunar eclipses in a row, and I thought, from the mathematical standpoint, how rare is that?" Biltz recalled. "I started researching it, and then as I was praying about it, I all of a sudden realized, 'Oh my goodness, I [have] to put these on the biblical calendar.'"[8]

That's when he realized that the moons were falling on the Jewish holidays and, after further research, he said, "The rest is history."[9]

"Now there are a lot of books and people theorizing what might happen, and that's theory, but the facts are that God did create them for signs on the feast days," Biltz said. "They have occurred on those feast days, and biblically, historically things have happened."[10]

— — — — — — —

In a 2013 interview with TheBlaze, Hagee also said that the premise of the blood moons theory is "confirmed by NASA" data. He argued that a series of four blood moons have appeared on Passover and Sukkot during the period of two consecutive years only a few times in history. And each time, Hagee said, something significant has happened concerning the Jewish people.[11]

Passover celebrates the Jews' liberation from Egyptian slavery, and Sukkot commemorates the Jews' forty-year wandering in the desert before reaching the Promised Land.

"This has happened only three times in over 500 years, so it's a very rare thing," Hagee said, adding that the dates during which the tetrads fell always began with "tears" and ended in "triumph" for the Jewish people.[12]

Some have, no doubt, scoffed at these ideas, but Hagee has a historical narrative that he said corroborates the theory.

Consider that in 1492, King Ferdinand and Queen Isabella "issued an edict of expulsion" kicking the Jews out of Spain. This happened during the Spanish Inquisition, which began in 1478, to rid the region of Jews and Muslims. According to NASA data, there was a tetrad from 1493 to 1494; there were three preceding tetrads that century as well, but they did not fall on Jewish holidays.[13]

There are other tetrads that Hagee links to Israel as well, as NASA data shows that yet another tetrad unfolded between 1949 and 1950, a key time for Israel's modern-day manifestation.[14]

"In 1948, that's the year Israel became a state," he explained. "The thing that happened prior to that was the tragedy of the Holocaust, which ended in the rejoicing of statehood."[15]

Another tetrad happened between 1967 and 1968, a period which saw the Six-Day War—a moment of "triumph" when Jerusalem was reunified and became "the eternal capital of the Jewish people once again," Hagee said.[16]

NASA data also shows that four blood moons emerged between the years 1909–1910, 1927–1928, and 1985–1986, but these also did not fall on the Jewish holidays and would, thus, not be counted among those with potential prophetic impact.[17]

Speaking more generally, the last tetrad to take place before the most recent 2014 and 2015 set of blood moons unfolded between 2003 and 2004, though the moons also did not fall on Jewish holidays as the most recent ones did.[18]

Hagee said that there would "not be anymore four blood moons in the future" that fall on these holidays—at least in the near-term—so he says the current tetrad could indicate the start of some major, earth-shattering events.[19]

NASA data does appear to show six others will happen this century, but none appear to have all four blood moons fall on both Passover and Sukkot.[20]

"I think the thing that people will take away from this is that it means, based on past history, that something is about to change in the Middle East concerning Israel that will affect the nations of [the] world and everyone on planet Earth," he said. "No one knows for sure what it will be, but based on the pattern of the past it will involve Israel. It will begin with tears and end in triumph and change the course of history forever."[21]

Hagee also appeals to Scriptures to corroborate the notion that God has traditionally communicated with mankind through celestial means and "is sending planet Earth signals from the heavens."[22] He cited Joel 2, Acts 2, and Luke 21. Here's the list of associated verses, including those found in Luke 21, which Biltz also cited:

- "The sun will be turned to darkness, and the moon to blood, before the great and awe-inspiring day of the LORD comes" (Joel 2:31).

- "There will be signs in the sun and the moon and the stars; and on the earth distress of nations, with perplexity, the sea and the waves roaring; men fainting from fear and expectation of what is coming on the inhabited earth. For the powers of heaven will be shaken. Then they will see the Son of Man coming in a cloud with power and great glory. When these things begin to happen, look up and lift your heads, for your redemption is drawing near" (Luke 21:25–28).

- "And I will show wonders in heaven above and signs on the earth below: blood, and fire, and vapor of smoke. The sun shall be turned into darkness, and the moon into blood, before that great and glorious day of the Lord comes" (Acts 2:19–20).

— — — — — — — —

Like other issues pertaining to prophecy or the end times, the blood moons phenomenon carries with it a great deal of controversy. Hank Hanegraaff is among the many critics of this theology, telling me in a 2014 interview for TheBlaze that the theory is both "appalling" and "deplorable."[23]

"What these purveyors of blood moon theology [are doing] is taking the natural use of the stars, which God ordains, and perverting it with superstitiousness which God disdains," Hanegraaff said. "The heavenly bodies are used for separating the night from the day... [for] marking seasons, from giving light on the Earth and so forth."[24]

Hanegraaff examined the verses Hagee cited, noting that he believes that there's no evidence that these scriptures are to be taken as future predictions in the modern era.

"Peter talks about the ultimate day of judgment... it pertains to the coming of the Lord... coming in judgment on Jerusalem and ultimately it pertains to a second coming as well, but there's no word whatsoever for taking the language of Joel and suggesting that somehow or other you can read from that language what is going to happen in the modern epic," Hanegraaff said.[25]

He also noted that, as stated, the Spanish Inquisition began fifteen years before the 1493 tetrad, though it is true that it wasn't until 1492 that the Jews were expelled from the region.[26]

Hanegraaff also pointed to some one-year differences as gaps in time that he said didn't make the tetrads reliable in terms of connecting them to biblical prophecy. Consider, for instance, that Israel was founded in May 1948, but the tetrad didn't start until 1949.

"Lunar eclipses are associated with Jewish events anyway," Hanegraaff said. "There should be no real surprise that you find these kinds of events happening."[27]

Kenneth L. Waters, associate dean and a New Testament professor at California's Azusa Pacific University, agreed that it's not entirely surprising that these dates would fall on Passover and Sukkot.

"[There] is nothing particularly extraordinary about these holy days coinciding with a full moon," he wrote in a 2014 CNN op-ed. "Jewish holy days are based upon a lunar calendar. Passover is always celebrated the first full moon after the vernal equinox and the Feast of Tabernacles is always the first full moon after the autumnal equinox."[28]

Ken Ham's Answers in Genesis provided an overview of how the calendar works, agreeing that there's nothing astounding about the dates lining up with Jewish holidays. The group even provided tables to show that it's not unique that eclipses sometimes fall on Jewish holidays, considering the Jewish calendar follows the moon.[29]

Dr. Danny Faulkner, an astronomer with Answers in Genesis, also noted that there are some limitations concerning where these blood moons were visible from during the 2014–2015 season.

"There also is a question of from what portion of the earth one ought to view these eclipses for them to constitute a sign," he wrote. "One might think that Jerusalem would be a key site, but the first three total lunar eclipses in 2014–2015 won't be visible from there, and only the beginning of the final eclipse will be. One must ask whether a sign that few people notice is much of a sign."[30]

EarthSky's Bruce McClure and Deborah Byrd explained in a blog post that the Jewish calendar is lunar and that in any given year "it's inevitable that a full moon should fall on or near the feasts of Passover…and Tabernacles," as they fall in the first and seventh months of the Jewish calendar.[31]

That said, the two confirm that, while full moons are common near the holidays, there have been only eight tetrads that meet the specifications that Hagee detailed over the course of the past twenty-one centuries. They fell in the following years (all AD): 162–163, 795–796, 842–843, 860–861, 1493–1494, 1949–1950, 1967–1968, and 2014–2015.[32]

— — — — — — — —

Considering the critiques surrounding the blood moons, Biltz sought to make a few clarifications in an interview for this book. Among them, he pushed back against the critique that a tetrad started in 1949 after Israel's founding the previous year.

"In May 1948 [Israel] declared independence, but they kept battling until 1949 when everything was actually solidified," he said. "Regardless of that, now all we can say is, what does it mean looking back? I think looking back, I look at it as here the UN thinks they discovered the state of Israel, and I think that God is saying, 'No, I'm the one who did this. This is My handiwork.'" Biltz continued, "I think He's just putting His handprints on it after the fact."[33]

And while he said that many people have attempted to forecast what's to come or have tied the blood moons phenomenon to the end of the world, he has not done so.

"A lot of people were saying things that I was saying that I wasn't saying, and other people were saying things were going to happen that were attributed to me that I never said," Biltz explained. "As far as theories go, I wasn't making a theory as much as looking at patterns. I said, 'Let's look [at] what happened in the past. Historically you see war with Israel.' That was the number one thing that I saw: something biblical with Israel."[34]

As for the biggest misconception surrounding his blood moons ideology, Biltz said that it's the mistaken notion that he argued that something would happen on the days that the blood moons in question took place. That said, he does believe that something could happen in relation to those moons in the near future.

As for another tetrad that matches the requirements to be part of the blood moons phenomenon, Biltz said that people will be in for quite a wait.

"The next time you have four blood moons in a row that also fall on Passover and Tabernacles isn't for about five hundred years," he said.[35]

In an interview for this book, Hagee mirrored these comments, saying that he believes that one of the major misconceptions about the four blood moons theory is that he was "predicting the date of the Messiah's return or some other specific 'end of days' event during the 2014–2015 triad of blood moons."[36]

This, he said, is patently false, as Hagee cited Matthew 24:36 to note that we cannot know the day or hour of Christ's return. Pointing back to the Old Testament story of Noah and his ark, Hagee said that though we cannot and do not know the day and hour, it is quite possible for us to know the "season."[37]

"We can know the season of Christ's return. The Bible says, 'But as the days of Noah were, so also will the coming of the Son of Man be' [NKJV]," Hagee said, citing Matthew 24:37. "Noah did not know the day or the hour that the floods of the deep would be released to destroy the world through the flood." He continued, "But he did know that when the boat was completely finished, that the animals were on the boat, and Noah and his family walked up the gangplank as God closed the door to the ark; there was no doubt the flood was near."[38]

Hagee said that prophecy provides certain signals that will unfold before Jesus's return, with the return of the Jews being cited among them.

"The return of the Jewish people from the nations of the world to form the nation of Israel is on that checklist," he said. "The four blood moons is on that checklist. The knowledge explosion of Daniel 12:4 is on that checklist. Something is about to change."[39]

Chapter 17

JESUS'S SECOND COMING IN LIGHT OF HIS FIRST

I T'S NO SECRET that Christians view the totality of the Old and New Testaments as a harmonious collective work that tells the story of Creation, offers guidelines for living a Christ-centered life, and explains God's redemptive plan for mankind. It's impossible—or at least monumentally difficult—to understand the core of the New Testament without comprehending the themes and contents embedded in the Old Testament. After all, without the latter texts, there could be no former, as the two are intensely interwoven to create a full picture of God's grace and mercy for humanity.

Perhaps Rick Lawrence, a longtime editor at *GROUP* magazine, said it best when he told me in an interview that "the Bible on its own is really about Jesus," before offering a concise and highly beneficial breakdown of the books' contents and their intended purposes: "The Old Testament points to the Messiah, the Gospels describe the Messiah, and the Epistles chronicle what a life centered around— orbiting around—Jesus is like," Lawrence said.[1]

Due to this collective nature of the Bible, most preachers pull lessons from both the Old and New Testaments in an effort to make moral points and affirm important spiritual lessons, meshing together verses to form concrete and life-transforming theological mosaics.

When it comes to the study of the end times, dispensational premillennialists, among others, believe that the premise is no different, seeing various portions of the Old Testament as relating to the eschatology that is present in the New Testament scriptures. What has resulted, as this book documents, are a variety of perspectives on Bible prophecy. It's a fascinating mix in which theologians proclaim that some of what's prophesied in both the Old and New Testaments has yet to be fulfilled.

"The Old Testament certainly contains many prophecies that have not yet come to pass, such as Isaiah 2:1–4 or Isaiah 11, among many others," Dr. Michael Brown explained. "In Acts 3 Peter said that the return of Jesus would correspond to the times of the restoration of all things, as described by the [Old Testament] prophets. That time has still not come."[2]

As we've discussed, not everyone embraces that there are still yet-to-be-fulfilled prophecies in the Old Testament, though, with some rejecting the cobbling together of scriptures from both sections of the Bible to form an overarching end-times paradigm. These critics argue that much, or at least some, of what is commonly attributed to the end times by dispensationalist premillennialists already came to pass centuries ago.

— — — — — — —

Let's consider some of the core beliefs surrounding prophecies pertaining to the Messiah.

Christians believe that Jesus's first coming was prophesied in Old Testament scriptures, with the fulfillment of those predictions coming to pass with Christ's birth, which came around four hundred to five hundred years after the penning of Malachi—the final book of the Old Testament.

Just as Christians believe that the Old Testament prophesied about the coming Jesus, so too do many Christians believe that both the Old and New Testaments prophesy about what's to come at the end of days.

Most Christians—aside from full preterists—believe that at least the events described in the final chapters of Revelation have not yet come to pass. So, there's not much of a question among the majority of Christians as to whether at least a small portion of the Bible is yet to be fulfilled; the debate, however, centers on just how much fulfillment remains, whether the Old and New Testaments both contain unfulfilled verses, and in what form these events will unfold.

And while many critics of futurist end-times theology would potentially scoff at such literal readings of many of these eschatological verses, Ron Rhodes made a thought-provoking point in his book *The 8 Great Debates of Bible Prophecy*, noting that the prophecies surrounding Jesus's coming were "fulfilled literally."[3] Following that paradigm, Rhodes argues that it is quite possible to expect that end-times prophecies also logically hold the same potential to have a literal fulfillment.

That's a sentiment that is shared by Tim LaHaye, who has shown through the Left Behind series, among his many other projects, what he believes will literally unfold during the biblical end times. He too sees important comparisons between Old Testament prophecies about Christ's birth and prophetic verses about the end times.

"I believe that God meant for the end-time prophecies to be a way of proving that He is supernatural," LaHaye told me. "When we spell out the events for the future, we're very dogmatic about the fact that we believe that Christ is going to come before the Tribulation and that He's going to save the church out of the Tribulation by the Rapture, and then the world will go through the Tribulation described basically in Revelation and outlined a little bit by Daniel."[4]

It is that unity of the Old and New Testaments that Jeff Kinley said is evident in exploring Messianic prophecies, with the author mentioning that he believes the predictions concerning the coming of the Messiah in the Old Testament were "fulfilled in Jesus Christ"—something he finds absolutely astounding.[5]

"The mathematical odds of that happening with one person are astronomical and should lead any rational, thinking person to amazement and intellectual belief in Jesus," he said. "But what it ultimately teaches us is that the Bible is batting 1,000 percent."[6]

— — — — — — —

Perhaps it's best to explain in a bit more detail just how interrelated the Testaments are to one another, specifically when it comes to the first coming of Christ.

To illustrate that point, consider a massive undertaking by Rick Lawrence and Ken Castor, editors of the *Jesus-Centered Bible*—a Bible edition that includes Old Testament text highlighted in blue letters to note the many references in the scriptures that are believed to have some relation to Christ. The concept is quite similar to the red-letter Bibles that highlight Jesus's words in the New Testament.

Lawrence told me in an interview that the Old Testament prophetic mentions of Christ were so prevalent and plentiful that he worked eighteen-hour-days alongside Castor for weeks in an effort to pinpoint each one, finding a total of nearly seven hundred.[7]

"We just discovered, as we went, so many connections to Jesus in the Old Testament," he told me. "There were so many moments where we just stopped, stared at each other and started crying."[8]

Lawrence continued, "[We] couldn't believe how seamless the Old and New Testaments are when you really slow down and consider."[9]

Author and attorney David Limbaugh agrees and is so passionate about the subject that he released a book titled *The Emmaus Code* in 2015—a text that documents Christ's presence throughout the Old Testament.

Limbaugh said that when he first became a Christian, it was the realization that there were Messianic prophecies in the Old Testament that were ultimately fulfilled in Christ that brought him "over the tipping point from skeptic to believer."[10]

He specifically cited three chapters in the Bible when speaking about the Old Testament scriptures that most impacted his perspective: Micah 5, Isaiah 53, and Psalm 22.

"[In] Micah 5:2—the prophet Micah in the Old Testament predicted the actual city of Jesus' Birth, Bethlehem," Limbaugh said.[11]

The verse, which is widely attributed to being a prophecy about Christ, reads: "But you, Bethlehem Ephrathah, although you are small among the tribes of Judah, from you will come forth for Me one who will be ruler over Israel. His origins are from of old, from ancient days."

And Isaiah 53:4–8 reads:

> Surely he has borne our grief and carried our sorrows; yet we esteemed him stricken, smitten of God, and afflicted. But he was wounded for our transgressions, he was bruised for our iniquities; the chastisement of our peace was upon him, and by his stripes we are healed. All of us like sheep have gone astray; each of us has turned to his own way, but the LORD has laid on him the iniquity of us all.
>
> He was oppressed, and he was afflicted, yet he opened not his mouth; he was brought as a lamb to the slaughter, and as a sheep before its shearers is silent, so he opened not his mouth. By oppression and judgment he was taken away, and who

shall declare his generation? For he was cut off out of the land
of the living; for the transgression of my people he was struck.

Limbaugh went on to discuss other Old Testament prophecies surrounding Jesus, saying that "Christ's life, death and resurrection is
revealed, is predicted." He continued, "No bones will be broken, he'll
be falsely accused, he will stand silent in the face of his accusers, he
will be ridiculed and scorned and mocked, his robe…they'll gamble
for his robe and his clothes. He'll be crucified along with the sinners,
the transgressors."[12]

━ ━ ━ ━ ━ ━ ━ ━

Theologians and Bible experts like Kinley, LaHaye, Brown, and
Rhodes would, again, argue that there can be parallels drawn between
prophecies surrounding the first coming of Jesus and eschatological
scriptures.

"Prophetically speaking, the Bible has never struck out or even
swung and missed, but rather has hit a home run with every single
prophetic word," Kinley said, explaining that, concerning Jesus,
"every Old Testament prophecy has come true, exactly and literally as
Scripture predicted."[13]

With that in mind, he wonders why people wouldn't assume that the
same would happen surrounding New Testament prophecies. "Such biblical reliability grounds our faith as we move forward in history and
God's prophetic timetable," Kinley said. "Therefore, if Scripture really
does talk about the end times, we should pay attention to it."[14]

Specifically speaking of the Second Coming, Brown said that
Christians can have "absolute confidence that Jesus will return
because He came the first time," saying that Christ's sacrifice radically
changed the world.[15]

"He fulfilled the key prophecies that had to be fulfilled before the
second temple was destroyed in AD 70, and the prophecies of the
growth of His people around the world continue to come to pass in
startling fashion," Brown added. "Of course He will come again and
finish what He started!"[16]

Once again, though, eschatological differences are rooted in differing
takes on interpretive method. Take, for instance, LaHaye's belief that a

true understanding of the purpose of eschatological verses is directly dependent upon how one views the authority of the Bible.

Paraphrasing Paul's words in 2 Timothy 3:16–17, he said, "All scripture is given by inspiration of God and is profitable for doctrine, reproof, and righteousness, that the man of God that really understands the word of God will be thoroughly furnished, thoroughly outfitted for all truth."[17]

The popular author said that many err in assuming that simply because someone goes to seminary that he or she is qualified to "speak for God," explaining instead that the true hallmark of biblical understanding is rooted in one's overarching stance on Scripture. "It's whether or not he believes in the authority of both the Old and New Testament and what God says has happened, is happening, and will happen in the future," LaHaye explained.[18]

Many premillennialists would clearly argue that one could look to prophecy predicting Jesus in the Old Testament as a guide to understanding eschatological scriptures. Since the Messianic verses later had a literal fulfillment, these individuals believe that the same is quite possible of end-times scriptures; they believe that these references too will have future fulfillment in a literal sense.

It's an intriguing argument, and one that deserves attention, though the refined details have clearly done little to dismiss the critiques that some biblical scholars have that much of the Old and New Testament content attributed to eschatology—even the majority of Revelation—has already been fulfilled.

Chapter 18

THE FAILURE OF
END-TIMES DATE SETTING

DESPITE THE SEEMINGLY never-ending barrage of disagreements over end-times theology, it seems like there are at least a few elements that most Christians can agree on. Extreme preterists aside, most believe that Jesus's second coming is impending, and the vast majority reject any sort of definitive eschatological date setting.

Yet, despite the widespread rejection of setting specific dates for events like the Rapture and the Second Coming, some Christians still continue—as they have throughout the ages—to try to pinpoint dates and times, with their followers coming along for the ride. Naturally those supporters end up profoundly disappointed when none of these promises come to pass.

As Dr. Randall Balmer, a religion professor at Dartmouth College, once wrote, "American history is littered with predictions about the end of the world." And yet, the world is still here—for now.[1]

The most highly publicized end-times prediction in recent years came from the late Harold Camping, founder of California-based Family Radio. If you recall, Camping launched a media firestorm and garnered global attention in 2011 when he told his followers that the world would come to a cataclysmic end on May 21 of that year. (He had previously erroneously pondered whether the world would end on September 6, 1994.[2])

When the day came and passed without incident, Camping had a choice: he could have apologized and moved on, but instead he forged on, claiming that he had miscalculated the original date and that the end would, instead, come on October 21, 2011.[3]

Camping said, after further reflection, that he realized that May 21 was simply the spiritual beginning of the end, but that the physical manifestation would come on October 21. A statement published to the

Family Radio website explained that God "accomplished exactly what He wanted to happen" on May 21, sending a warning that His "salvation program" had come to completion on that day.[4]

Over the next five months leading up to October, Camping said that everyone—aside from believers—would be under "God's final judgment." He explained that part of the confusion over the original prediction was rooted in a misunderstanding (Camping said that the meaning was "withheld from true believers") of the following phrases: "the completion of God's salvation program" and "God's final judgment."[5]

Seeing the former phrase as being associated with the "Rapture" and the latter with an "earthquake," Camping called for a new understanding of these words in light of his then-updated October 21 date, seemingly indicating that he and his supporters had suffered a profound misunderstanding while crafting their May 21 prediction. Rather than a physical earthquake, Camping said that it appeared as though the fear that many felt after media picked up the original May 21 story constituted a spiritual earthquake of sorts.[6]

"Therefore we have learned from our experience of last May 21 what actually happened," the statement continued. "All of mankind was shaken with fear. Indeed the earth (or mankind) did quake in a way it had never before been shaken. God had come spiritually to bring judgment upon the whole world."[7]

As for the Rapture reference, Camping said that, although no one was physically caught up on May 21, that date was essentially a cut-off of sorts, indicating that no one else who had not accepted Jesus by that date would be able to afterward; those who did were "eternally safe with God in Heaven," though, he argued.

And the tough language about what would befall nonbelievers continued with Camping saying in the statement that the rest of the world would be "annihilated together" as well as with the physical world on October 21 of that year.[8]

"On that day the true believers (the elect) will be raptured," he said. "We must remember that only God knows who His elect are that He saved prior to May 21."[9]

Again, October 21 came and went with no Rapture, no annihilation, and no indication that Camping's definitive date setting held any merit. Some laughed at these predictions or angrily dismissed them, with either reaction proving appropriate to most rational observers, especially considering the repetitious outcome.

As for Camping, he released a statement a few days after the failed doomsday prophecy, outlining the difficulties that he was having pinpointing the end: "We're living in a day when one problem follows another. And when it comes to trying to recognize the truth of prophecy, we're finding that it is very, very difficult," he said. Concluding that it "seems embarrassing for Family Radio," the statement went on to encourage people not to lose faith in God.[10]

It wasn't until March 2012, though, that a letter was posted from Camping on the Family Radio website, apologizing for all that had unfolded, calling the date setting "incorrect and sinful."[11]

Signed by Camping and his staff, the letter conceded that Matthew 24:36 and Mark 13:32 are correct in cautioning that no man will know when Christ will return.

"We must also openly acknowledge that we have no new evidence pointing to another date for the end of the world," the letter read, in part. "Though many dates are circulating, Family Radio has no interest in even considering another date.... We tremble before God as we humbly ask Him for forgiveness for making that sinful statement."[12]

As far as we know, Camping's original end-times date setting reportedly first ramped up in 1994 when dozens of his followers gathered together, while holding their Bibles up to the sky, on September 6 of that year, as they expected—based on Camping's teachings—to witness Christ's return. When it didn't come, Camping said that he had made a mathematical error and then spent years running new calculations, which resulted in the failed 2011 dates, as the *San Francisco Chronicle* widely documented.[13]

Without getting too deep into the methods that Camping used to predict the end times, it can be noted that the evangelist saw significance in biblical numbers, believing that there was a reason for their inclusion in the text. It was through a complex equation that he ended up landing on his failed predictions, seeing the number five as meaning "atonement," ten as indicating "completeness," and seventeen as meaning "heaven," according to the *Chronicle*.[14]

Here's how this all played out: he started with Jesus dying on April

1, AD 33, and counted through April 1, 2011, which is 1,978 years. Then, he multiplied that number by 365.2422, which is the number of days in a solar year. From April 1 through May 21 is then 51 days, which can be added to the previous equation, which had come to about 722,449. The total was then 722,500.[15]

And since (5 x 10 x 17) x (5 x 10 x 17) = 722,500, Camping felt he had really stumbled upon something. Of that equation, he told the *Chronicle* back in 2010, "Five times 10 times 17 is telling you a story. It's the story from the time Christ made payment for your sins until you're completely saved."[16]

If your head is spinning, you're not alone. Despite the confusion surrounding the biblical prediction as well as verses seemingly cautioning against such a notion, some people believed wholeheartedly in what Camping was saying and it appears—at least from his own statements and his refusal to back down until he was forced to—that he bought into it as well.

On the surface, the end result was most certainly embarrassing for Camping, but there is another disturbing level worth exploring: the impact that it had on his followers, as the date setting reportedly came along with some real-life tragedy. Some who truly believed that the end would come to fruition reportedly sold their homes and belongings back in 2011 in anticipation.

"There were a lot of people who sold their houses, who gave up their life savings," former Family Radio employee Matt Tuter once told VICE. "And Harold thought it was funny. He would come into my office and say, 'So-and-so called me. They're broke, but I'm not giving their money back.'" He went on to call Camping "a very twisted man."[17]

Reports at the time of Camping's May 2011 prediction claimed that Robert Fitzpatrick of Staten Island, New York, had spent $140,000 of his own savings to help buy ads supporting the end-times claims. He told media after May 21 came and went without incident that he did not "understand" why the prediction was wrong.[18]

Fitzpatrick later spoke to Reuters after Camping's 2013 death, explaining that he believes that some of what Camping said was, indeed, true.

"Amazingly, when I go back and look at some of these things in the Bible, I have to conclude that he was largely correct," Fitzpatrick said, noting that he still believes the end will come at some point. "I know that his teaching has been discredited in the eyes of the world."[19] Money, though, wasn't the only thing that was purportedly lost after the failed end-times prophecy. A fourteen-year-old girl from Russia was reportedly so scared over the initial prediction that she killed herself so that she wouldn't be left behind to suffer calamity.[20]

Camping died on December 15, 2013, at age ninety-two, just two years after his end-times predictions made him an international phenomenon.[21]

— — — — — — —

The evangelist is far from the only individual to make failed doomsday end-times predictions throughout the ages.

Consider William Miller, a nineteenth-century farmer and religious leader who attracted one hundred thousand followers with an end-times theory of his own. Miller promised that Christ would return in 1843, and, like Camping, he readjusted that date to 1844 when a mass exodus failed to take place on the original date he predicted.[22]

Bible professor Dr. L. Michael White once explained in an article for PBS's *Frontline* that Miller believed that Christ's return in 1843 would usher in a millennial reign, with the events of Revelation then unfolding. Miller's views then spread through pamphlets and lectures, effectively garnering both support and skepticism.[23]

Drawing parallels between Camping and Miller, Balmer wrote in a Religion Dispatches piece that Miller's predictions were seemingly based on the dating of Noah's flood, with the preacher devising "a complex numerological formula based, at least in part, on the reign of Artaxerxes and the 'seventy weeks' mentioned in the book of Daniel in the Hebrew Bible."[24]

These computations led to a belief that Christ's return would come between March 21, 1843, and March 21, 1844. When this failed to happen, a new date was set. Then when the recalculation also later failed, Miller's followers—who had also given up possessions—were heartbroken. The failure came to be known as the Great Disappointment, with some of his followers going on to form the Seventh-Day Adventist Church, according to Balmer.[25]

The Seventh-Day Adventist Church hasn't shied away from

discussing Miller's failed prophetic proclamations, either, including the details in official church historical information.

"When Baptist preacher William Miller said Jesus was coming back on October 22, 1844, many Americans weren't just surprised that he had set a date," reads an article on the denomination's website. "The notion that Christ was literally returning was in itself a radical idea."[26]

Disillusioned followers split into three groups: some felt the date was indeed wrong, others said Christ had returned in a spiritual sense, and a third group said that the date was right, but that the event was something other than Christ's return.

It was on October 22—Miller's failed second date—that they believed "Jesus had begun the last phase of his atoning ministry in the heavenly sanctuary," according to the denomination.[27]

What followed was a denominational structure that emphasizes a relationship with Christ, with more than 18 million members worldwide, according to 2014 statistics.[28]

Second-Day Adventist historian David Trim said that it is notable that, despite failed apocalyptic predictions, Miller's followers were able to go on and form a successful denomination.

"That Adventists did so—it's not proof that God is on your side, but it is proof that you have intelligent, rational leaders," Trim said.[29]

We can go through a plethora of other similar stories, though Camping and Miller account for two of the most well known. Balmer is most certainly correct that American history is characterized by these predictions, though I'll explore one last example that extends much further back into the early Christian church.

Consider the second-century Montanism movement, which was predicated upon the beliefs of Montanus, who told his followers that Christ would soon be coming. According to *Encyclopaedia Britannica*, Montanus was apparently so convincing that people left their homes and ascended to a field in between the villages of Pepuza and Tymion—villages in modern-day Turkey—to wait for a new Jerusalem to emerge from heaven and rest upon the earth.[30]

Montanus claimed that he was speaking under the influence of the Holy Spirit and was joined by two women—Maximilla and another named either Priscilla or Prisca, according to *Encyclopaedia Britannica*.[31]

"The Montanists...emphasized an imminent, premillennial escha-tology. While this apostolic expectation for Jesus' return was not new (Mark 9:1), the general feeling had been lost by the second century Christians who felt that the stability of the church would be lasting," Jim Liang wrote in Western Seminary's *Transformed* blog. "The Montanists recaptured the eschatological longing and hope of the ear-liest disciples."[32]

Also known as New Prophecy, the Montanism movement eventu-ally died out, with mainstream Christian leaders shunning it.

━ ━ ━ ━ ━ ━ ━ ━

In the end, date setting is nothing new, as intrigue and anticipation over the end times often boil over, leading some to take their interest a step too far.

But, despite the many individuals who have claimed to have known the date and time, thus far none of their predictions have checked out, which proves biblical scholar Dr. Michael Heiser's point that date set-ting is a "colossal waste of time."[33]

"Then I mentally move from that to, just another occasion to mock the church, because that's what it's really going to turn out to be," he said of those whose predictions fail. "People are going to get deceived. They probably won't give up the faith. Although I guess that could happen."[34]

In the end, though, it's the mockery that he said is most problematic.

"It just makes it so easy for people to point at Christians and go, 'What silly, unsubstantial, vacuous, shallow people,' when people do stuff like this," Heiser said.[35]

Chapter 19

WHERE PEOPLE STAND ON THE END TIMES

ONSIDERING THE NEW Testament's clear indication that Jesus will one day return, it should come as no surprise that polling finds that the vast majority of Bible believers in America embrace the idea that Christ's second coming will one day unfold.

According to research conducted by Shibley Telhami, a fellow at the Brookings Institution's Center for Middle East Policy and a professor for peace and development at the University of Maryland, 72 percent of Christians and 81 percent of Evangelicals, more specifically, professed a belief in the end times and the Second Coming, though they expressed uncertainty about when these events will unfold. Only 5 percent of Christians and 12 percent of Evangelicals told researchers in the 2015 survey that they believed that this key, end-times event would happen in their lifetime.[1]

These small proportions aren't surprising in light of Jesus's warning in Matthew 24:36 and Mark 13:32 that the "day or hour no one knows." Despite the uncertainty, though, there is a sense among many Christians that the end times—regardless of how far off the final conclusion ends up being—are upon us.

Respondents in a separate 2010 Pew Research Center poll were asked to provide their views on whether Christ will return by 2050. While 48 percent of Christians said that He will definitely or probably (27 percent and 20 percent, respectively) return in the next forty years, others weren't so sure; 38 percent said that it would definitely or probably not happen (10 percent and 28 percent, respectively).[2]

Clearly, it's a mixed bag, as Christians balance the feelings of unease that many have in light of world events with Christ's proclamation in Mark 13:32 that "not even the angels in heaven, nor the Son" know exactly when the end will come.

But perhaps the most telling research done on the subject of the end times came in 2013 when the Barna Group asked respondents, "Do you, personally, believe that the world is currently living in the 'end times' as described by prophecies in the Bible, or not?"

The results were stunning, with 41 percent of Americans answering affirmatively. More specifically, 54 percent of Protestants and 77 percent of Evangelicals felt that humanity was living in the last days. Catholics, however, took a very different view, with 73 percent rejecting such a notion. On the flip side, 45 percent of practicing Catholics said at the time that we are now living in the end times.[3]

On the racial front, there were also some intriguing breakdowns worth briefly noting. While 39 percent of white Americans said that we're living in the end times, 48 percent of Hispanics and 54 percent of African Americans said the same.[4]

Differences were also observed among married people and families when compared to views among the general populace. Those who were married (46 percent) and families with kids at home (47 percent) said that they believed that we are living in the end times, with both of these latter statistics coming in higher than the national average (41 percent).[5]

— — — — — — — —

As we've explored in previous chapters, many biblical experts believe that the troubling events unfolding in the Middle East directly relate to prophecy and, interchangeably, the end times.

LifeWay Research got a bit more specific on the eschatological front, finding in another 2013 study that one in three respondents believed that the ongoing crisis in Syria is "part of the Bible's plan for the end times." Now, it should be noted that the question underpinning this finding was quite specific, as researchers asked for agreement or disagreement with the following statement: "I believe the battles in Syria are all part of the prophecies of the Book of Revelation." While 32 percent agreed, 49 percent disagreed, with the statistics carrying some weight, considering the specificity of the inquiry. Those who attended church once or twice a month were more likely to see this tie.[6]

And that wasn't the only question that specifically invoked the Book of Revelation, with LifeWay asking whether respondents believed that

US military involvement in the Syria crisis could lead to the Battle of Armageddon, as it is highlighted in the final book of the Bible; 26 percent agreed that it could.[7]

Additionally, one in five (18 percent) expressed their belief that the world would end during their lives, though 70 percent rejected such a notion.[8]

— — — — — — — —

Telhami and the Center for Middle East Policy at Brookings spent quite a bit of effort discerning where Christians and, more specifically, Evangelicals stand on these issues. The professor, who has been studying public opinion about the Middle East for quite some time, said that he embarked on the research after noticing the intense interest that Evangelicals have in the region—an interest that is, no doubt, tied to theological views about the end times.

"Over the past two years, it's very clear that the focus on the Middle East is principally among Evangelicals in ways that really supersede any community in the United States, including Jewish Americans," Telhami told me. "It's very clear that this has become a key constituency for the Middle East in America."[9]

The researcher said that he spent much time diving deep into who Evangelicals are and what they believe, contending that many past polls have simply lumped together Evangelicals and born-again Christians into a singular group, explaining that isn't necessarily the most accurate way to explore the data.

"People assume they're very similar and people assume that also; that helps with enhancing the size of the sample, particularly doing a national sample of all Americans," Telhami explained. "It turns out there [are] really important differences."[10]

While 90 percent of Evangelicals say that they are also born again, the same doesn't come to fruition when assessing the opposite dynamic, as nearly half who say that they are born again don't call themselves Evangelical. By dividing these groups, Telhami felt that he was able to yield more representative results.[11]

On the political front, he noted that Evangelicals make up 23 percent of the Republican Party, but that if one sets them aside and measures the remainder of party affiliates, he or she would recognize that "the rest of the Republican party—on matters related to Israel and the Middle East—is not different from the rest of the population."[12]

Evangelicals, thus, hold unique views, with religious faith and devotion driving some of their perspectives on international affairs—opinions that are likely shaped and impacted by what they believe will come to fruition during the end times.

"When you inquire further into the theological aspects with end times and the belief in end times and the relationship, their expectation of...the biblical interpretation of prophecy—whether it's literal or not—you find that there's a huge correlation between those who believe that end times will happen, and some roughly 17 percent believe it's going to happen in this century," Telhami said.[13]

Showcasing just how differently Evangelicals think about the end times from their non-Evangelical Christian cohorts, consider that the vast majority of Evangelicals—79 percent—believe that violence across the Middle East "is a sign that the end times are nearer," with only 43 percent of non-Evangelical Christians saying the same.[14]

While Telhami wasn't surprised that Evangelicals would place more of a focus on prophecy than "traditional Christians," he said that the sweeping proportion of Evangelicals who embraced various eschatological views stunned him. "What surprises [me is] how large a majority of Evangelicals believes in this, that this really is a sign and that something is going to happen in Israel, things are going to turn against Israel as you get closer to end times," he said.[15]

Telhami said that he isn't sure whether the influx of negative news coming from the Middle East is exacerbating end-times beliefs, or whether they have historically been this pointed, though he plans to keep exploring the subject.[16]

As for some of the more specific findings involving the Middle East, Telhami's research found that the majority of Christians (55 percent) and Evangelicals (75 percent) believe that certain events must happen concerning Israel before Jesus's return—sentiment that is commonly derived from Old and New Testament analysis, as explored throughout this book.[17]

Probing deeper, he found that one of the key events would be the ability of Israel to include all of the land that was once promised to the Israelites in the Old Testament, with the larger umbrella group of

Christians surveyed differing from the Evangelical cohort. Overall, 51 percent of non-Evangelical Christians and 63 percent of Evangelicals said that they believe this is essential before the Rapture or Second Coming can unfold, according to the survey results.[18]

Also, concerning Israel, 73 percent of Evangelicals posited that the world would turn against Israel as the end times approach, with just 49 percent of non-Evangelical Christians agreeing. Those proportions in mind, it isn't at all surprising, then, that Evangelicals expressed more favorable views toward the Jewish state. Overall, 45 percent of Americans sampled said that they believe that the modern-day Jewish people are God's "chosen people," though 49 percent disagreed; 55 percent of Republicans answered affirmatively, with just 33 percent of Democrats saying the same.[19]

On a final note, there was another question in the survey that might point to just how much modern-day Israel is a part of the Evangelical fabric. When Telhami asked in an open-ended question which "national or world leader" they admire most, 16 percent of Evangelicals named Israeli prime minister Benjamin Netanyahu—the most chosen individual among that cohort—with Ronald Reagan (11 percent) and Barack Obama (10 percent) following. Among Republicans as a whole, Netanyahu and Reagan tied with 12 percent; only 1 percent of Democrats chose Netanyahu.[20]

Now that we have an understanding of where Christians stand on these issues, it's important to explore the opinions of American faith leaders.

Chapter 20

WHERE PROTESTANT PASTORS, PRIESTS, AND MINISTERS STAND ON THE END TIMES

IT'S CERTAINLY VALUABLE to survey members of the general public about their end-times beliefs, but with so many questions and so much contention surrounding eschatology, I decided to dig a bit deeper by looking to pastors and ministers for their take on some of the most hotly debated eschatological perspectives.

Polls routinely ask parishioners about their end-times beliefs, but there's very little information about what, exactly, members of the clergy believe about the Rapture, the Millennium, the Antichrist, and other related biblical themes.

So, in preparation for this book, we commissioned a poll through LifeWay Research, asking one thousand senior pastors, ministers, and priests—all Protestants who self-identified as either Evangelical, mainline, or "neither"—across America to tell us what they believe.[1] It was an effort that yielded some fascinating results about where individuals who are on the front lines of the Christian faith stand on biblical prophecy, with notable differences emerging between different denominations, theological perspectives, ages, and levels of education.

Respondents were presented with three questions; the first focused in on which Rapture view best represents their perspective. As you learned earlier on in this book, the Rapture is the belief that God will supernaturally rescue Christians from chaos and destruction at some point before—or during—the end times.

Pastors in the survey were presented with the following options: the Rapture already occurred, a future pre-Tribulation Rapture will occur, a future mid-Tribulation Rapture will take place, a pre-wrath

Rapture will occur, a post-Tribulation Rapture is impending, or that
the Rapture isn't meant to be taken literally.

Many Evangelicals have long suspected that the largest percentage
of Christians overall would support a pre-Tribulation view, an idea
that was corroborated by the data, as the largest share of pastors—36
percent—reported believing in that Rapture paradigm. The second
largest proportion was the 25 percent who agreed that "the concept of
the Rapture is not to be taken literally."

Furthermore, 18 percent selected a post-Tribulation paradigm, with
smaller proportions for mid-Tribulation (4 percent), pre-wrath (4 percent), preterist ideals (1 percent), and none of the options presented
(8 percent). (For more information on these views, consult the definitions of each that were presented in chapter 2 of this book.) See the
graph below for a visual representation of these views.

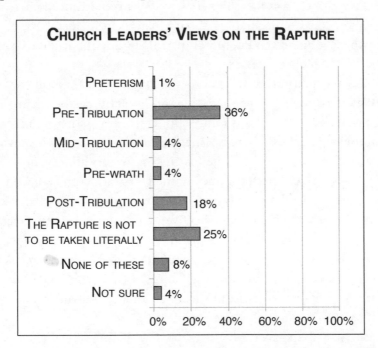

The proportions begin to take more intriguing shape when one
starts extrapolating based on specific doctrinal and denominational views. For instance, while 43 percent of Evangelical pastors
selected a pre-Tribulation Rapture, just 31 percent of mainline pastors agreed; Evangelicals were also more likely (21 percent) to choose a

post-Tribulation worldview than their mainline counterparts (15 percent). In the end, 36 percent of mainline pastors said that "the concept of the Rapture is not to be taken literally," compared to just 17 percent of Evangelicals.

The LifeWay poll also yielded some intriguing comparisons between pastors from Baptist, Lutheran, Methodist, Pentecostal, and Presbyterian/Reformed traditions, finding that Pentecostals were the most likely—73 percent—to embrace a pre-Tribulation Rapture. Baptists came in second with 61 percent, though just 1 percent of Lutherans selected that theological framework.

There were also some notable differences among various age cohorts, with only 28 percent of pastors in the eighteen to forty-four age range category accepting a pre-Tribulation Rapture—the least likely when compared to those in the forty-five to fifty-four, fifty-five to sixty-four, and the over sixty-five age ranges.

On the education front, those with no college degree were the most likely to embrace a pre-Tribulation Rapture (60 percent), with only 26 percent of individuals with a master's degree agreeing. Meanwhile, 33 percent of those with a master's degree and 29 percent of those with a doctoral degree expressed belief that the Rapture concept shouldn't be taken literally, compared to just 6 percent of pastors without a degree and 16 percent of those who have a bachelor's degree.

These statistics provide a fascinating lens into what is likely being preached and taught at various churches across the country. What is clear is that there is no consensus—not one of the Rapture views crosses or even nears 50 percent.

— — — — — — — —

In addition to asking for pastors' views on the Rapture, the survey also inquired about their perspective on the Millennium as it is described in Revelation 20. The Millennium is a period of time that some believe will consist of Jesus's literal one-thousand-year rule on earth; others take either a symbolic view or see it as the period of time between Christ's first and second comings, among other perspectives.

Faith leaders were presented with a variety of options in the survey, including the amillennial belief that there is no literal one-thousand-year Millennium and that Jesus is currently reigning spiritually and in the hearts of Christians; the postmillennial view that the Millennium is not a literal one thousand years, but is an era in which the world grows more Christian before Jesus's return; and the premillennial view that it is a literal one-thousand-year period during which Jesus will rule on earth after His second coming.

For this question, the results were even more pronounced, with premillennialism—the belief in the literal one-thousand-year period— resonating among nearly half (48 percent) of the pastors surveyed. Additionally, 31 percent opted for amillenialism, with only 11 percent selecting postmillennialism and a collective 12 percent selecting "none of these" or saying that they were unsure. See the graph below for a visual representation of these views.

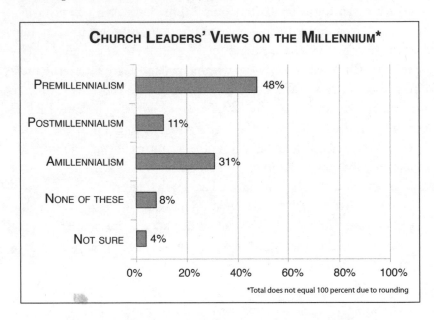

The results were also more pronounced when digging deeper into smaller theological circles under the Christian umbrella. Similar to the Rapture results, 57 percent of Evangelical pastors selected premillennialism, compared to only 38 percent of mainline preachers; an additional 38 percent of mainline faith leaders selected amillennialism, compared to just 24 percent of Evangelicals.

For this particular question, there were also some sweeping differences in terms of education, with 41 percent of those with a master's degree selecting amillennialism versus just 9 percent of those with no degree. Additionally, 71 percent of those with no degree and 63 percent with a bachelor's degree selected premillennialism, while only 36 percent with a master's degree and 46 percent with a doctoral degree said the same.

Denominational affiliations also offered up some notable differences, with 84 percent of Pentecostals and 75 percent of Baptists selecting premillennialism versus just 21 percent of Methodists, 14 percent of Presbyterian/Reformed, and 5 percent of Lutherans. On the flip side, 71 percent of Lutherans selected amillennialism, as did 52 percent of Presbyterian/Reformed and 37 percent of Methodists—but just 13 percent of Baptists and 4 percent of Pentecostals said the same.

Postmillennial views, on the other hand, are most prevalent among Methodists (27 percent) and Presbyterian/Reformed (20 percent).

There's still a great deal of debate over the Millennium, though there was a larger share embracing a single worldview under the diverse umbrella of ideas than there was when it came to the Rapture.

— — — — — — — —

In addition to seeking pastoral beliefs on the Rapture and the Millennium, we asked faith leaders to select a statement that most aligned with their views on the Antichrist. The options given included that the Antichrist is a figure who will arise in the future, a figure who arose in the past, that there is no individual Antichrist, that he is a personification of evil, and that he is an institution rather than a person. Here too nearly half of the pastors surveyed (49 percent) aligned with the literal (or dispensationalist premillennial) view that proclaimed that the Antichrist "will arise sometime in the future."

Interestingly, there were no notable proportions when it came to other proposals about what the verses commonly attributed to the Antichrist could be referencing. While 14 percent selected a "personification of evil," 12 percent opted for "there is no individual Antichrist." Additionally, 7 percent said that the Antichrist is an institution and not a person, with 6 percent describing the individual as having "already arose sometime in the past." See the graph below for a visual representation of these results.

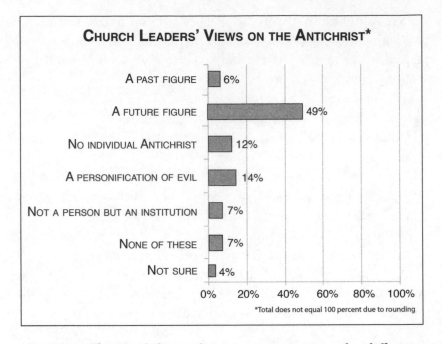

On the educational front, there are some noteworthy differences. Sixty-eight percent of those with no college degree believe that "he is a figure who will arise sometime in the future," much higher than those with a master's degree (39 percent) or a doctoral degree (49 percent). And only 5 percent of those who have no degree would agree with the idea that the Antichrist is simply a "personification of evil," with 18 percent of those with master's degrees and 16 percent of those with doctorates saying the same.

Mainline pastors were more likely to select "there is no individual Antichrist" than their Evangelical counterparts (15 percent versus 8 percent). They were also more likely to select that he is a "personification of evil" than Evangelicals (19 percent versus 10 percent) and that he is "not a person but an institution" (9 percent versus 6 percent).

Faith leaders are clearly divided on these matters, as are parishioners. There are a variety of reasons for these theological splits in perspective, though this chapter can do little more than present that data and allow readers to explore and ponder it. But one thing is certain: without a consensus, it is clear that the mysterious nature of eschatology—which is fueled, in part, by the lack of clarity in Scripture and the divergent ideas being taught in churches—isn't poised to be cleared up anytime soon.

Conclusion

WHEN IT COMES to debate over end-times theology, concluding that "it's complicated" is most certainly an understatement. Before embarking on this ever-fascinating book journey, I knew that there were various points of eschatological contention; what I didn't know, however, was just how multifaceted, complex, and even heated these disagreements can be.

Growing up in an Evangelical home, I was more than familiar with the premillennial, pre-Tribulation view, as that is exactly what has been preached by most of the pastors I've personally encountered throughout my spiritual walk.

That said, writing *The Armageddon Code* forced me to look, quite honestly, at perspectives that I not only knew very little about but also that I previously had no idea existed inside modern Evangelical and—more generally—Christian circles. For instance, the notion that Christ's return essentially unfolded in AD 70—an idea that is embraced by full preterists—was totally foreign to me. Also, the proposal that a future Rapture could potentially be one and the same with the Second Coming was also something that I admittedly had never spent a great deal of time pondering prior to this project.

— — — — — — — —

It's important that I note the somewhat limited lens through which I presented each chapter in this book. After all, some of the topics warrant—or at least invite—the potential for volumes of exploration. I attempted to frame the overarching arguments and events for each point of discussion, though what is presented is hardly exhaustive, because the array of end-of-days theories, perspectives, and alternative ideas are seemingly never ending.

The Armageddon Code tackles the broader debate over eschatology and provides an overview of some of the most common views out there surrounding the Rapture, the Tribulation, and the millennial kingdom, among other subjects. To be clear, it was virtually impossible to explore every single tidbit of the end-times discussion within the scope and confines of these pages; thus there are additional theories and ideas that were not included in this book. The broader scriptural themes within Revelation were touched upon, though each of the chapters in this book offer up a wealth of information and material that deserves far more attention and time.

— — — — — — —

As I wrap up this book, though, I must look back at one idea that was presented by Dr. Michael Heiser—a point of advice that I found to be among the most compelling and worthwhile for those attempting to study and definitively understand the end times. It was a proclamation that can help each of us properly frame and stay the course when confronted with prophetic and eschatological texts.

As you'll recall, Heiser proposed that it's important to realize that prophecy tends to be better understood after events have concluded, when human beings have had a chance to look back to see for themselves how the pieces of the puzzle came together in specific and profound ways.

Using the example of Old Testament prophecies about Jesus's first coming, he said that it is much clearer for us to look back today to see how Christ fulfilled those predictions than it was for people living in Bible times to do so in real time. In a sense, he cautioned that it's easier to see the narrative after the fact and conclude, "Oh, yeah. That makes sense now," than it is to cobble pieces together and make definitive conclusions before prophetic events have taken place.

As I previously stated, Heiser sees the same sort of dynamic when it comes to the Bible's outlining of the end times, claiming that it will likely "only be comprehensible after the fact."[1]

"All of the elements that we're familiar with as Christians as far as the role of the Messiah, what He would do, what He would say, where He would go, where He'd be from, all this stuff is just scattered across the Old Testament," Heiser said. "It's never put together. It's fragmented, and it's deliberate."[2]

Regardless of where one stands on eschatology, though, it makes sense that, considering the murkiness of the details, that finite conclusions can't and won't come until much later—and, quite possibly, after it all unfolds.

It appears that there's so much we don't—and can't—know at this juncture, but that doesn't mean that we shouldn't each embark on a personal quest to dive deeper into end-times scriptures and tradition to try and frame viable conclusions. This, after all, is an act that was and continues to be undertaken by many of the subjects in this book. And while many have come to very different conclusions, perhaps those differences are due to uncertainties in prophetic understanding.

— — — — — — — —

Some will likely wonder where I stand on the Rapture, the Millennium, and all of the proposed events in between, especially after extensive interviews with experts and theologians. I would like to avoid diving too deep into my stances, as it is truly up to the reader to craft a personal and thoughtful reaction to each eschatological claim. If anything, it is my hope that this book will, at the least, inspire you to set out on that journey of understanding—to dive deeper into Scripture and tradition to further assess the Bible's role, not only in humanity's past and present, but also our future.

That said, I do have a few notes. Admittedly, the Rapture has been one of the more difficult elements for me, as I have been sympathetic to both sides of the debate (most pointedly, those who accept and reject a pre-Tribulation Rapture). A pre-Tribulation event doesn't appear to be blatantly spelled out in Scripture, and, more specifically, it isn't overtly present in the Book of Revelation, as many critics contend. But does that mean it is unscriptural? Not necessarily.

On one hand, I understand the idea that God would rescue believers from His wrath, and we have examples in the biblical narrative that show God doing just that. After all, there's Noah and his well-known ark. It's not a bizarre notion to consider that the Lord would shield His people, though it is also perfectly acceptable and accurate to argue that Christians are absolutely not promised to be automatically buffered from any and all persecution, pain, and tribulation in the world, as we've seen exhibited throughout history and in the modern era.

I remain open to different Rapture possibilities, but in the end, it seems to be a lesser debate when compared to other points of contention. More pointedly—as many interview subjects have told me—it's not a salvation issue.

Another major issue that I feel compelled to briefly discuss here is the modern state of Israel. I'm absolutely fascinated by the fact that the Jews went nearly two millennia without a homeland.

While many ancient cultures and nations have perished and are long-lost figments of history past, this is not the case when it comes to Jews and Israel, with the Jewish people astonishing many by returning to the Holy Land in 1948. It is hard for me, intellectually and conceptually, to look at that fact—a development that was precipitated by the Holocaust—and not conclude that the return to the land is prophetic or, at the least, was brought about in some way by the Lord.

I found Joel Rosenberg's comments on the matter truly compelling, specifically his breakdown of the length of time during which the Jews were absent from the land. As I illustrated, he dubbed their shocking return as a remarkable development.

"For nineteen hundred years, it didn't happen. Think about that...maybe you could not be discouraged as a people for the first five hundred years, but like six hundred, seven hundred, nine hundred, one thousand years go by and nothing happens," Rosenberg said. "That's why the church abandoned these prophecies."

On a related note, it is quite fascinating to me that Ezekiel 38:5–6 mentions Persia, among other nations, as being part of the Gog and Magog invasion into Israel—an event that many prophecy experts believe has yet to take form. While the nation to the "far north" isn't named in the text, Persia—which is modern-day Iran—is mentioned, along with the nations of Cush, Put, Gomer, and Beth Togarmah. Those latter countries aside, it is notable that Ezekiel—a prophet who penned his book around twenty-five hundred years ago—is discussing an alliance involving Persia, a country that is known today as Iran.

Anyone paying even a miniscule amount of attention to the news knows that Iranian officials have routinely called for Israel to be wiped off the map.

At the least, this should cause some raised eyebrows. After all, it's curious that twenty-five hundred years after Ezekiel discussed an event that many prophecy experts believe has yet to unfold, the very nations described in those scriptures are currently at odds. Sure, it could all be by chance. But it's certainly a bit curious.

That, mixed with the overall chaos in the Middle East, gives me great pause and leads me to listen closer to what many biblical experts who see unfulfilled events in the Old and New Testaments have to say.

Then there's the debate and discussion over the proposed future Antichrist. Some look at the Scriptures and predict a central, diabolical figure who will rise to power and deceive the world. Others believe that the Antichrist and false prophet were figures who were represented by past leaders or forces in existence centuries ago.

Did the Antichrist and false prophet in Revelation already come to pass? Are the beasts merely symbolic? These are just some of the questions that experts will most certainly continue to hash out.

It's also important to look back to the Old Testament when discussing the Antichrist, as some dispensational premillennialists would contend that Daniel 9:27 is part of the narrative that predicts a future diabolical figure who will rise to power.

Critics reject this, believing that the chapter offers an already fulfilled prediction involving Antiochus Epiphanes, who later defiled the temple and, thus, satisfied the conditions described in that prophecy.

Premillennialists don't reject this, per se, but they see Antiochus as a foreshadowing of sorts of the Antichrist to come—a "type" of the Antichrist who gives a lens into the characteristics of the figure that is to come.[3]

It's important to note that Jesus Himself, in Matthew 24:15 as well as Mark 13:14, references the "abomination of desolation" that is present in Daniel 9; this is two centuries after Antiochus Epiphanes's actions. Clearly this extends beyond the text in Daniel and seemingly points to the fact that Christ is speaking about something that is unfulfilled—at least at the time that He is uttering His comments on the matter.

And then there's Paul's mention of a "man of lawlessness" and "man of sin" in 2 Thessalonians 2. In the end, it appears that there is a theme throughout the Scriptures, making it seem plausible that John is presenting yet another layer of this repeated pattern in Revelation when he mentions the beasts.

Whether this means that there will be a future antichrist or not remains to be seen, but considering the increasing chaos that is unfolding throughout the world—uncertainty that could be stemmed by a figure who promises peace, particularly when it comes to the Middle East—it's understandable how people land there, theologically speaking.

I could go on and on in my assessment of these elements. In the end, it's hard for me to look at all that is unfolding—all of the unraveling, all of the chaos, all of the signs that seem to be indicators of a march toward what the Bible describes of the end of days—and assume that there's simply nothing to see.

While I cannot be definitively certain how it will all shake down, what I think the vast majority of Christians can embrace is a future second coming of Christ along with a new heaven and a new earth, as detailed in Revelation.

— — — — — — —

At the end of my interview with Pastor Greg Laurie, I asked him if there were any points about the end times that we hadn't yet discussed, but that he wanted to be sure people heard. What followed was a pointed message urging unity.

"I would just say that I do believe that it's important that we believe that Christ could come back at any time," Laurie said. "He told us to watch and be ready."[4]

But the Harvest Crusades founder also said that there needs to be a sense of unity even in the midst of eschatological debate, explaining that he believes Bible believers can have their differences but "not break fellowship over it."[5]

"We want to remember that the most important thing is that we turn from our sin and put our faith in Christ and are ready to meet Him," he said. "One day, it's all going to be revealed. If I'm wrong, I would be happy to admit to my preterist friends, but I really think when we're in heaven we won't care about things like that."

He concluded with a call to people that I would like to not only advance but also endorse: regardless of where people stand on the end times, studying and understanding Revelation is key.

"We hold our views, we hold our views with great passion, but I do believe, as I already said, there's a great blessing promised to those that read, study, and keep the words of the Book of Revelation, and I think, principally, on the topic of Bible prophecy as well," Laurie said.

"So I hope that people will begin to study this book, especially in light of all the things that are happening in our world today, because there's a lot of questions, and people are frightened, and the fact is, the Bible gives answers."[6]

With that, I say, "Amen."

Notes

Introduction: Our Obsession With the End of Days

1. Lindsay Rothfeld, "Why We're So Obsessed With Zombies," Mashable, March 12, 2015, accessed January 25, 2016, http://mashable.com/2015/03/12/zombie-obsession/#sUfDQfvSpkqj.

2. Ibid.

3. Ibid.

4. Kelsey Geiser, "Stanford Scholar Explains Why Zombie Fascination Is Very Much Alive," *Stanford Report*, February 20, 2013, accessed January 26, 2016, http://news.stanford.edu/news/2013/february/why-zombie-fascination-022013.html.

5. Ibid.

6. Ibid.

Chapter 1: Why There's So Much Debate Over the End Times

1. Michael Heiser, in discussion with the author, October 29, 2015.

2. Joel Rosenberg, in discussion with the author, September 11, 2015.

3. Ibid.

4. Michael Brown, in discussion with the author, December 12, 2015.

5. Ibid.

6. Ibid.

7. Ibid.

8. Rosenberg, discussion.

9. Ibid.

10. Ron Rhodes, in discussion with author, September–November 2015.

11. Ibid.

12. Ibid.

13. Ibid.

14. Heiser, discussion.

15. Ibid.

16. Ibid.

17. Ibid.

18. Ibid.

19. Ibid.

20. Ibid.

21. Ibid.

22. Jeff Kinley, interview by Billy Hallowell, *The Church Boys*, TheBlaze, audio, December 4, 2015, accessed February 2, 2016, https://soundcloud.com/thechurchboys/ep-47-trying-to-be-wrong.

23. Ibid.
24. Ibid.
25. Ibid.
26. Ed Hindson, in discussion with the author, September 4, 2015.
27. Ibid.
28. Kinley, interview.
29. Ibid.
30. Ibid.
31. Tim LaHaye, in discussion with the author, November 28, 2015.
32. Ibid.
33. Greg Laurie, in discussion with the author, December 16, 2015.
34. Ibid.
35. Ibid.
36. Ibid.

CHAPTER 2: THE RAPTURE AND WHETHER IT'S BIBLICAL

1. Pew Research Center, "Global Survey of Evangelical Protestant Leaders," June 22, 2011, accessed January 7, 2011, http://www.pewforum.org /2011/06/22/global-survey-of-evangelical-protestant-leaders/.
2. Rhodes, discussion.
3. Jeff Kinley, *Wake the Bride* (Eugene, OR: Harvest House Publishers, 2015), 57.
4. Mark Hitchcock, in discussion with the author, September 9, 2015.
5. Mary Fairchild, "What Is the Rapture?", About.com, August 5, 2015, accessed February 2, 2016, http://christianity.about.com/od/faqhelpdesk/a /whatisrapture.htm.
6. Ibid.
7. Hitchcock, discussion.
8. Jennifer LeClaire, "Despite Popular Theology, Apologist Says Rapture Movies Are Not Biblical," *Charisma News*, August 5, 2014, accessed February 2, 2016, http://www.charismanews.com/culture/44904-despite-popular -theology-apologist-says-rapture-movies-are-not-biblical.
9. Ibid.
10. Ibid.
11. *Christianity History*, "John Nelson Darby," ChristianityToday.com, August 8, 2008, accessed February 2, 2016, http://www.christianitytoday.com /ch/131christians/pastorsandpreachers/darby.html?start=2.
12. Ibid.
13. Matt Perman, "What Does John Piper Believe About Dispensation-alism, Covenant Theology, and New Covenant Theology?", desiringGod.org, January 23, 2006, accessed February 2, 2016, http://www.desiringgod.org /articles/what-does-john-piper-believe-about-dispensationalism-covenant -theology-and-new-covenant-theology.
14. LeClaire, "Despite Popular Theology, Apologist Says Rapture Movies Are Not Biblical."

15. William Lane Craig, in discussion with the author, September 23, 2015.

16. Ibid.

17. Ibid.

18. Billy Hallowell, "Does the Bible Predict God's End-Times Destruction of Syria—and Is Prophecy About to Unfold Before Our Eyes?", TheBlaze, June 17, 2013, accessed February 2, 2016, http://www.theblaze.com/stories /2013/06/17/does-the-bible-predict-gods-end-times-destruction-of-syria-and -is-prophesy-about-to-unfold-before-our-eyes/.

19. Hank Hanegraaff, in discussion with the author, October 2, 2015.

20. Ibid.

21. Ibid.

22. Heiser, discussion.

23. Billy Hallowell, "Is the Rapture Biblical—and Will Non-Christians Really Be 'Left Behind'? Theologians Battle Over End Times Prophecy," The-Blaze, September 29, 2014, accessed February 2, 2016, http://www.theblaze .com/stories/2014/09/29/is-the-rapture-really-biblical-theologians-battle-over -end-times-prophecy/.

24. Kinley, *Wake the Bride*.

25. Craig, discussion.

26. Billy Hallowell, "End Times Expert Breaks Down Revelation—and Reveals Why He's Convinced There Will Be a 'Rapture,'" TheBlaze, December 4, 2014, accessed February 2, 2016, http://www.theblaze.com/stories/2015/12 /04/this-is-a-powder-keg-authors-end-times-warnings-about-chaos-in-the -middle-east-the-antichrist-and-the-rapture/.

27. Ibid.

CHAPTER 3: DIGGING DEEPER: PRE-TRIBULATION RAPTURE THEORY

1. Rosenberg, discussion.

2. Ibid.

3. Hitchcock, discussion.

4. Rosenberg, discussion.

5. Ibid.

6. Rosenberg, discussion.

7. Hitchcock, discussion.

8. Ibid.

9. Ibid.

10. Rhodes, discussion.

11. Hindson, discussion.

12. Ibid.

13. Ibid.

14. Hitchcock, discussion.

15. Hindson, discussion.

16. Rosenberg, discussion.

17. Ibid.

18. Ibid.

19. Ibid.
20. Kinley, *Wake the Bride*, 65.

CHAPTER 4: OTHER IDEAS ABOUT THE RAPTURE

1. Hanegraaff, discussion.
2. Ibid.
3. Ibid.
4. Ibid.
5. Ibid.
6. Brown, discussion.
7. John Piper, "Definitions and Observations Concerning the Second Coming of Christ," desiringGod.org, August 30, 1987, accessed February 2, 2016, http://www.desiringgod.org/articles/definitions-and-observations -concerning-the-second-coming-of-christ.
8. Ibid.
9. Ibid.
10. Ron Rhodes, *The 8 Great Debates of Bible Prophecy* (Eugene, OR: Harvest House Publishers, 2014).
11. Millard J. Erickson, *Christian Theology*, second edition (Grand Rapids, MI: Baker Academic, 1998), 1214.
12. Ibid., 1230.
13. Ibid.
14. Steve W. Lemke, "The Biblical Case for Mid-Tribulationalism," New Orleans Baptist Theological Seminary, accessed February 2, 2016, http://www.nobts.edu/faculty/itor/lemkesw/personal/midtribulationism.html.
15. Brown, discussion.
16. Rhodes, *The 8 Great Debates of Bible Prophecy*, 113.
17. Erickson, *Christian Theology*, 1230.
18. Rhodes, *The 8 Great Debates of Bible Prophecy*, 119.
19. Ibid., 121.
20. Sam Storms, in discussion with the author, November 2015.
21. Ibid.
22. Ibid.
23. Ibid.
24. Ibid.
25. Ibid.
26. Ibid.
27. Ibid.
28. Douglas Wilson, in discussion with the author, November 2015.
29. Ibid.
30. Ibid.

CHAPTER 5: THE TRIBULATION

1. LaHaye, discussion.
2. Tim Lahaye Ministries, "Pre-Trib FAQ," accessed January 6, 2016, http://timlahaye.myshopify.com/pages/pre-trib-faq.
3. Ibid.
4. John Noē, "An Exegetical Basis for a Preterist-Idealist Understanding of the Book of Revelation," *Journal of the Evangelical Theological Society* 49, no. 4 (December 2006).
5. LaHaye, discussion.
6. Hindson, discussion.
7. LaHaye, discussion.
8. Ibid.
9. Rhodes, *The 8 Great Debates of Bible Prophecy*, 139.
10. Ibid., 140.
11. Ibid.
12. Ibid.
13. Heiser, discussion.
14. Ibid.
15. Ibid.
16. Storms, discussion.
17. Ibid.

CHAPTER 6: THE ANTICHRIST

1. Rosenberg, discussion.
2. Hitchcock, discussion.
3. Brown, discussion.
4. LaHaye, discussion.
5. Gregory H. Harris, "The Wound of the Beast in the Tribulation," *Bibliotheca Sacra* 156 (October–December 1999): 459.
6. Brown, discussion.
7. Hanegraaff, discussion.
8. LaHaye, discussion.
9. Rosenberg, discussion.
10. Hitchcock, discussion.
11. Rosenberg, discussion.
12. Ibid.
13. Hitchcock, discussion.
14. Ibid.
15. Rosenberg, discussion.
16. Hitchcock, discussion.
17. Ibid.
18. Stephen J. Nichols, "Prophecy Makes Strange Bedfellows: On the History of Identifying the Antichrist," *Journal of the Evangelical Theological Society* 44, no. 1 (March 2001): 87–105.

19. Rosenberg, discussion.
20. Nichols, "Prophecy Makes Strange Bedfellows: On the History of Identifying the Antichrist," 75.
21. Ibid.
22. Ibid., 79.

Chapter 7: The Debate Over the Nature of the Beasts

1. Storms, discussion.
2. Ibid.
3. *Encyclopaedia Britannica*, s.v. "Arius," last modified April 9, 2014, accessed February 3, 2016, http://www.britannica.com/biography/Arius.
4. Storms, discussion.
5. Ibid.
6. *Encyclopaedia Britannica*, s.v. "Antiochus IV Epiphanes," by Hans Volkmann, last modified May 5, 2014, accessed February 3, 2016, http://www.britannica.com/biography/Antiochus-IV-Epiphanes.
7. Rhodes, *The 8 Great Debates of Bible Prophecy*, 144.
8. LaHaye, discussion.
9. Ibid.
10. Storms, discussion; *Encyclopaedia Britannica*, s.v. "Titus," last modified February 7, 2014, accessed February 3, 2016, http://www.britannica.com/biography/Titus.
11. Storms, discussion.
12. Hanegraaff, discussion.
13. Ibid.
14. Ibid.
15. Ibid.
16. Ibid.
17. Hank Hanegraaff, "Who Is the Antichrist?" Christian Research Institute, June 10, 2009, accessed February 3, 2016, http://www.equip.org/article/who-is-the-antichrist/.
18. Hanegraaff, discussion.
19. Hank Hanegraaff, *The Complete Bible Answer Book*, collector's edition (Nashville: Thomas Nelson, 2009), 163.
20. Hanegraaff, discussion.
21. Ibid.
22. Ibid.
23. Shane Wood, in discussion with the author, November 2015.
24. Ibid.
25. Ibid.
26. Ibid.
27. Heiser, discussion.
28. Ibid.
29. Storms, discussion.
30. Ibid.

31. Ibid.

32. LaHaye, discussion.

33. Harris, "The Wound of the Beast in the Tribulation."

34. Ibid., 461.

35. Ibid., 462.

36. Ibid., 462.

37. Ibid., 463.

38. Charlie Restivo, "Revelation 13:11–18," sermon, Calvary Chapel of Westchester County, November 2, 2014, MP3 format, http://www.calvary chapelwestchester.org/index.php?option=com_biblestudy&view=studieslist &t=1&Itemid=156#.

39. *Merriam-Webster Online*, s.v. "gematria," accessed January 11, 2016, http://www.merriam-webster.com/dictionary/dispensation.

40. Roger Barrier, "What Is the Meaning of '666' in Revelation?", Cross walk.com, November 4, 2013, accessed February 3, 2016, http://www.cross walk.com/church/pastors-or-leadership/ask-roger/what-is-the-meaning-of -666-in-revelation.html.

41. Rhodes, discussion.

42. Ibid.

43. Restivo, "Revelation 13:11–18."

44. Ibid.

45. Ibid.

46. Harris, "The Wound of the Beast in the Tribulation," 467.

47. Wood, discussion.

CHAPTER 8: THE GREAT MILLENNIAL DEBATE

1. Wilson, discussion.

2. Ibid.

3. Rosenberg, discussion.

4. Ibid.

5. Noē, "An Exegetical Basis for a Preterist-Idealist Understanding of the Book of Revelation," 771.

6. Ibid.

7. Rhodes, *The 8 Great Debates of Bible Prophecy*, 241.

8. Ibid.

9. William Lane Craig, "Doctrine of the Last Things (Part 10): Views on the Millennium," transcript, September 10, 2014, *Defenders Podcast*, Reasonable Faith, accessed February 3, 2016, http://www.reasonablefaith.org /defenders-2-podcast/transcript/s13-10.

10. Storms, discussion.

11. Noē, "An Exegetical Basis for a Preterist-Idealist Understanding of the Book of Revelation."

12. Laurie, discussion.

13. Ibid.

14. Ibid.

15. Ibid.

16. John Hagee, in discussion with the author, December 2015.

17. Ibid.

18. Craig, "Doctrine of the Last Things (Part 10): Views on the Millennium."

19. Storms, discussion.

20. Ibid.

21. Ibid.

22. Ibid.

23. Ibid.

24. Sam Storms, "The Amillennial View of the Kingdom of God," Sam Storms.com, March 15, 2007, accessed February 3, 2016, http://www.sam storms.com/all-articles/post/the-amillennial-view-of-the-kingdom-of-god/.

25. Craig, "Doctrine of the Last Things (Part 10): Views on the Millennium."

26. Ibid.

27. Storms, "The Amillennial View of the Kingdom of God."

28. Noë, "An Exegetical Basis for a Preterist-Idealist Understanding of the Book of Revelation," 780.

29. Wilson, discussion.

30. Rhodes, discussion.

31. Ibid.

32. R. Fowler White, "Agony, Irony, and Victory in Inaugurated Eschatology: Reflections on the Current Amillennial-Postmillennial Debate," *Westminster Theological Journal* 62, no. 2 (Fall 2000): 162.

33. Storms, "The Amillennial View of the Kingdom of God."

34. Craig, "Doctrine of the Last Things (Part 10): Views on the Millennium."

35. Bill Bright, "Catch Excitement for the Gospel," Cru.org, accessed January 7, 2016, http://www.cru.org/train-and-grow/transferable-concepts /help-fulfill-the-great-commission.html.

36. Craig, discussion.

37. Wilson, discussion.

38. Ibid.

39. Ibid.

40. Ibid.

41. Ibid.

42. Ibid.

43. Ibid.

44. Ibid.

45. Craig, discussion.

46. Hanegraaff, discussion.

47. Ibid.

48. Ibid.

49. Ibid.

50. Ibid.

51. Ibid.

CHAPTER 9: UNDERSTANDING SCRIPTURE AND ESCHATOLOGY

1. Wayne McDill, "7 Principles of Biblical Interpretation," LifeWay.com, March 12, 2014, accessed February 3, 2016, http://www.lifeway.com/pastors /2014/03/12/7-principles-of-biblical-interpretation/.

2. Ellen White, "Defining Biblical Hermeneutics," *Bible History Daily*, October 13, 2014, accessed February 3, 2016, http://www.biblicalarchaeology .org/daily/biblical-topics/bible-interpretation/defining-biblical-hermeneutics/.

3. McDill, "7 Principles of Biblical Interpretation."

4. White, "Defining Biblical Hermeneutics."

5. "What Is Biblical Hermeneutics?", gotQuestions.org, accessed January 8, 2016, http://www.gotquestions.org/Biblical-hermeneutics.html.

6. *Encyclopaedia Britannica*, s.v. "Hermeneutics," accessed January 8, 2016, http://www.britannica.com/topic/hermeneutics-principles-of-biblical -interpretation.

7. *Encyclopaedia Britannica*, s.v. "Biblical Literature," last modified September 28, 2015, accessed February 3, 2016, http://www.britannica.com /topic/biblical-literature/The-critical-study-of-biblical-literature-exegesis -and-hermeneutics.

8. LaHaye, discussion.

9. Ibid.

10. *Encyclopaedia Britannica*, s.v. "Biblical Literature."

11. Ibid.

12. Perman, "What Does John Piper Believe About Dispensationalism, Covenant Theology, and New Covenant Theology?"

13. Ibid.

14. Rhodes, *The 8 Great Debates of Bible Prophecy*, 22.

15. Ibid., 23.

16. Perman, "What Does John Piper Believe About Dispensationalism, Covenant Theology, and New Covenant Theology?"

17. *Merriam-Webster Online*, s.v. "dispensation," accessed January 8, 2016, http://www.merriam-webster.com/dictionary/dispensation.

18. Rhodes, *The 8 Great Debates of Bible Prophecy*, 20–22.

19. Perman, "What Does John Piper Believe About Dispensationalism, Covenant Theology, and New Covenant Theology?"

20. Jeff Kinley, in discussion with the author, November–December 2015.

21. Ibid.

22. Ibid.

23. Ibid.

24. Rhodes, discussion.

25. H. Wayne House, "The Future of National Israel," *Bibliotheca Sacra* 166 (October–December 2009): 473.

26. Darrell Bock, in discussion with the author, October 2015.

27. Ibid.

28. Ibid.

29. Frederic R. Howe, "Does Christ Occupy David's Throne Now?", *Journal of the Grace Evangelical Society* (Spring 2006): 65.

30. House, "The Future of National Israel," 468–469.

31. Rhodes, *The 8 Great Debates of Bible Prophecy*, 27.

32. Ibid., 26.

33. Perman, "What Does John Piper Believe About Dispensationalism, Covenant Theology, and New Covenant Theology?"

34. Rhodes, *The 8 Great Debates of Bible Prophecy*, 26.

35. Perman, "What Does John Piper Believe About Dispensationalism, Covenant Theology, and New Covenant Theology?"

36. Kinley, discussion.

37. Larry D. Pettegrew, "The New Covenant and New Covenant Theology, *The Master's Seminary Journal* (Fall 2007): 181.

38. Ibid., 182.

39. Perman, "What Does John Piper Believe About Dispensationalism, Covenant Theology, and New Covenant Theology?"

40. Kinley, discussion.

41. Ibid.

42. Ibid.

43. LaHaye, discussion.

CHAPTER 10: UNDERSTANDING REVELATION

1. Bock, discussion.

2. Denny Burk, "Jim Hamilton on His New Revelation Commentary," DennyBurk.com, January 11, 2012, accessed February 4, 2016, http://www.dennyburk.com/jim-hamilton-on-his-new-revelation-commentary/.

3. Bock, discussion.

4. Ibid.

5. Ibid.

6. Brown, discussion.

7. Ibid.

8. Laurie, discussion.

9. Ibid.

10. Wilson, discussion.

11. Cornelis Venema, "Interpreting Revelation," *Tabletalk*, January 1, 2012, accessed February 4, 2016, http://www.ligonier.org/learn/articles/interpreting-revelation/.

12. Ibid.

13. Ibid.

14. Wilson, discussion.

15. Venema, "Interpreting Revelation."

16. Laurie, discussion.

17. Richard L. Mayhue, "Jesus: A Preterist or a Futurist?" *The Master's Seminary Journal* 14, no. 1 (Spring 2003): 10.

18. Wilson, discussion.

19. Venema, "Interpreting Revelation."
20. Wilson, discussion.
21. Hanegraaff, discussion.
22. Ibid.
23. Wood, discussion.

CHAPTER 11: PRETERISTS

1. Mayhue, "Jesus: A Preterist or a Futurist?", 10.
2. Riley O'Brien Powell, "What's Preterism?" LivingtheQuestion.org, accessed January 8, 2016, http://livingthequestion.org/resources/.
3. Noē, "An Exegetical Basis for a Preterist-Idealist Understanding of the Book of Revelation."
4. Mayhue, "Jesus: A Preterist or a Futurist?", 10.
5. Ibid.
6. Ibid.
7. Ibid.
8. Ibid., 13.
9. Noē, "An Exegetical Basis for a Preterist-Idealist Understanding of the Book of Revelation," 767.
10. *Christian History*, "A.D. 70 Titus Destroys Jerusalem," ChristianityToday.com, October 1, 1990, accessed February 4, 2016, http://www.christianitytoday.com/ch/1990/issue28/2808.html?start=1.
11. Noē, "An Exegetical Basis for a Preterist-Idealist Understanding of the Book of Revelation," 768.
12. Riley O'Brien Powell, "Coming of God," LivingtheQuestion.org, accessed January 11, 2016, http://livingthequestion.org/coming-of-god/.
13. Wood, discussion.
14. Ibid.
15. Stanley D. Toussaint, "A Critique of the Preterist View of the Olivet Discourse," *Bibliotheca Sacra* 161 (October–December 2004).
16. Ibid.
17. Ibid., 470.
18. Ibid., 484.
19. Mayhue, "Jesus: A Preterist or a Futurist?", 20.
20. Toussaint, "A Critique of the Preterist View of the Olivet Discourse," 484.
21. Ibid., 470.
22. Ibid., 487–488.
23. Powell, "Coming of God."
24. Don Preston, in discussion with the author, October 2015–January 2016.
25. Ibid.
26. Ibid.
27. Powell, "Coming of God."

28. Toussaint, "A Critique of the Preterist View of the Olivet Discourse," 489.

29. Mayhue, "Jesus: A Preterist or a Futurist?", 17.

30. Noë, "An Exegetical Basis for a Preterist-Idealist Understanding of the Book of Revelation."

31. Hank Hanegraaff, "Who or What Is the Great Prostitute of Revelation 17?", Christian Research Institute, April 13, 2011, accessed February 4, 2016, http://www.equip.org/bible_answers/who-or-what-is-the-great-prostitute-of-revelation-17/.

32. Ibid.

33. Powell, "What's Preterism?"

34. Ibid.

35. Billy Hallowell, "Does the Bible Predict End Times Destruction in Syria? Expert's Key Question About 'Prophetic Implications' Involving Russia and Iran," TheBlaze, October 2, 2015, accessed February 4, 2016, http://www.theblaze.com/stories/2015/10/02/does-the-bible-predict-end-times-destruction-in-syria-experts-key-question-about-prophetic-implications-involving-russia-and-iran/.

36. Ibid.

37. Powell, "What's Preterism?"

38. Preston, discussion.

39. Ibid.

40. Ibid.

41. Wilson, discussion.

42. Ibid.

43. Ibid.

44. Ibid.

Chapter 12: The End Times Are Upon Us, According to Some

1. Laurie, discussion.

2. Ibid.

3. Billy Hallowell, "Are the End Times Upon Us? Author Says 'Unrestrained Immorality' Mirrors 'Pandemic Godlessness' Seen in the Bible," TheBlaze, May 2, 2014, accessed February 4, 2016, http://www.theblaze.com/stories/2014/05/02/are-the-end-times-upon-us-author-says-unrestrained-immorality-mirrors-pandemic-godlessness-seen-in-the-bible/.

4. Hindson, discussion.

5. Ibid.

6. Ibid.

7. Ibid.

8. Hallowell, "Are the End Times Upon Us? Author Says 'Unrestrained Immorality' Mirrors "Pandemic Godlessness' Seen in the Bible."

9. Ibid.

10. Ibid.

11. Ibid.

12. Ibid.

13. Rosenberg, discussion.

14. Rhodes, discussion.

15. Rosenberg, discussion.

16. Billy Hallowell, "Author Reveals the Five Signs That He Says Are 'Flashing Warning Lights' That the End Times Could Be Nearing," TheBlaze, June 22, 2015, accessed February 4, 2016, http://www.theblaze.com/stories /2015/06/22/author-reveals-the-five-signs-that-he-says-are-flashing-warning -lights-that-the-end-times-could-be-nearing/.

17. Ibid.

18. Ibid.

19. Ibid.

20. Hindson, discussion.

21. Kinley, interview.

22. Hindson, discussion.

23. Kinley, interview.

24. Ibid.

CHAPTER 13: GOG, MAGOG, AND THE REESTABLISHMENT OF ISRAEL

1. Joel Rosenberg, "With Russian & Iranian Forces Now Engaged in Combat in Syria, People Are Asking, 'What Is the War of Gog & Magog?' Here's the Answer, Part One," *Joel C. Rosenberg's Blog*, October 8, 2015, accessed February 4, 2016, https://flashtrafficblog.wordpress.com/2015/10/08 /with-russian-iranian-forces-now-engaged-in-combat-in-syria-people-are -asking-what-is-the-war-of-gog-magog-heres-the-answer-part-one/.

2. James Rochford, "The Regathering of Israel," Evidence Unseen, accessed January 14, 2016, http://www.evidenceunseen.com/articles/prophecy /the-regathering-of-israel/.

3. *Encyclopaedia Britannica*, s.v. "Babylonian Exile," last modified November 25, 2014, accessed February 4, 2016, http://www.britannica.com /event/Babylonian-Exile.

4. Jeff Kinley, in discussion with author, November–December 2015.

5. Ibid.

6. Ibid.

7. Ibid.

8. Ibid.

9. Aryeh Spero, in discussion with the author, December 2015.

10. Ibid.

11. Ibid.

12. Ibid.

13. Ibid.

14. Heiser, discussion.

15. Ibid.

16. Ibid.

17. Ibid.

18. Ibid.

19. Ibid.

20. Joel Rosenberg, "What Is the War of Gog and Magog? Part Three—the Good News," *Joel C. Rosenberg's Blog*, May 12, 2011, accessed February 4, 2016, https://flashtrafficblog.wordpress.com/2011/05/12/what-is-the-war-of-gog-and-magog-part-three-the-good-news/.

21. Joel Rosenberg, "What Is the 'War of Gog and Magog'? Part One," *Joel C. Rosenberg's Blog*, May 9, 2011, accessed February 4, 2016, https://flashtrafficblog.wordpress.com/2011/05/09/what-is-the-war-of-gog-and-magog-part-one/.

22. Ibid.

23. Ibid.

24. Ibid.

25. Rhodes, discussion.

26. Ibid.

27. Rosenberg, "What Is the 'War of Gog and Magog'? Part One."

28. Hindson, discussion.

29. Joel Rosenberg, "What Is The War of Gog and Magog? Part Two," *Joel C. Rosenberg's Blog*, May 11, 2011, accessed February 4, 2016, https://flashtrafficblog.wordpress.com/2011/05/11/what-is-the-war-of-gog-and-magog-part-two-as-we-remember-israels-63rd-day-of-independence-is-this-prophetic-war-close-at-hand/.

30. Rhodes, discussion.

31. Hindson, discussion.

32. Rhodes, discussion.

33. Rosenberg, discussion.

34. Joel Rosenberg, "Answers to the Most Frequently Asked Questions About the 'War of Gog & Magog.' Part Four in Our Series on the Prophecies of Ezekiel 38–39," *Joel C. Rosenberg's Blog*, October 15, 2015, accessed February 4, 2016, https://flashtrafficblog.wordpress.com/2015/10/15/answers-to-the-three-most-frequently-asked-questions-about-the-war-of-gog-magog-part-four-in-our-series-on-the-prophecies-of-ezekiel-38-39/.

35. Ibid.

36. Kinley, discussion.

37. Ibid.

38. Ibid.

39. Laurie, discussion.

40. Ibid.

41. Ibid.

42. Ibid.

43. Sam Storms, "Revelation 20:1–15—Part I," SamStorms.com, April 21, 2007, accessed February 5, 2016, http://www.samstorms.com/all-articles/post/revelation-20:1-15---part-i.

44. Ibid.

45. Ibid.

46. Sam Storms, "Armageddon (What and When?)," SamStorms.com, September 28, 2013, accessed February 5, 2016, http://www.samstorms.com/enjoying-god-blog/post/armageddon--what-and-when-.

47. Kinley, discussion.

CHAPTER 14: ISRAEL'S ROLE IN THE END TIMES

1. Rosenberg, discussion.

2. *Encyclopaedia Britannica*, s.v. "Israel," accessed January 12, 2016, http://www.britannica.com/place/Israel.

3. Rosenberg, discussion.

4. Rhodes, *The 8 Great Debates of Bible Prophecy*, 33.

5. Ibid., 34.

6. Wilson, discussion.

7. Ibid.

8. Ibid.

9. Rhodes, *The 8 Great Debates of Bible Prophecy*.

10. Hank Hanegraaff, "Who Started Replacement Theology?, and Q&A," *Bible Answer Man*, audio, August 28, 2015, accessed February 5, 2016, http://streaming.integrationworks.com:3000/archive/BAM20150828.mp3.

11. Ibid.

12. Ibid.

13. Ibid.

14. Ibid.

15. Hanegraaff, discussion.

16. Ibid.

17. Ibid.

18. Ibid.

19. Ibid.

20. Ibid.

21. Ibid.

22. Ibid.

23. R. Scott Clark, "Covenant Theology Is Not Replacement Theology," *The Heidelblog* (blog), August 21, 2013, accessed February 5, 2016, http://heidelblog.net/2013/08/covenant-theology-is-not-replacement-theology/.

24. Ibid.

25. Ibid.

26. Wilson, discussion.

27. Ibid.

28. Heiser, discussion.

29. Ibid.

30. Rhodes, discussion.

31. Laurie, discussion.

32. Ibid.

33. Ibid.

34. LaHaye, discussion.

35. Rhodes, *The 8 Great Debates of Bible Prophecy*.

36. Ibid.

37. Kinley, discussion.

38. Ibid.

39. Ibid.

40. Ibid.

41. Ibid.

42. Ibid.

43. Ibid.

44. Rhodes, *The 8 Great Debates of Bible Prophecy*.

45. Ibid.

46. LaHaye, discussion.

47. Ibid.

48. Ibid.

49. Hagee, discussion.

50. Ibid.

51. Ibid.

52. "Will all Israel Be Saved in the End Times?" gotQuestions.org, accessed January 19, 2016, http://www.gotquestions.org/all-Israel-saved.html.

53. Ibid.

54. Ibid.

55. Wilson, discussion.

56. Kinley, discussion.

57. Ibid.

58. Ibid.

59. Ibid.

60. Ibid.

61. LaHaye, discussion.

62. Ibid.

CHAPTER 15: SYRIA'S CURRENT UNRAVELING AND ITS TIE TO BIBLICAL PROPHECY

1. Rosenberg, discussion.

2. "Pentagon Weighing Use of Military Force to Protect U.S. Trained Syrian Rebels If They've Come Under Fire by Russia," TheBlaze, October 2, 2015, accessed February 5, 2016, http://www.theblaze.com/stories/2015/10/02/pentagon-weighing-use-of-military-force-to-protect-u-s-trained-syrian-rebels-if-theyve-come-under-fire-by-russia/.

3. Joel Rosenberg, "Putin Orders Russian Military Forces Into Combat in Syria, Just Miles From Northern Border of Israel. Russian Forces Working Closely With Iran. Here's the Latest," *Joel C. Rosenberg's Blog*, October 1, 2015, accessed February 5, 2016, https://flashtrafficblog.wordpress.com/2015/10/01/putin-orders-russian-military-forces-into-combat-in-syria-just-miles-from-northern-border-of-israel-russian-forces-working-closely-with-iran-heres-the-latest/.

4. "Russia Kills US-Backed Syrian Rebels In Second Day of Air Strikes as Iran Prepares for Ground Offensive," *Telegraph*, October 2, 2015, accessed February 5, 2016, http://www.telegraph.co.uk/news/worldnews/europe /russia/11903702/Russias-Vladimir-Putin-launches-strikes-in-Syria-on-Isil -to-US-anger-live-updates.html.

5. Rosenberg, "Putin Orders Russian Military Forces Into Combat in Syria, Just Miles From Northern Border of Israel. Russian Forces Working Closely With Iran. Here's the Latest."

6. Laurie, discussion.

7. Ibid.

8. Ibid.

9. Billy Hallowell, "Does the Bible Predict God's End-Times Destruction of Syria—and Is Prophecy About to Unfold Before Our Eyes?", TheBlaze, June 17, 2013, accessed February 5, 2016, http://www.theblaze.com/stories /2013/06/17/does-the-bible-predict-gods-end-times-destruction-of-syria -and-is-prophesy-about-to-unfold-before-our-eyes/.

10. Yasmine Hafiz, "Isaiah 17:1 Is Syria War Part of Jesus' Second Coming? Christians and Muslims Quote Scripture," *Huffington Post*, August 29, 2013, accessed February 5, 2016, http://www.huffingtonpost.com/2013/08/29 /syria-jesus-second-coming_n_3830214.html?utm_hp_ref=religion.

11. Joel Rosenberg, "Does Bible Prophecy Foretell the Destruction of Damascus?", *Joel C. Rosenberg's Blog*, June 28, 2012, accessed February 5, 2016, https://flashtrafficblog.wordpress.com/2012/06/28/does-bible-prophecy -foretell-the-destruction-of-damascus/.

12. Ibid.

13. Ibid.

14. Hallowell, "Does the Bible Predict God's End-Times Destruction of Syria—and Is Prophecy About to Unfold Before Our Eyes?"

15. Ibid.

16. Hank Hanegraaff, "Metaphorical Descriptions of Heaven, and Q&A," *Bible Answer Man* with Hank Hanegraaff, audio, June 19, 2013, accessed February 5, 2016, http://www.oneplace.com/ministries/bible-answer-man /player/questions-and-answers-350263.html.

17. Ibid.

18. Ibid.

19. Ibid.

20. Ibid.

21. Ibid.

22. Candida Moss, "Sorry, Evangelicals, Syria Will Not Spur the Second Coming," The Daily Beast, September 5, 2013, accessed February 5, 2016, http://www.thedailybeast.com/articles/2013/09/05/sorry-evangelicals-syria -will-not-spur-the-second-coming.html.

23. Ibid.

CHAPTER 16: THE BLOOD MOONS BATTLE

1. Bruce McClure and Deborah Byrd, "What Is a Blood Moon?", EarthSky.org, September 22, 2015, accessed February 5, 2016, http://earthsky.org/space/what-is-a-blood-moon-lunar-eclipses-2014-2015#tetrad.

2. Liz Klimas, "See the Awesome Pictures and Video of Last Night's First of Four 'Blood Moons," TheBlaze, April 15, 2014, accessed February 5, 2016, http://www.theblaze.com/stories/2014/04/15/see-the-awesome-pictures-and-video-of-last-nights-first-of-four-blood-moons/.

3. Religion News Service, "This Sunday's Fourth 'Blood Moon'—What Is God's Divine Billboard Saying?", news release, September 24, 2015, accessed February 5, 2016, http://pressreleases.religionnews.com/2015/09/24/this-sundays-fourth-blood-moon-what-is-gods-divine-billboard-saying/.

4. Billy Hallowell, "Is the Coming 'Blood Moon' a Biblical Sign From God That Something Earth-Shattering Is About to Happen to Israel?", The Blaze, September 25, 2015, accessed February 5, 2016, http://www.newsjs.com/url.php?p=http://www.theblaze.com/stories/2015/09/25/is-the-coming-blood-moon-a-biblical-sign-from-god-that-something-earth-shattering-is-about-to-happen-to-israel/.

5. Amazon.com, "Four Blood Moons: Something Is About to Change," accessed February 5, 2016, http://www.amazon.com/Four-Blood-Moons-Something-Change/dp/1617952141/ref=sr_1_1?ie=UTF8&qid=139205904 1&sr=8 1&keywords=Four Blood+Moons%3A+Something+Is+About+to +Change.

6. Mark Biltz, in discussion with the author, December 19, 2015.

7. Ibid.

8. Ibid.

9. Ibid.

10. Ibid.

11. Hallowell, "Is the Coming 'Blood Moon' a Biblical Sign From God That Something Earth-Shattering Is About to Happen to Israel?"

12. Ibid.

13. National Aeronautics and Space Administration, "Five Millennium Catalog of Lunar Eclipses: 1401 to 1500 (1401 CE to 1500 CE)," NASA Eclipse Web Site, accessed January 13, 2016, http://eclipse.gsfc.nasa.gov/LEcat5/LE1401-1500.html.

14. National Aeronautics and Space Administration, "Five Millennium Catalog of Lunar Eclipses: 1901 to 2000 (1901 CE to 2000 CE)," NASA Eclipse Web Site, accessed January 13, 2016, http://eclipse.gsfc.nasa.gov/LEcat5/LE2001-2100.html.

15. Hallowell, "Is the Coming 'Blood Moon' a Biblical Sign From God That Something Earth-Shattering Is About to Happen to Israel?"

16. Ibid.

17. Ibid.; National Aeronautics and Space Administration, "Five Millennium Catalog of Lunar Eclipses: 1901 to 2000 (1901 CE to 2000 CE)."

18. Hallowell, "Is the Coming 'Blood Moon' a Biblical Sign From God That Something Earth-Shattering Is About to Happen to Israel?"

19. Ibid.

20. National Aeronautics and Space Administration, "Five Millennium Catalog of Lunar Eclipses: 1901 to 2000 (1901 CE to 2000 CE)."

21. Hallowell, "Is the Coming 'Blood Moon' a Biblical Sign From God That Something Earth-Shattering Is About to Happen to Israel?"

22. Ibid.

23. Ibid.

24. Ibid.

25. Ibid.

26. Ibid.

27. Ibid.

28. Kenneth L. Waters Sr., "Does the Bible Predict the Blood Moon'?" *Belief* (blog), CNN.com, April 14, 2014, accessed February 5, 2016, http://religion .blogs.cnn.com/2014/04/14/whats-up-with-the-blood-moons-prophecies/.

29. Danny Faulkner, "Will Lunar Eclipses Cause Four Blood Moons in 2014 and 2015?", Answers in Genesis, July 12, 2013, accessed February 5, 2016, https://answersingenesis.org/astronomy/moon/will-lunar-eclipses-cause-four -blood-moons-in-2014-and-2015/.

30. Ibid.

31. McClure and Byrd, "What Is a Blood Moon?"

32. Ibid.

33. Biltz, discussion.

34. Ibid.

35. Ibid.

36. Hagee, discussion.

37. Ibid.

38. Ibid.

39. Ibid.

CHAPTER 17: JESUS'S SECOND COMING IN LIGHT OF HIS FIRST

1. Billy Hallowell, "They Did Something to the Bible That Had Never Been Done Before. And It Was So Powerful That It Left Them in Tears," TheBlaze, October 12, 2015, accessed February 5, 2016, http://www.theblaze .com/stories/2015/10/12/they-did-something-to-the-bible-that-had-never -been-done-before-and-it-was-apparently-so-powerful-that-it-left-them-in -tears/.

2. Brown, discussion.

3. Rhodes, *The 8 Great Debates of Bible Prophecy*, 42.

4. LaHaye, discussion.

5. Kinley, discussion.

6. Ibid.

7. Hallowell, "They Did Something to the Bible That Had Never Been Done Before. And It Was So Powerful That It Left Them in Tears."

8. Ibid.
9. Ibid.
10. Billy Hallowell, "Famous Author Reveals Biblical Prophecies That Pushed Him Over the 'Tipping Point from Skeptic to Believer,'" TheBlaze, November 17, 2015, accessed February 5, 2016, http://www.theblaze.com /stories/2015/11/17/famous-author-reveals-biblical-prophecies-that-pushed -him-over-the-tipping-point-from-skeptic-to-believer/.
11. Ibid.
12. Ibid.
13. Kinley, discussion.
14. Ibid.
15. Brown, discussion.
16. Ibid.
17. LaHaye, discussion.
18. Ibid.

CHAPTER 18: THE FAILURE OF END-TIMES DATE SETTING

1. Randall Balmer, "The Great Disappointment: When the World Fails to End on Schedule," Religion Dispatches, May 25, 2011, accessed February 5, 2016, http://religiondispatches.org/the-great-disappointment-when-the -world-fails-to-end-on-schedule/.
2. Billy Hallowell, "'It Seems Embarrassing': Failed doomsday Preacher Harold Camping Offers an Apology...Sort of," TheBlaze, November 1, 2011, accessed February 5, 2016, http://www.theblaze.com/stories/2011/11/01/it -seems-embarrassing-failed-doomsday-preacher-harold-camping-offers-an -apology-sort-of/.
3. Ibid.
4. "What Happened on May 21?", Family Radio, Internet Archive, accessed January 13, 2016, http://web.archive.org/web/20111019171607 /http://www.familyradio.com/x/whathappened.html.
5. Ibid.
6. Ibid.
7. Ibid.
8. Ibid.
9. Ibid.
10. Nicola Menzie, "Family Radio Founder Harold Camping Repents, Apologizes for False Teachings," *Christian Post*, October 30, 2011, accessed February 5, 2016, http://www.christianpost.com/news/family-radio -founder-harold-camping-repents-apologizes-for-false-teachings-59819 /#r3YxHuRiyeEiu5bW.99.
11. "An Important Letter From Mr. Camping—March 2012" Family Radio, Internet Archive, accessed January 13, 2016, https://web.archive.org/web /20120311172055/http:/www.familyradio.com/announcement2.html?keep This=true&TB2_iframe=true&height=440&width=611.
12. Ibid.

13. Justin Berton, "Biblical Scholar's Date for Rapture: May 21, 2011," SFGate.com, January 1, 2010, accessed February 5, 2016, http://www.sfgate .com/bayarea/article/Biblical-scholar-s-date-for-rapture-May-21-2011 -3204226.php.

14. Ibid.

15. Ibid.

16. Ibid.

17. Rick Paulas, "Life After Doomsday," VICE.com, November 7, 2014, accessed February 5, 2016, http://www.vice.com/read/life-after-dooms day-456.

18. BBC News, "'Rapture': Believers Perplexed After Prediction Fails," May 22, 2011, accessed February 5, 2016, http://www.bbc.com/news/world -us-canada-13489641.

19. Steve Gorman, "California Doomsday Prophet Harold Camping Dead at 92," Reuters, December 17, 2013, accessed February 5, 2016, http://www .reuters.com/article/us-usa-doomsday-prophet-idUSBRE9BG16320131217.

20. Elena Garcia, "Fearful Teen Commits Suicide Due to Harold Camp-ing's Judgment Day Prediction," *Christian Post*, May 26, 2011, accessed Feb-ruary 5, 2016, http://www.christianpost.com/news/fearful-teen-commits -suicide-on-eve-of-harold-campings-rapture-50542/.

21. Paulas, "Life After Doomsday."

22. Rachel Cole, "10 Failed Doomsday Predictions," *Encyclopaedia Britannica*, accessed January 13, 2016, http://www.britannica.com/list/10 -failed-doomsday-predictions.

23. L. Michael White, "Prophetic Belief in the United States: William Miller and the Second Great Awakening," PBS.org, accessed January 13, 2016, http://www.pbs.org/wgbh/pages/frontline/shows/apocalypse/explanation /amprophesy.html.

24. Balmer, "The Great Disappointment: When the World Fails to End on Schedule."

25. Ibid.

26. Elizabeth Lechleitner, "Seventh-Day Adventist Church Emerged From Religious Fervor of 19th Century," Seventh-Day Adventist Church, accessed January 13, 2016, https://www.adventist.org/en/information/history/article /go/0/seventh-day-adventist-church-emerged-from-religious-fervor-of-19th -century/.

27. Ibid.

28. Seventh-Day Adventist Church, "Seventh-Day Adventist World Church Statistics 2014," accessed January 13, 2016, https://www.adventist.org/en /information/statistics/article/go/0/seventh-day-adventist-world-church -statistics-2014/.

29. Lechleitner, "Seventh-Day Adventist Church Emerged From Religious Fervor of 19th Century."

30. Cole, "10 Failed Doomsday Predictions."

31. *Encyclopaedia Britannica,* s.v. "Montanism," accessed January 13, 2016, http://www.britannica.com/topic/Montanism.

32. Jim Liang, "5 Things to Know About Montanism," *Transformed* (blog), Western Seminary, January 7, 2014, accessed February 5, 2016, http://www.westernseminary.edu/transformedblog/2014/01/07/5-things-to-know-about-montanism/.

33. Heiser, discussion.

34. Ibid.

35. Ibid.

Chapter 19: Where People Stand on the End Times

1. Shibley Telhami, "American Attitudes Toward the Middle East and Israel," Center for Middle East Policy at Brookings, December 3, 2015, accessed February 5, 2016, http://www.brookings.edu/~/media/Research/Files/Reports/2015/12/04-american-public-opinion-israel-middle-east-telhami/2015-Poll-Key-Findings-Final.pdf?la=en.

2. Pew Research Center, "U.S. Christians' Views on the Return of Christ," Pew Research Center, March 26, 2013, accessed February 5, 2016, http://www.pewforum.org/2013/03/26/us-christians-views-on-the-return-of-christ/.

3. Religion News Service, "Shock Poll: Startling Numbers of Americans Believe World Now in the "End Times," press release, September 11, 2013, accessed February 5, 2016, http://pressreleases.religionnews.com/2013/09/11/shock-poll-startling-numbers-of-americans-believe-world-now-in-the-end-times/.

4. Ibid.; Billy Hallowell, "Are the Bible's End Times Prophecies Coming True? Here Are the Stunning Stats Showing What Americans Think," The Blaze, September 12, 2013, accessed February 5, 2016, http://www.theblaze.com/stories/2013/09/12/shocking-number-of-americans-believe-were-now-living-in-the-end-times-as-described-in-the-bible-poll-finds/.

5. Ibid.

6. LifeWay Research, "Many Americans Link U.S. Military Strike in Syria to End Times," September 13, 2013, accessed February 5, 2016, http://www.lifewayresearch.com/2013/09/13/many-americans-link-u-s-military-strike-in-syria-to-end-times/.

7. Ibid.

8. Ibid.

9. Shibley Telhami, interview by Billy Hallowell, *The Church Boys*, The Blaze, audio, December 23, 2015, accessed February 5, 2016, https://soundcloud.com/thechurchboys/ep-50-soi-guess-this-would-be-our-christmas-show-then.

10. Ibid.

11. Ibid.

12. Ibid.

13. Ibid.

14. Telhami, interview by Billy Hallowell; Telhami, "American Attitudes Toward the Middle East and Israel."

15. Ibid.

16. Ibid.

17. Telhami, "American Attitudes Toward the Middle East and Israel."

18. Ibid.

19. Ibid.

20. Ibid.

CHAPTER 20: WHERE PROTESTANT PASTORS, PRIESTS, AND MINISTERS STAND ON THE END TIMES

1. This survey, sponsored by Charisma Media, was conducted by LifeWay Research through phone interviews between January 8 and January 22, 2016. One thousand senior pastors, ministers, or priests were randomly selected from a list of all Protestant churches to participate in the survey.

CONCLUSION

1. Heiser, discussion.

2. Ibid.

3. "The Daniel 11 Prophecy: Antiochus to Antichrist," Joel's Trumpet, August 1, 2012, accessed February 10, 2016, http://www.joelstrumpet.com /?p=3722.

4. Laurie, discussion.

5. Ibid.

6. Ibid.

ABOUT THE AUTHOR

THROUGH JOURNALISM, MEDIA, public speaking appearances, and the blogosphere, Billy Hallowell has worked as a journalist and commentator for more than a decade. He has been published and featured in political and cultural books, textbooks, articles, and websites that focus on the youth of America and their role in the future of our world.

Hallowell is the faith editor and an assistant editor at TheBlaze, and he has contributed to *The Washington Post*, *Human Events* (blog), *The Daily Caller*, *Mediaite* (blog), and *The Huffington Post*, among other news sites. He has also appeared on Fox News, FOXNews.com LIVE, and HuffPo Live, among others.

Hallowell's career in journalism and commentary began at an early age. Following the Columbine shooting in 1999, the then fifteen-year-old launched Teen Web Online, a website intended to address violence, discrimination, and other social issues facing America's young generation. In 2002 he founded Pathufind Media, an ongoing project that subcontracts affordable speakers to colleges and community groups. In 2003 Hallowell was selected to represent the United States at the World Bank's conference on youth development in Paris, France.

Following this experience, he was honored by the International Youth Foundation with the YouthAction Net Fellowship. On the educational front, he was a Rhodes Scholar nominee in 2006 and the recipient of the prestigious Clark Fellowship during the same year. In addition to these honors, Hallowell has received a number of journalism and community awards for his work.

Hallowell was educated at the College of Mount Saint Vincent in Riverdale, New York, and graduated with a BA in communications, with concentrations in broadcasting, corporate and journalism, and a minor in writing. In June 2008 he completed his MS in social research from Hunter College in Manhattan, New York. You can follow him on Twitter (@BillyHallowell).